INTERNATIONAL RESPONSES TO ISSUES OF CREDIT AND OVER-INDEBTEDNESS IN THE WAKE OF CRISIS

Markets and the Law

Series Editor:
Geraint Howells, University of Manchester, UK

Series Advisory Board:
Stefan Grundmann – Humboldt University of Berlin, Germany
Hans Micklitz – Bamberg University, Germany
James P. Nehf – Indiana University, USA
Iain Ramsay – York University, Canada
Charles Rickett – University of Queensland, Australia
Reiner Schulze – Münster University, Germany
Jules Stuyck – Katholieke Universiteit Leuven, Belgium
Stephen Weatherill – University of Oxford, UK
Thomas Wilhelmsson – University of Helsinki, Finland

Markets and the Law is concerned with the way the law interacts with the market through regulation, self-regulation and the impact of private law regimes. It looks at the impact of regional and international organizations (e.g. EC and WTO) and many of the works adopt a comparative approach and/or appeal to an international audience. Examples of subjects covered include trade laws, intellectual property, sales law, insurance, consumer law, banking, financial markets, labour law, environmental law and social regulation affecting the market as well as competition law. The series includes texts covering a broad area, monographs on focused issues, and collections of essays dealing with particular themes.

Other titles in the series

EU and US Competition Law: Divided in Unity?
The Rule on Restrictive Agreements and Vertical Intra-brand Restraints
Csongor István Nagy
ISBN 978 1 4094 4230 1

Financial Regulation in Africa
An Assessment of Financial Integration Arrangements in
African Emerging and Frontier Markets
Iwa Salami
ISBN 978 0 7546 7985 1

The Tobacco Challenge
Legal Policy and Consumer Protection
Geraint Howells
ISBN 978 0 7546 4570 2

International Responses to Issues of Credit and Over-indebtedness in the Wake of Crisis

Edited by

THERESE WILSON
Griffith University, Australia

Routledge
Taylor & Francis Group

LONDON AND NEW YORK

First published 2013 by Ashgate Publishing

2 Park Square, Milton Park, Abingdon, Oxfordshire OX14 4RN
52 Vanderbilt Avenue, New York, NY 10017

Routledge is an imprint of the Taylor & Francis Group, an informa business

First issued in paperback 2020

British Library Cataloguing in Publication Data
Wilson, Therese.
  International responses to issues of credit and
  over-indebtedness in the wake of crisis. – (Markets and
  the law)
  1. Credit – Law and legislation. 2. Restraint of trade.
  3. Antitrust law.
  I. Title II. Series
  343'.07–dc23

The Library of Congress has cataloged the printed edition as follows:
Wilson, Therese, Dr.
  International responses to issues of credit and over-indebtedness in the wake of crisis /
By Therese Wilson.
    p. cm.—(Markets and the law)
  Includes bibliographical references and index.
  ISBN 978-1-4094-5522-6 (hardback) 1. Consumer credit—Law and legislation. 2.
Global Financial Crisis, 2008–2009. 3. Financial services industry—Law and legislation.
I. Title.
  K1096.W55 2013
  332.7'43—dc23

2012035942

ISBN 978-1-4094-5522-6 (hbk)
ISBN 978-0-367-60173-7 (pbk)

Contents

List of Figures and Tables

Figures

Tables

List of Contributors

Justin Malbon is a Professor of Law at Monash University Law School, Melbourne, Australia.

Hans-W. Micklitz is a Professor of Law and the Jean Monnet Fellow at the European University Institute, Florence, Italy.

Luke Nottage is a Professor of Law at the University of Sydney, Sydney, Australia.

Christopher L. Peterson is most recently Senior Counsel for Enforcement Strategy for the US Consumer Financial Protection Bureau; however, at the time of writing he was the John J. Flynn Endowed Professor of Law at the S.J. Quinney College of Law, University of Utah, USA.

Iain Ramsay is a Professor of Law at the University of Kent, Canterbury, UK.

Eileen Webb is a Professor of Law at the University of Western Australia, Perth, Australia.

Toni Williams is a Professor of Law at the University of Kent, Canterbury, UK.

Therese Wilson is a Senior Lecturer at Griffith Law School and a member of the Socio-Legal Research Centre, Griffith University, Brisbane, Australia.

Preface

This book arose out of a symposium held in Tasmania, Australia, in January 2012, at which the authors discussed issues of credit and over-indebtedness, and international responses to them, in the wake of the global financial crisis.

Sincere thanks are due to the contributing authors not only for their chapters which appear in this book, but also for their stimulating contributions to our discussions in Tasmania and for their excellent company.

The symposium was made possible by the generous support of Griffith Law School and the Socio-Legal Research Centre, Griffith University, Brisbane, Australia. In particular, thanks are due to the Dean of Griffith Law School, William Macneil, and the Deputy Dean Research, Brad Sherman, for their commitment to encouraging quality research. Thanks are also due to the wonderful Carol Ballard and her assistant Madonna Adcock, for amazing administrative and organizational support.

Finally, sincere thanks to my husband, Chris, for his good humour and company in Tasmania, and for his love and support always.

Therese Wilson
Brisbane, Australia

PART I
Introduction

Chapter 1

Credit and Over-indebtedness: Current Context, Regulatory Responses and Future Possibilities

Therese Wilson

1 Introduction

The global financial crisis occurred in a context of relaxed financial regulation, which enabled market conduct such as the spreading of risk through secondary trading, including trading in residential mortgage-backed securities.[1] This context, which might be described as a neoliberal, economic consumerist context, has persisted in Western liberal democracies since the crisis and has influenced the regulatory responses to it.

Neoliberalism might be described as *economic* liberalism – a political philosophy which ostensibly favours free markets and limited regulatory intervention in the operation of those markets.[2] Two aspects of the assertion that the current political and economic context is neoliberal should be highlighted here: first is the argument that neoliberalism is not in fact concerned with free markets and limited regulation, but is actually concerned with 'giant firms' and regulating in their interests;[3] and the second is that a neoliberal environment tends to be supportive of protecting economic consumer interests, as opposed to consumer protection interests and producer interests.[4]

Crouch argues that when neoliberals refer to markets, they really mean corporations – that 'markets' are really large, multinational firms that wield significant economic and political power, and accordingly enjoy the allegiance of state governments.[5] In the wake of the global financial crisis, their power and influence – including the power and influence of giant financial firms whose conduct caused the crisis – continues. Crouch explains that '[t]he combination

---

1   See discussion in Colin Crouch, *The Strange Non-Death of Neoliberalism* (Polity Press 2011) 98.

2   Ibid 5–8.

3   Ibid 52, 145.

4   See discussion in James Whitman, 'Consumerism versus Producerism: A Study in Comparative Law' (2007) 117 Yale Law Journal 340, 365–367.

5   Crouch, *The Strange Non-Death of Neoliberalism* (n 1) 52, 145.

of economic and political forces behind this agenda is too powerful for it to be fundamentally dislodged from its predominance'.[6]

In terms of the protection of economic consumer interests within the neoliberal paradigm, this assertion draws on Whitman's comparative law thesis regarding 'consumerism versus producerism'.[7] Whitman describes a twentieth-century move away from a producerist legal order towards a consumerist legal order, particularly in the US. The producerist legal order is one that focuses on the rights and interests of producers of goods, such as workers and competitors, while the consumerist legal order focuses on the rights and interests of consumers of those goods. An important distinction is made, however, between the economic rights and interests of consumers within a consumerist legal order and consumer protection rights. Economic consumerism is concerned with ensuring that consumers can access goods at competitive prices. It embraces the free competitive market and the primacy of consumer choice. The consumer protection interest is more closely aligned with the producer interest, in that it is more paternalistic and welfarist. The consumer protection interest is also said to be compatible with the producer interest, whereas the economic consumer interest is not. A legal order concerned with the consumer protection interest may well limit choice and give rise to higher prices, through seeking to eliminate harmful products from the market. A legal order concerned with the producer interest may, not inconsistently, seek to eliminate unfair competition in the market (for example, through large firms producing cheap but inferior and possibly harmful goods) and to protect the rights of workers involved in production. The economic consumerist legal order may well overlook the consumer protection interest and the producer interest in the quest for choice and low prices.[8] Applying these concepts to consumer credit, it is argued that the dominant neoliberal, economic consumerist legal order would be concerned with facilitating easy access to credit and consumer choice, such as through mortgage securitization models, whereas a legal order concerned with consumer protection would seek to remove harmful credit products from the market, including predatory mortgage loans made possible through the separation of risk from the mortgage transaction under the mortgage securitization model.

There remains a reluctance to interfere with consumer choice in the interests of consumer protection. One suggestion that has been made to overcome the regulatory inability to intervene too radically in speculative financial services has been a two-tiered regulatory system, where the consumer protection interest at least has influence on the regulation of financial intermediaries entrusted with 'ordinary' consumers' savings and investments. Under this system, those firms entrusted with deposits and investments of 'ordinary' people would be heavily regulated, while a lightly regulated, high-risk financial sector would continue

---

6   Ibid 175.

7   Whitman, 'Consumerism versus Producerism' (n 4).

8   Ibid 340–368.

to exist, for those consumers who 'choose' to engage with that sector.[9] Piciotto recommends such an insulation of savings from financial speculation by 'treating banks and other managers of savings essentially as public utilities'.[10]

This and other recommendations for consumer protection reform, including some which will be explored in this book, have not as yet been embraced by regulators.

This book commences with an exploration of the political, economic and regulatory context in which credit regulation is taking place in the wake of the global financial crisis. It then moves to apply these considerations in a critique of particular regulatory responses, including current approaches to interest-rate ceilings, the role of credit-rating agencies, approaches to housing finance, and responsible lending. Possible new strategies and directions for consumer credit regulation will then be explored. These include the possibility of extending responsible lending regimes to protect small-business borrowers, the adoption of product safety regulatory concepts in relation to unsafe credit products, a recognition of the relationship between corrupt structures and corrupt practices and a consideration of the role of private sector actors, such as banking corporations, in consumer protection.

2 The international context

Chapter 1 by Toni Williams, 'Continuity Not Rupture: The Persistence of Neoliberalism in the Internationalization of Consumer Finance Regulation', notes the pre-crisis assumptions that financial transactions were both private transactions affecting only the financial institution and customer involved and parochial transactions contained within national boundaries. Therefore, national – as opposed to international or global – regulation was seen as appropriate. One impact of the global financial crisis has been a recognition that integrated, international financial consumer protection policies are necessary in order to strengthen financial stability. The chapter argues, however, that the integrated, international regulation being contemplated adopts the neoliberal national regulatory models that have sorely failed consumers in their relevant jurisdictions. It is noted, for example, that the G20's financial stability model embraces neoliberalism's financial consumer, who is responsible for, and capable of, protecting herself, and who is engaging with neoliberalism's 'competitive, resilient and disciplined' markets. This model, it is argued, ignores the complex and opaque nature of consumer finance products that deny consumers a basis on which to make choices in an allegedly competitive market. It further ignores both the behavioural biases that affect consumer choice and the size and influence of transnational firms that enable them to create entry

---

9   Crouch, *The Strange Non-Death of Neoliberalism* (n 1) 122.

10   Sol Piciotto, 'Disembedding and Regulation: The Paradox of International Finance' (The Social Embeddedness of Transnational Markets conference, Bremen, February 2009).

barriers to potential competitors and design products and services to suit them and their shareholders rather than consumers.

Consistent with neoliberalism's economic consumerist approach, Williams finds it telling that at the G20 summits held between November 2008 and November 2011, financial consumer *protection* was discussed in aspirational terms only, rather than in terms of concrete regulatory action to be taken in order to achieve it. Similarly, the Organization for Economic Development and Cooperation (OECD), entrusted by the G20 with the task of developing high-level principles for financial consumer protection, has demonstrated in those principles a clear preference for 'market-enabling regulation in the form of information-based consumer rights and remedies'.

Williams hypothesizes that the G20 model is likely to fail in protecting consumers, given the failure of national neoliberal regulatory models to effectively protect consumers from harmful products. The example used is the regulatory model implemented in the UK and Australia to deal with payment protection insurance ('PPI'), which has not prevented the exploitation of consumers who, notwithstanding the regulatory emphasis on financial literacy and disclosure, continue to be sold PPIs in circumstances where they do not understand the product and it is of no benefit to them.

Micklitz's chapter on 'Access to, and Exclusion of, European Consumers from Financial Markets after the Global Financial Crisis' considers the international context in which European consumers have found themselves as a result of credit access or exclusion from safe credit access. The chapter identifies three categories of consumer who have been differently affected by the global financial crisis on the basis of economic conditions in their nation-states: the 'normal consumer' who has not been adversely affected; the 'consumer at risk' of being adversely affected; and the 'affected consumer'. Those adversely affected as a result of having entered into consumer credit agreements will not find the market as forgiving of them as it has been of financial institutions and nation-states which, consistently with Crouch's neoliberal regulation for the 'giant firm', have been excused from their debts. Micklitz notes, by contrast, that individual consumers will be held to their liabilities under consumer credit contracts, lose their homes and face bankruptcy.

Micklitz then goes on to discuss the pre-crisis global ideology of 'easy access to consumer credit' and the 'democratization of credit' which, as explained above, fits neatly within the neoliberal, economic consumerist paradigm. The irony is that while such a creed should have led to a focus on solutions to financial exclusion, it failed to do so because of a lack of 'social regulation', such as consumer protection regulation, which would protect consumers from harmful credit products and facilitate access to safe credit. Instead, the credit access that was 'opened up' was often harmful and predatory. The consequences of this lead Micklitz to conclude that 'European law does not really care about the socially and financially excluded'.

3 Current responses

In Part III, current regulatory responses to issues of credit and over-indebtedness in the wake of the global financial crisis are considered in light of the international context outlined in Part II above.

In 'Culture or Politics? Models of Consumer Credit Regulation in France and the UK' Iain Ramsay focuses on consumer credit regulation in France and in the UK because they 'represent distinct approaches' and have resulted in lower levels of consumer credit in France. In this regard Ramsay describes the French political economy as incorporating a distrust of credit and neoliberal models of regulation and adopting a producerist model of consumer credit protection, evidenced, for example, in the opposition to credit *gratuit* (interest-free credit offered by retailers) by the banks on the basis that it represents unfair competition in the credit market. Whereas in the UK there is an economic consumerist emphasis on consumer choice, in France the emphasis is on consumer protection per se. Ramsay notes that these differences are evident not only in legislation, but also in the approaches taken by the courts: whereas English courts have shown a reluctance to interfere with contractual obligations under credit contracts, French courts have demonstrated a willingness to impose duties and responsibilities on the lender beyond the scope of the credit contract itself.

With respect to credit ratings agencies and the information collected by them, in France only negative information pertaining to defaults is kept on record, whereas the UK has positive credit reporting. An explanation given for the French reluctance to embrace positive credit reporting is the French suspicion and distrust of the collection of information which may infringe on the human dignity inherent in privacy. The UK has favoured positive credit reporting on the basis of increasing consumer choice and managing risk. Turning to interest-rate ceilings, Ramsay notes that since the Second World War France has consistently maintained price ceilings on credit. This might be attributable to the influence of labour in France and a distrust of credit as exploitative of workers. The question of interest-rate ceilings remains a hotly debated topic in the UK due to concerns that they would serve to restrict choice and exacerbate financial exclusion. Finally, mortgage-lending practices are more conservative in France than the UK, which has resulted in lower default rates in France. This can be contrasted with the greater propensity for risky home mortgage lending in the UK.

While these examples do seem to fit neatly within the neoliberal, economic consumerism versus consumer protection/producerism/welfarism dichotomy, Ramsay cautions against generalizations, noting that '[t]he French approach might be explained by "French exceptionalism", a hold-out against the increased global domination of a neoliberal capitalism of "mindless consumerism" stoked by consumer credit and credit cards'. He points out that France has certainly embraced aspects of neoliberalism and would have embraced them more enthusiastically if not for the global financial crisis, which tilted the balance back towards a recognition of the dangers of credit. It remains the case, however, that there are clear differences between the two countries in their approaches to credit regulation. Ramsay concludes that this makes it difficult to isolate and identify a 'European model of credit regulation'.

Therese Wilson's chapter on 'The Responsible Lending Response' draws on the neoliberal context outlined by Williams and analyses responsible lending regimes in Australia, the US, Europe and South Africa. Consumer protection imperatives, it is argued, have to some extent been hijacked by a 'financial stability' imperative, looking to the protection of markets rather than people. Drawing on Crouch's thesis concerning the 'non-death of neoliberalism', Wilson argues that the focus on financial market protection is partly attributable to the financial sector's ability to persuade government that it needs to be protected because state economies are dependent on its survival. The chapter refers to the 'reactive' rather than 'proactive' nature of responsible lending regimes, where responsible lending has been a reaction to the actual 'free market' failure that has occurred and does not seek to guard the consumer against other possible failures that might arise. The US focus on responsible lending for residential mortgages only, rather than on consumer credit more generally, is given as a clear example of this. Wilson also highlights the evidence in some responsible lending regimes of the 'responsibilization' of the consumer, whereby the regime focuses on irresponsible borrowing rather than on irresponsible lending. This is clearly the case with the South African regime, where a borrower's failure to make full and truthful disclosure of their financial position gives rise to a complete defence to creditors in response to any allegation of 'reckless' lending. Similarly, reference to 'creditworthiness' in the EU directives contains, it is argued, an implicit judgement of blameworthiness, which feeds 'responsibilization'. A major concern regarding the 'responsible borrower' approach is that it ignores both structural causes of over-indebtedness, including lack of real choice for some consumers, and theories of behavioural bias, which hold that consumers will display overoptimism and overconfidence when entering credit agreements. The chapter argues that an effective responsible lending regime should: (1) focus on responsible lending, rather than responsible borrowing, in order to avoid over-indebtedness; (2) focus on consumer credit in general, not limited to residential mortgage loans; (3) encourage flexible, individualized credit assessment practices; and (4) involve a regulatory agency charged with enforcement, which is adequately resourced to properly monitor and enforce compliance with market conduct regulation, including responsible lending obligations.

4 Possible future initiatives

Part IV concludes with four chapters that outline new approaches and directions for consumer credit regulation, in the wake of the global financial crisis. Eileen Webb's chapter on 'Extending Responsible Lending to Small Business: A "Consumer" Categorization?' argues that because of the vulnerable position in which small business borrowers can find themselves, consumer protections afforded to individual credit consumers should be extended to small business credit consumers. It is argued that this is particularly necessary in the wake of the global financial crisis, given the impact of the crisis on small businesses. Webb notes that small business borrowers in many jurisdictions, including Australia, are limited in terms of consumer protection and the legal avenues open to them to pursue lenders who behave in a manner which would give rise to legal action in the event of such conduct on the part of an individual consumer. In Australia, for example, small business borrowers are not protected by responsible lending provisions, variations in the event of hardship, or the opportunity to set aside an unjust transaction. The chapter considers arguments that small businesses be categorized as consumers for the purposes of consumer protection legislation. Notably, just as there is concern regarding intrusive regulation exacerbating financial exclusion for individuals who will find it harder to access credit, the same argument is made with respect to small businesses. The counterargument is that irresponsible lending is undesirable even if it does restrict choice, and Webb is puzzled by the resistance to this extension of regulation by the banks, which should have nothing to fear if their small business lending is already meeting the responsible lending criteria.

Given that small business is a significant employer and contributor to the economy, it should be supported, including through access to consumer credit protections, particularly where economies are struggling to recover from the global financial crisis. Certainly, to the extent that consumer protection has been about protecting vulnerable consumers from the excesses of the marketplace, those vulnerabilities can be identified in small business borrowers. Webb points out that this is not to say that a consumer needs to be constitutionally 'vulnerable' to be considered such, but rather that vulnerability is situational, and a small business is just as likely as an individual consumer to be situationally vulnerable when entering into a credit transaction.

In 'Innovating for "Safe Consumer Credit": Drawing on Product Safety Regulation to Protect Consumers of Credit' Luke Nottage notes that the 'free market' does not protect against risky products, and 'consumer choice' does not mean that risky products will be avoided. In the wake of the global financial crisis, Nottage calls for 'fundamental re-evaluations of the empirical and theoretical grounds for credit regulation', arguing that public regulation (as opposed to reliance on markets or private-law regulation through the courts) is justified where such consumer credit services are harmful, in the same way that public regulation is justified where tangible consumer products are unsafe. This is particularly relevant where there is a high probability of harm and grave consequences, as may be the case with short-term fringe credit products, such as payday loans.

One regulatory proposal is a requirement of disclosure of risk. Just as in some jurisdictions suppliers of goods must disclose to the regulator safety issues that arise with respect to their products, Nottage argues that 'consumer credit suppliers should disclose abnormal problems arising with their borrowers'. One example is where there are 'unusually high' (under industry standards) numbers of suicides or insolvencies among their borrowers. Such disclosure would then stimulate regulatory intervention – for example, an examination of lending practices and a consideration of whether obligations such as responsible lending have been breached. Nottage asserts that taking a 'more holistic approach to financial markets regulation – open to insights from various product markets, international experiences and theories – offers more hope for avoiding future global economic crises'.

In 'Bank–Community Development Finance Institution Partnerships as a Means for Addressing Financial Vulnerability' Justin Malbon considers the roles of Community Development Finance Institutions (CDFIs) and banks to address financial exclusion through a partnership model. CDFIs are not-for-profit financial institutions that exist for the social purpose of addressing financial exclusion, and in some jurisdictions they enjoy the support of banks through cross-sectoral partnership arrangements. Malbon argues that, to the extent that such partnerships currently rely on corporate social responsibility programmes within banks, they are unlikely to achieve the necessary scale to have a real impact, and policy-makers need to consider the issue of financial exclusion more broadly rather than settle on bank–CDFI partnerships as the solution.

Finally, in his chapter on 'Mortgage Racketeering: The American Home Mortgage Foreclosure Crisis and the UN Convention against Corruption', Christopher Peterson argues that it would be desirable to draw upon private sector anti-corruption regulation in considering mortgage industry reform. He outlines the business structure adopted by the American mafia and likens it to that adopted by the mortgage industry through its securitization model – a model that facilitates corruption. Peterson describes the mafia model whereby the risk of public law enforcement is overcome by isolating the mafia 'family' from that risk by using expendable 'soldiers' for illegal activity. The 'soldiers' or 'front-line participants' in mortgage securitization were the mortgage originators and mortgage brokers. Peterson argues that, like the front-line mafia soldiers who would expect to serve prison terms as part of their apprenticeships, the mortgage originators and brokers who breached underwriting standards and consumer protection laws expected to 'shed their corporate identity through insolvency ... only to reappear in another business form ... [and] the boom-and-bust cycle of mortgage originators allowed the home finance industry to discard origination companies that attracted the attention of law enforcement'. Peterson describes the disaggregation of responsibility and liability in mortgage lending through the complex arrangements between the many parties involved in these transactions.

Peterson refers to the UN Convention Against Corruption which in article 12, among other things, prohibits the establishment of 'off-the-books' accounts and the making of 'off-the books' or inadequately identified transactions. He notes that 'while the drafters of the UN Convention probably did not intend to include securitization within the scope of "off-the-books", it was precisely the off-balance-sheet nature of securitization that enabled thinly capitalized originators to churn out so many ill-advised loans'. The corruption-prone organizational structure of mortgage securitization is therefore worthy of regulatory attention.

5 Conclusion

Consumer credit regulation in Western liberal democracies continues to be conceptualized within a neoliberal, economic consumerist context. This brings with it a strong focus on consumer choice and the 'responsibilization' of the consumer through financial education and information disclosure. Just as these strategies have not served the cause of consumer protection well under national regulation, they are unlikely to effectively protect consumers under international strategies such as the G20 financial stability model. They certainly do not address the problem of financial exclusion, which at the very least requires a focus on protection from harmful, high-cost, exploitative credit products as well as strategies to overcome market discrimination against consumers who are perceived as 'unprofitable'.

This book analyses current responses to issues of consumer credit and over-indebtedness, and then explores possible regulatory responses that might sit outside the neoliberal model. Proactive consumer protection policies which seek to protect consumers from harm and move beyond 'choice', financial education and disclosure are essential if we are to avoid another global financial crisis.

PART II
International Context

Chapter 2

Continuity, not Rupture: The Persistence of Neoliberalism in the Internationalization of Consumer Finance Regulation

Toni Williams[1]

1 Introduction

The banking crisis that began in 2007 has disrupted dominant beliefs about the efficiency, resilience and the capacity for self-correction of global financial markets. These beliefs rested on assumptions that 'global financial firms', whatever their taste for risk, act rationally to ensure their survival; that the most significant threats to global financial stability stem from volatile 'emerging market economies'; and that policy-makers in rich economies have sufficient prescience and adequate policy tools to contain the fall-out when overinflated asset bubbles burst.[2]

Of particular interest to this chapter are the assumptions that dealings between financial firms and retail consumers of financial products and services, including credit, insurance, mortgages, savings and investments, are essentially private and parochial. These dealings are assumed to be private in that they advance the self-defined economic goals of individual consumers, producers and retail market intermediaries, rather than engage broader public or collective interests. They are assumed to be parochial in that the consumer interest in financial products – particularly credit and credit-related products – is thought to be limited and local in scope and purpose and, correspondingly, financial firms, however transnational their operations and cosmopolitan their brands, nonetheless are assumed to conduct their businesses as if each national market that they service were discrete, narrow and self-contained.[3] These assumptions of privacy and parochialism contributed

1   This chapter benefited substantially from the comments of colleagues at the Tasmania workshop from which this book is derived. I would also like to thank participants in the Regulation Discussion Group at the University of Oxford, whose comments and questions clarified some key elements of the argument and Iain Ramsay for his perceptive comments and criticisms. Responsibility for any remaining errors or misinterpretations is mine.

2   Peter Gowan 'Crisis in the Heartland' (2009) 55 New Left Review 5; Adair Turner, *The Turner Review: A Regulatory Response to the Global Banking Crisis* (FSA 2009).

3   Writing in 1999, Picciotto and Haines remarked on the persistence of local institutions, markets and traditions in globalized finance: Sol Picciotto and Jason Haines,

to a perspective that placed the regulation of consumer financial markets outside the remit of global financial policy-making.[4] This perspective persisted into the twenty-first century even as regional trading blocs such as the EU and international organizations such as the World Bank and the OECD adopted policies to advance the interests of financial firms in the widening and deepening of consumer finance markets.[5]

After rampant mortgage mis-selling in the US triggered a crisis with consequences that continue to reverberate around the world, the perspective on financial consumption and its regulation as a local and domestic matter, detached from the world of global financial policy-making, has increasingly appeared anachronistic. While much of the global debate about reforming the regulatory architecture of global finance focuses on conventional prudential regulatory techniques such as capital adequacy standards, surveillance and orderly resolution mechanisms for failed and failing firms, there has emerged a distinct strand of policy discussion about the contribution of financial consumer protection reform to the safety and soundness of the global financial system. At the November 2011 meeting of the G20, which is reported to have ended in 'bitter acrimony'

'Regulating Global Financial Markets' (1999) 26(3) Journal of Law and Society 351.

4   See, for example, Garicano's and Lastra's observation that '[f]inancial stability is the ultimate goal of supervision, regulation and crisis management. Yet, supervision is designed to meet other goals, too, such as consumer protection …': Luis Garicano and Rosa M Lastra, 'Towards a New Architecture for Financial Stability: Seven Principles, (2010) 13(3) Journal of International Economic Law 597.

5   In addition to its general consumer protection measures such as the directives on unfair terms in consumer contracts, (Directive 93/13/EEC) and unfair commercial practices (Directive 2005/29/EC), and its formal support for financial education, 'Communication from the Commission of 18 December 2007: Financial Education', COM(2007) 808, the EU has sought to harmonize regulatory arrangements and substantive norms of markets for consumer financial products: for example, Directive 2002/65/EC of 23 September 2002 concerning distance marketing of consumer financial services, Directive 2007/64/EC of 13 November 2007 on payment services in the internal market, Directive 2008/48/EC of 23 April 2008 on credit agreements for consumers, Directive 2002/92 on insurance mediation, and Directive 2004/39/EC of 21 April 2004 on markets in financial instruments and investment services. For examples of the OECD's pre-crisis policy oriented towards expanding markets for financial services, see the OECD's financial education project, summarized at: <http://www.oecd.org/document/42/0,3343, fr_2649_15251491_25696983_1_1_1_1,00.html> accessed 31 May 2012; OECD, *Open Markets Matter: The Benefits of Trade and Investment Liberalisation*, (OECD 1998); OECD, *GATS: The Case for Open Services Markets* (OECD 2002). For examples of the World Bank's work on market expansion, see Brigit Helms, *Access for All: Building Inclusive Financial Systems* (World Bank 2006); Anjali Kumar, *Access to Financial Services – Brazil* (World Bank 2005); and World Bank, *Good Practices for Consumer Protection and Financial Literacy in Europe and Central Asia – Consultative Draft* (World Bank 2008).

over the euro crisis of that year,[6] the leaders were nonetheless able to agree that 'integration of financial consumer protection policies into regulatory and supervisory frameworks contributes to strengthening financial stability'[7] and to approve a blueprint for global cooperation and development of consumer financial market regulation.[8]

This chapter analyses the arrival of financial consumer protection on the policy agenda of the G20 and considers the implications of this development for consumers of financial products and services. With its justification for consumer protection regulation framed in terms of securing global financial stability, the central goal of the G20's consumer protection work seems quite different from those of established projects of internationalizing consumer law, such as the objective stated in the UN General Assembly's 1985 'Guidelines for Consumer Protection': 'To facilitate production and distribution patterns responsive to the needs and desires of consumers.'[9] As this chapter shows, however, the relationship between the G20 model and national instruments of financial consumer protection tends to reflect continuity with with pre-crisis model rather than rupture.

Arguing that the G20's financial stability model represents further internationalization of a variant of a familiar neoliberal model of financial consumer protection,[10] the chapter questions the capacity of the financial stability model to shift contractual power from financial firms to consumers or, more generally, to benefit financial consumers. This question is explored through a case study of the regulation of payment protection or consumer credit insurance sales in two jurisdictions – Australia and the UK – that were early adopters of the neoliberal model of financial consumer protection. The case study shows that exploitation and mistreatment of financial consumers thrived in jurisdictions that had adopted the consumer protection model that is now undergoing internationalization under the umbrella of financial stability enhancement. This finding is a salutary reminder of the limited protection that the dominant market failure paradigm of neoliberalism offers financial consumers and serves also as a stimulus or invitation

---

6 For example, James Chapman, 'Euro Crisis Risks UK Double Dip, Warns PM as Global Leaders Break up amid Acrimony and Indecision' *Daily Mail* (5 November 2011) <http://www.dailymail.co.uk/news/article-2057835/Euro-crisis-risks-UK-double-dip-warns-PM-global-leaders-break-amid-acrimony-indecision.html#ixzz1gq5zZwYk>.

7 G20 Information Centre, *Cannes Summit Final Declaration: Building Our Common Future: Renewed Collective Action for the Benefit of All* (G20 Cannes Summit 2011).

8 OECD, *G20 High Level Principles on Financial Consumer Protection* (OECD 2011).

9 Objective 1(b) United Nations Guidelines for Consumer Protection 1985 A/RES/39/248.

10 This argument is developed in more depth in Iain Ramsay and Toni Williams, 'The Crash that Launched a Thousand Fixes – Regulation of Consumer Credit after the Lending Regulation and the Credit Crunch' in Kern Alexander and Niamh Moloney (eds), *Law Reform and Financial Markets* (Elgar Financial Law, Edward Elgar 2011).

to financial consumer protection scholars to imagine other regulatory institutions and practices that might do more to enhance the protection of financial consumers.

The next section of the chapter outlines central elements of the model of neoliberalism that appears in financial sector policy-making discourses and initiatives, including those of the G20. Section 3 then traces the entry of financial consumer protection on to the financial stability agenda of global policy-makers in the wake of the financial crisis. This section describes references to consumer protection in the declarations published at the end of the six crisis-driven driven summits of G20 leaders held from 2008 to 2011 and discusses the reports of the Financial Stability Board (FSB) and the Organization for Economic Cooperation and Development (OECD) on options and high-level principles for financial consumer protection that were endorsed by the G20 in November 2011.

Section 4 is the comparative case study on sales regulation of payment protection/consumer credit insurance in the UK and Australia. The case study outlines the normative architectures of consumer protection that the two jurisdictions have adopted and describes regulators' findings about the persistence of the problems that the regulation was intended to eliminate. The chapter concludes with reflections on the implications of the case study for thinking about the G20's financial stability model and a brief discussion about whether other reforms proposed by the G20 in furtherance of its financial stability objectives may potentially create new opportunities for the development of consumer finance regulation.

2 Elements of neoliberalism and its implications for consumer finance markets

A substantial theoretical and policy literature analyses neoliberalism in various ways: as epistemology, as ideology, as politics, as a programme of development, as institutional reform and as social and economic policy. In David Harvey's influential work, neoliberalism consists of political–economic practices based on the theory that 'human well-being can best be advanced by liberating individual entrepreneurial freedoms and skills within an institutional framework characterised by strong private property rights, free markets and free trade'.[11] This institutional framework is constituted by the freedoms and restraints created by the private-law norms of contract, tort and property and the competition law regimes that structure the ability of firms to grow and to dominate markets for their products. In addition to the work of creating and sustaining these institutions, which are the foundation of contract power in a market society, neoliberal states also have opened up new markets for suppliers of consumer financial products through strategies of privatizing and marketizing public services. These strategies have eviscerated the social services that comprised much of the social wage, and, when

---

11   David Harvey, *A Brief History of Neoliberalism* (OUP 2005).

coupled with the post 1970s stagnation of labour market incomes, have delivered financial consumers to firms as a new site of retail business opportunity for credit, insurance and savings products.[12]

One often-noted paradox of neoliberalism is the extent to which this ideology that 'holds the market sacred'[13] masks the active role of the state in constituting the conditions of market society. Neoliberalism thus contributes to a politics that privileges Hayekian claims about freedom and the spontaneity and self-regulating capacity of markets. Such claims not only emphasize the implicit disciplining of the individual by the market and the market by the individual, but also highlight both the optimism that neoliberal ideology once fostered about the capacity of the market to meet people's wants and the beliefs that it promoted in the desirability of a limited, apparently non-interventionist, role for the state in social and economic provisioning. Internalized by individuals and incorporated into human consciousness, neoliberalism's subordination of 'principles of social justice to those of perceived economic imperatives'[14] is thus understood not as a consequence of the elimination of social safety nets, but instead as a manifestation of consumer choice.

How neoliberalism shapes subjectivity and consciousness is a theme of the Foucauldian governmentality literature. Here, neoliberalism refers to decentred technologies of 'governing-at-a-distance'[15] and calculative rationalities that are deployed in meta-regulation – that is, regulating the 'conduct of conduct'.[16] This strand of neoliberal theorizing associates market tropes of entrepreneurialism and competition with the disciplining of individuals through risk, self-governance and responsibilization at a wide range of sites, including sexualities, bodies, families and professions as well as financial markets and products.[17] One of its central

---

12   Aldo Barba and Massimo Pivetti, 'Rising Household Debt: Its Causes and Macroeconomic Implications – a Long-period Analysis' (2009) 33(1) Cambridge Journal of Economics 113; Paulo L Dos Santos, 'On the Content of Banking in Contemporary Capitalism' (2009) 17 Historical Materialism 180.

13   Stephanie Lee Mudge, 'What is Neo-Liberalism?' (2008) 6(4) Socio-Economic Review 703.

14   Colin Hay, 'The Normalizing Role of Rationalist Assumptions in the Institutional Embedding of Neoliberalism' (2006) 33(4) Economy and Society 500.

15   David Garland, 'The Limits of the Sovereign State: Strategies of Crime Control in Contemporary Society' (1996) 36(4) British Journal of Criminology 445.

16   This phrase is usually attributed to Foucault, as his characterization of the core problem of the exercise of governmental power, but it is not easy to find in translated versions of his work. The French quotation is 'L'exercice du pouvoir consiste à "conduire des conduites"' in Michael Foucault, *Dits et écrits* IV (Gallimard 1994) 237. According to a post on the foucault.info website, an English version of the discussion is available in Michael Foucault, 'The Subject and the Power' in Hubert Dreyfus and Paul Rabinow (eds), *Michel Foucault: Beyond Structuralism and Hermeneutics* (University of Chicago Press 1982) 208.

17   See generally Nikolas Rose, 'Government, Authority and Expertise in Advanced Liberalism' (1993) 22(3) Economy and Society 283; Nikola Rose, *Powers of Freedom:*

contributions concerns the technologies of ruling or governance, especially as they shape individuals' sense of agency and their performance of decision-making. Viewed through this lens, the measures to improve financial literacy that have recently become policy priorities of international organizations, transnational firms and national governments appear as a neoliberal governance technology for responsibilizing individuals to manage the risk of economic insecurity and fostering a quasi-entrepreneurial subjectivity among financial consumers that enables the market to exert discipline over firms. Confident of their ability to protect themselves, neoliberalism's self-governing financial consumers are the ideal-type subjects of its imaginary competitive, resilient and disciplined markets.[18]

Just as the ideal-type financial consumer of neoliberalism may bear little resemblance to typical consumers of credit, insurance and savings products, with their behavioural quirks, biases and blinkers, so, too, may the financial firm operating in real consumer markets differ considerably from its neoliberal prototype. That prototype is the firm as 'price-taker', one among a multitude offering similar products and competing for the custom of discerning and informed financial consumers in a high-volume market with insignificant barriers to entry and exit. Neoclassical economic theory posits that firms cannot survive in such markets unless they offer products that consumers demand at attractive prices that consumers will pay. Acknowledging that successful firms are likely to grow, the theory, somewhat complacently, imagines the risk of domination as manageable through competition-enhancing regulation that encourages the entry of other firms and fosters an economy of active, assertive and capable consumers who continuously search, compare, switch and complain.

In practice, consumer financial markets under neoliberalism may be constituted quite differently from the neoclassical model, for several reasons. Many consumer finance products are long-term, complex and opaque, often possessing 'experience' or 'credence' characteristics such that consumers are unable to observe the quality – and sometimes the price – before obtaining and 'consuming' the products. Exploiting this unobservability and the unequal holding of other pertinent information, financial firms may market consumer finance products as highly differentiated, thwarting the comparisons that are the basis of competitive market discipline.[19] In any event, consumers may be unlikely to exert discipline because their transactions with financial firms are occasional purchases and consumer

---

Reframing Political Thought (CUP 1999); Wendy Larner, 'Neo-liberalism: Policy, Ideology, Governmentality' (2000) 63 Studies in Political Economy 5.

18   This point is elaborated in more detail in Toni Williams, 'Empowerment of Whom and for What? Financial Literacy Education and the New Regulation of Consumer Financial Services' (2007) 29(2) Law & Policy 226. See also Ramsay and Williams, 'The Crash that Launched a Thousand Fixes' (n 10).

19   This point is elaborated in Steffen Huck, London Economics et al, *Consumer Behavioural Biases in Competition: A Survey of the Office of Fair Trading* (OFT 2011) 1.11.

decision-making is vulnerable to behavioural biases.[20] Finally, consumer finance markets are dominated by giant transnational firms whose distribution networks may operate as entry barriers protecting them against competition, whose political influence may secure firm-friendly ground rules for the markets they supply, and whose organizational power over the design, marketing and contractual terms of financial products enables them to subordinate the consumer interest to those of the firm's managers and shareholders.[21]

Crouch's illuminating analysis of neoliberalism advances the thesis that 'actually existing ... neoliberalism is nothing like as devoted to free markets as is claimed. It is, rather, devoted to the dominance of public life by the giant corporation'[22] – that is, the firm that is active in multiple jurisdictions and 'sufficiently dominant within its markets to be able to influence the terms of those markets by its own actions, using its organizational capacity to develop market-dominating strategies'.[23] The ability of the giant corporation to influence governments and, through them, the regulation of markets by regime shopping, lobbying, networking and political campaign funding has been well documented in political economy research since the early years of neoliberal restructuring.[24] Studies of international business law and regulation have explored the ways in which giant firms may participate in international standard-setting and norm development processes as non-state actors in fields such as corporate governance,

---

20   There is a considerable literature on this topic. The Huck study, ibid, provides a recent thematic literature review, which also links behavioural biases to the conditions under which 'competition' may be harmful to real consumers, as opposed to the agents in the economic models.

21   On competition problems and large firm dominance of UK markets for important consumer finance products, see Don Cruickshank, *Competition in UK Banking: A Report to the Chancellor of the Exchequer* (HMSO 2000); *Office of Fair Trading, Personal Current Accounts in the UK: An OFT Market Study* (OFT 2008); Office of Fair Trading, *Review of Barriers to Entry, Expansion and Exit in Retail Banking* (OFT 2010); Andrew Tyrie, *Competition and Choice in Retail Banking: Ninth Report of Session 2010–11*, Vol. 1: *Report, Together with Formal Minutes* (The Stationery Office 2010); Cruickshank reported a Herfindahl-Hirschmann Index market concentration score for current accounts of 1,330. By 2007 the index score had risen to 1,410 and in 2010 it was reported to be 1,736. According to recent OFT/Competition Commission (CC) merger guidelines, a market with an HHI measure exceeding 1,000 could be characterized as 'concentrated' whilst a market with HHI measures exceeding 2,000 could be characterized as 'highly concentrated': Tyrie (2010) 12.

22   Colin Crouch, *The Strange Non-Death of Neoliberalism* (Polity 2011), preface p. viii.

23   Ibid 49.

24   See, for example, Martin Rhodes, '"Subversive liberalism"': Market integration, globalization and the European welfare state' (1995) 2(3) Journal of European Public Policy 384; Anne Gray, 'New labour – new discipline' (1998) 20 (65) Capital & Class 1; for a contemporary overview of this literature see Crouch The Strange Non-Death of Neoliberalism (n 22).

environmental law and labour law,[25] and the problem of regulating firms that are 'too-big-to-fail' currently preoccupies financial-sector policy-makers. Relatively little scholarly attention has been paid to the role of giant financial firms in the regulation and governance of consumer finance markets, however, and this may be indicative of the power of the assumptions about the privacy and parochialism of transactions in these markets.

Giant firm dominance of particular financial consumer markets may result in classic oligopolistic practices, including tacit collusion among suppliers and the supply of high-priced, low-value products, as, for example, in the UK's doorstep lending market.[26] But the complexity and opacity of consumer financial transactions create additional opportunities for giant firms to deploy their organizational capacity to dominate financial consumers through product development, marketing and sales processes, and product characteristics such as excessive fees, hidden charges and unfair terms.[27] That same organizational capacity also allows giant financial firms to build their reputational capital and establish the network externalities that keep entry barriers high. Such entry barriers may not be insurmountable by other transnational giants and smaller firms that are able to find a niche, but new entrants have little incentive to disrupt the 'firm-friendly' structure and practices of a market equilibrium that generates large surpluses to providers of financial products. Consequently, in a market where established practice has become organized around firms taking advantage of information asymmetry and exploiting consumers' short-term biases – typical problems in retail finance markets – competition may have the effect of further embedding domination by financial firms.[28]

---

25   For recent case studies and theoretical contributions that illustrate a variety of analytical and critical approaches, see, for example, Ben Cashore, Graeme Auld and Deanna Newsom, *Governing Through Markets: Forest Certification and the Emergence of Non-State Authority* (Yale University Press 2004); Magali A Delmas and Oran R Young, *Governance for the Environment: New Perspectives* (Cambridge University Press 2009); Walter Mattli and Ngaire Woods, *The Politics of Global Regulation* (Princeton University Press 2009); Luc Fransen, *Corporate Social Responsibility and Global Labor Standards: Firms and Activists in the Making of Private Regulation* (Routledge 2012); Peter Utting, Darryl Reed et al, *Business Regulation and Non-State Actors: Whose Standards? Whose Development?* (Routledge 2012).

26   Competition Commission, *Home Credit Market Investigation* (Competition Commission 2006).

27   Dos Santos, 'On the Content of Banking in Contemporary Capitalism' (n 12); *Office of Fair Trading v Abbey National plc and Others* [2009] UKSC 6, [2009] EWCA 116, [2008] EWHC 875 (Comm).

28   The essence of the analysis, which is a variant of Akerlof's 'market for lemons', is that in such a market a 'good corporate citizen' firm is unable reliably to signal to consumers that its products offer consumers better value: Michael Barr, Sendhil Mullainathan and Eldar Shafir, *Behaviorally Informed Financial Regulation* (New America Foundation 2008); Huck et al, *Consumer Behavioural Biases in Competition* (n 20); George Akerlof,

The findings of a 2008 market study of UK personal current accounts market illustrate the persistence of a firm-friendly equilibrium in a 'moderately concentrated' market populated by four giant firms (according to Crouch's definition) supplying 65 per cent of current accounts and some 18 smaller banks.[29] This study showed how the banks exploited product complexity and opacity to focus consumers' attention and competition 'almost exclusively on more visible fees', such as monthly fees and ATM charges, when most of their revenues from current accounts are generated by lower-visibility costs to consumers such as foregone interest and insufficient funds charges.[30] These bank revenues were substantial, estimated at £8.3 billion in 2006 or £152 per active bank account, higher than the combined revenues from credit cards and savings accounts, and the banks targeted insufficient funds charges 'as an attractive way to generate additional revenue without affecting demand for their accounts'.[31] Moreover, this firm-friendly equilibrium occurred and was sustained in a market for a financial product that is widely held by consumers and, as such, relatively familiar to them and in a market in which the study found some degree of competition. It is thus no surprise that market studies of less widely held consumer finance products, where firms may exercise even greater control over product development and marketing, have found evidence of extremely high revenues, firm-friendly equilibria and other indications of financial firms' dominance over consumers.[32]

Several important contributions to consumer law and policy literature critically examine the application of ideas stemming from neoliberalism theory to consumer transactions, particularly the theoretical construction of the confident capable consumer as sovereign of the competitive market, but there has been little engagement with the general implications of neoliberal models of the economy

---

'The Market for "Lemons": Quality Uncertainty and the Market Mechanism' (1970) 84 Quarterly Journal of Economics 488.

29   Office of Fair Trading, *Personal Current Accounts in the UK: an OFT Market Study* (OFT 2008).

30   Ibid. 'In 2006 the aggregate revenue of banks from current accounts was approximately £8.3 billion. PCAs generate more revenue for banks than savings and credit cards combined: 31 per cent compared with 17 per cent and 13 per cent respectively. Banks earned over 85 per cent of their revenues on PCAs from two sources: net interest income from credit and debit balances (£4.6 billion), and levying charges associated with insufficient funds (£2.6 billion)': Executive Summary 3.

31   The OFT report cites to anonymized bank 'internal documents on the level of charges that include statements such as: "in order to maximise fee revenue, whilst maintaining our competitive position, selective increases in [insufficient funds charges] are proposed", and "Increasing [insufficient funds] charges will have less impact on our marketing position ... due to its lower visibility".' Ibid: Executive Summary footnote 8.

32   Office of Fair Trading, Review of High Cost Credit (OFT 2010); Competition Commission, *Home Credit Market Investigation* (n 25).

for the structuring of consumer markets.[33] A recent contribution by Ramsay and Williams responds to this gap with an analysis of the core institutions associated with the recent international project of restructuring consumer credit markets: credit bureaux, disclosure obligations on firms, financial literacy initiatives for consumers and financial ombudsmen.[34] According to their advocates, which include the World Bank and the OECD, these four institutions, taken together, will strengthen consumer confidence and equip them with the requisite information resources and decision-making skills to exert marked disciplinary pressures on firms. In markets dominated by giant firms, however, credit bureaux may facilitate market segmentation through the targeting of consumers who will pay excessive charges and fees; product disclosure may be used to deceive, confuse and mislead; and financial education may consist of little more than disguised product marketing that exacerbates consumers' behavioural biases.[35]

This brief overview of neoliberalism theory illuminates its key elements as a form of regulatory restructuring that positions the market – conceived as a 'non-political, non-cultural, machine like entity'[36] – as the supreme, if not exclusive, mode of social organization, and deliberately deploys law and regulation to facilitate market expansion, including measures that ostensibly aim to strengthen the market's capacity to discipline firms. Notwithstanding this apparent commitment to the tenets of competition, neoliberalism's consumer finance markets may be dominated by the giant transnational firm, no longer performing simply as an anonymous actor on the supply side of the market as per neoclassical models of competition, but instead emerging as a distinctive resource-allocating economic agent that may act as rival to. and collaborator with, both the market and the state.[37]

---

33   For critical analysis of the concept of the confident consumer see, for example, Thomas Wilhelmsson, 'The Abuse of the "Confident Consumer" as a Justification for EC Consumer Law' (2004) 27(3) Journal of Consumer Policy 317. A search for the term 'neoliberalism' in the online database of the flagship Journal of Consumer Policy generated only 15 instances of authors using the terms 'neo-liberal' or 'neoliberal', and in most instances the reference was fleeting such that it did not even warrant a sources citation. A search of the Hein online database of legal scholarship generated 25 sources that included the terms 'neoliberal', 'law' and 'consumer', but most of the articles are about neoliberalism's purported transformation of the individual from 'citizen' into 'consumer' rather than consumer law.

34   Ramsay and Williams, 'The Crash that Launched a Thousand Fixes' (n 10).

35   See discussion and references in Ronald Mann, *Charging Ahead: The Growth and Regulation of Credit Card Markets* (Cambridge University Press 2006); Lauren Willis, 'Against Financial Literacy Education' (2008) 94 Iowa Law Review 197; Steffen Huck and Jidong Zhou, 'Consumer Behavioural Biases in Competition: A Survey' (2011) *Working Papers 11–16*, New York University; Ramsay and Williams, 'The Crash that Launched a Thousand Fixes' (n 10).

36   Mudge, 'What is Neo-liberalism?' (n 13).

37   Crouch *The Strange Non-Death of Neoliberalism* (n 22).

3 Incorporation of consumer protection into the global financial stability policy agenda

Towards a financial stability model of consumer protection: the G20 summits

Between November 2008 and November 2011, the leaders of the G20 states held six summit meetings on the resolution of the financial crisis and regulatory reforms to prevent the recurrence of such a large-scale economic collapse. These meetings marked something of a shift in the geopolitical order, as the self-assumed global economic leadership shifted from the G7 to a larger, albeit still exclusive, association of 19 rich and middle-income countries plus the EU.[38] Over the course of these summits the G20 leaders developed a scheme of regulatory restructuring that aligns financial consumer protection regulation with global financial stability goals. This alignment departs from historical justifications of consumer protection as contesting the distribution of market power or responding to consumer vulnerability. Elements of this alignment bear more than a passing resemblance, however, to the pre-crisis neoliberalization of consumer protection, with its framing of problems in consumer markets as remediable failures correctable through competition and information remedies.

All but one of the summit communiqués link the enhancement of financial consumer protection to the international diffusion of regulation to strengthen the financial sector and improve financial stability. But there is no elaboration of the standards, institutions and practices that a financial stability model of financial consumer protection entails until after the Seoul summit at the end of 2010. Nonetheless, it is useful to briefly review key elements of the earlier summits as

---

38 The G20 was established after the late 1990s crises in Asia, Brazil and Russia, on the assumption that the major threat to global financial stability emanates from fast-growing emerging economies. The idea was to open up dialogue between these economies and the established global behemoths of the G7/8. The membership is Argentina, Australia, Brazil, Canada, China, France, Germany, India, Indonesia, Italy, Japan, Mexico, Russia, Saudi Arabia, South Africa, South Korea, Turkey, the United Kingdom, the United States and the EU, as represented by the presidents of the European Council and the European Central Bank. That this broader membership has not answered the significant questions about the legitimacy of this type of global governance institution is evidenced by the violent state reactions to protest at the sites of G20 meetings. For discussion and analysis of the violence at the Toronto 2010 summit see Debra Parkes and Meaghan Daniel, 'Political Protest, Mass Arrests, and Mass Detention: Fundamental Freedoms and (Un) Common Criminals' (2012) http://ssrn.com/abstract=2038359. These questions have become more urgent since the G20 arrogated to itself the role of global and economic policy-maker. For differing evaluations of this geopolitical role see Susanne Soederberg, 'The Politics of Representation and Financial Fetishism: The Case of the G20 Summits' (2010) 31(4) Third World Quarterly 523; and Douglas Arner, 'Adaptation and Resilience in Global Financial Regulation' (2011) 89 North Carolina Law Review, 101.

this political and institutional setting provides the context for the model of financial consumer protection that the G20 ultimately endorsed at the Paris 2011 summit.[39]

At the first crisis summit held in Washington in November 2008, a scant two months after the bankruptcy of Lehman Brothers and amidst bank rescue operations in the US, the UK and other Western states, the leaders declared their faith in the capacity of the neoliberal model of economic development to achieve their goals of global growth and financial-sector reform. The summit declaration reports 'a shared belief [in] market principles, open trade and investment regimes,'[40] and 'a commitment to free market principles, including the rule of law, respect for private property, open trade and investment, competitive markets and efficient, effectively regulated financial systems'.[41] Responding to the 'global scope' of financial markets, the leaders agree on a need for international coordination over their regulation, but this need is juxtaposed to the assertion that '[r]egulation is first and foremost the responsibility of national regulators who constitute the first line of defense against market instability'.[42] Thus, the global regulatory approach is to be institutionalized through regulatory cooperation and consistent implementation within the neoliberal paradigm rather than through an international treaty organization such as the WTO.[43] In aid of cooperation and consistency, the global leaders commit to ensuring that regulatory restructuring in their home jurisdictions 'supports market discipline, avoids potentially adverse impacts on other countries, including regulatory arbitrage, and supports competition, dynamism and innovation in the marketplace'.[44]

Financial consumer protection makes a fleeting appearance in the Washington summit declaration as an element of 'integrity in financial markets', one of five principles of financial markets reform that the leaders undertake to pursue,[45] but it is not elaborated in the summit's work plan or follow-up action points.

---

39   For a comprehensive account of the development of the entire financial regulatory restructuring agenda through the first five summits, see Arner, 'Adaptation and Resilience in Global Financial Regulation' (n 37); for a more critical analysis of the summits, see Soederberg, 'The Politics of Representation and Financial Fetishism' (n 37).

40   G20, 'Declaration of the G20 Summit on Financial Markets and the World Economy' (G20 Summit, Washington, 2008).

41   Ibid para 12.

42   Ibid para 8.

43   Ibid para 8. For discussion of a more integrated and formal structure for international regulation of global finance, see Lance Taylor and John Eatwell, Global Finance at Risk: The Case for International Regulation (Polity Press 2000); Luis Garicano and Rosa Lastra, 'Towards a New Architecture for Financial Stability: Seven Principles' (2010) 13(3) Journal of International Economic Law 597.

44   G20, 'Declaration of the G20 Summit on Financial Markets and the World Economy' (n 39) para 8.

45   Ibid. The other principles endorsed by statement are: strengthening transparency and accountability, enhancing sound regulation, reinforcing international cooperation and reforming international financial institutions.

Initiatives that are highlighted for further development, however, include reforms that potentially may have important consequences for financial consumers such as the measures to increase regulatory surveillance of the so-called systemically important financial institutions (SIFIs), the giant financial firms whose failures may have destabilizing effects on the global economy. This aspect of the summit declaration and follow-up action plans focuses on safeguards against the macro-prudential and spill-over risks posed by global SIFIs rather than on their conduct in consumer finance markets. Nonetheless, the intensification of SIFI supervision creates a new international site of regulatory practice at which to engage with the protection of financial consumers against the giant financial firms.

In April 2009 the G20 leaders met in London to agree a 'Global Plan for Recovery and Reform'. Characterizing the financial crisis as 'the greatest challenge to the world economy in modern times',[46] the summit declares that the leaders' goals of 'sustainable globalisation and rising prosperity for all' are to be achieved through 'an open world economy based on market principles, effective regulation, and strong global institutions'.[47] Consumer protection appears on a laundry list of measures to improve stability through strengthening financial regulation, but again there is no substantive discussion of regulatory measures or institutions or of how financial consumer protection relates to other dimensions of strengthened financial regulation.[48] This lack of development of the consumer protection goal is striking because this summit's declaration tempers the leaders' support for a neoliberal 'open world economy based on market principles' with commitments on job growth, social protection of the poorest and most economically vulnerable populations, and sustainable economic development.[49] Omitted from these distributional aspirations, financial consumer protection remains but a minor theme of the summit's proposals to stabilize and strengthen the global financial system.

There appears to be more enthusiasm for international regulatory norms at the London summit than in Washington in that the summit declaration characterizes strong domestic regulatory systems as necessary, but not sufficient, to ensure global stability. Thus, the leaders supplement their commitments to 'much greater consistency and systematic cooperation between countries' with an agreement to establish 'the framework of internationally agreed high standards that a global financial system requires'.[50] In part to facilitate consistency, cooperation and international agreement on global standards, the G20 decided to rename and

---

46   G20, 'The Global Plan for Recovery and Reform' (G20 Summit. London, 2009).

47   Ibid para 3.

48   'Regulators and supervisors must protect consumers and investors, support market discipline, avoid adverse impacts on other countries, reduce the scope for regulatory arbitrage, support competition and dynamism and keep pace with innovation in the marketplace' (para 14).

49   Ibid paras 25–28.

50   Ibid para 14.

reform the Financial Stability Forum, another organization established after the financial crises of the late 1990s. Now called the Financial Stability Board (FSB), this international financial policy think-tank and standard-setter has been endowed with a larger membership and a strengthened mandate to enhance its capacity to promote global financial stability policies.[51] As well as taking on general functions of researching risks, vulnerabilities and regulatory standards in the global financial system, facilitating information exchange and collaborating with regulatory standard-setters, the FSB acquired responsibility for selecting the global SIFIs (G-SIFIs) that warrant special regulatory surveillance, and for supporting the international supervisory colleges that serve as G-SIFI regulators, including through the creation of guidelines.[52]

By the time of the September 2009 Pittsburgh summit, the G20 leaders, buoyed by IMF predictions of 3 per cent economic growth in 2010,[53] felt sufficient optimism to describe the global economy as in transition 'from crisis to recovery'[54] and, building on that perceived success, to 'designate the G-20 as the premier forum for our international economic cooperation'.[55] After discussing the matters on which the leaders believed G20 initiatives to have resulted in 'substantial progress' on strengthening the global financial system (prudential oversight, risk management in financial firms, transparency, market integrity, international cooperation and the SIFIs' supervisory college scheme), the summit communiqué acknowledges that financial consumer protection, while still on the agenda of financial stability reform, remains an area in which 'far more needs to be done'.[56] But, once again, the leaders' commitment seems largely aspirational as there is no indication that further action is under consideration to improve the regulation of financial consumer protection or align it with other elements of the global financial system.

Notably, the Pittsburgh summit declaration refers to consumer protection and financial services a second time in its discussion of the G20's economic development objectives. In furtherance of these objectives, the leaders agreed to launch a Financial Inclusion Experts Group and pledged to increase the poor's access to sustainable scalable financial services.[57] This pledge and its associated

---

51   G20, 'The Global Plan for Recovery and Reform' (n 45). The FSB membership includes the FSF the G20 countries, Spain and the European Commission. For information about the work of the FSB see <http://www.financialstabilityboard.org>.

52   Ibid.

53   G20, 'Leaders Statement: The Pittsburgh Summit' (G20 Summit. Pittsburgh, 2009) in reference to International Monetary Fund; IMF, 'World Economic Outlook, Sustaining the Recovery' (IMF 2009).

54   G20, 'Leaders Statement: The Pittsburgh Summit' (n 52).

55   Ibid para 50.

56   Douglas Arner and Joseph Norton, 'Building a Framework to Address Failure of Complex Global Financial Institutions' (2009) 39 Hong Kong Law Journal 95.

57   Ibid. The role of the Financial Inclusion Experts Group is to 'identify lessons learned on innovative approaches to providing financial services to these groups, promote

infrastructure of cooperation with the International Financial Corporation of the World Bank and the Consultative Group to Assist the Poor (CGAP), illustrates continuity with the pre-crisis neoliberal project of expanding markets for financial services, especially through micro-finance programmes.[58] The G20's endorsement of this project is particularly striking in light of the growing evidence of individual and household over-indebtedness problems generated by micro-finance programmes.[59] In contrast to the over-indebtedness created through the non-micro-financial systems of rich countries, however, a high level of debt among micro-finance users in poor countries is not constructed as potentially destabilizing in its effects on global finance, which perhaps accounts for the G20's lack of attention to the risks to micro-finance users of its market expansion policies.

The Toronto summit declaration of June 2010 does not mention protection of financial consumers. But the leaders' agreement on the 'four pillars' of financial-sector reform to improve resilience and stability outlines an institutional framework for regulation that may be significant to the future development of international regulatory arrangements on financial consumer protection.[60] The first reform pillar imagines interjurisdictional policy transfer through international adoption of model regulatory standards, a model that is fairly typical of the international policy networks of neoliberal globalization. The other pillars focus on the implementation and enforcement of the higher standards through the activation of meta-regulatory processes affecting firms and national regulatory orders. Thus, the leaders pledged to enhance the capacities of domestic supervisors and regulators to oversee financial markets and firms, including their capacities 'proactively to identify and address risks' and to intervene early and effectively.[61] They agreed to strengthen international peer review and assessment of national regulatory systems and financial sectors through the established IMF/World Bank Financial Sector Assessment Programme and to enhance their capacity for mutual surveillance of financial-sector regulation in their own states through the

---

successful regulatory and policy approaches and elaborate standards on financial access, financial literacy, and consumer protection.'

58   See, for example, Anjali Kumar, *Access to Financial Services in Brazil* (World Bank Publications 2005); Brigit Helms, *Access for All : Building Inclusive Financial Systems* (World Bank Publications 2006); Ash Demirgüç-Kunt and Thorsten Beck, *Finance for All? Policies and Pitfalls in Expanding Access* (World Bank Publications 2008).

59   See, for example, David Hulme, 'Is Microdebt Good for Poor People? A Note on the Dark Side of Microfinance' in Thomas Dichter and Malcolm Harper (eds), What's Wrong with Microfinance? (Practical Action Publishing 2007) 19–22; Malcolm Harper (ed), *Microfinance: Evolution, Achievements and Challenges* (Practical Action Publishing 2003); Jessica Schicks, 'Microfinance Over-indebtedness: Understanding its Drivers and Challenging the Common Myths' (2010) Bruxelles: Centre Emilee Bergheim, Solvay School of Business, CEB Working Paper (10/048).

60   G20, 'G20 Toronto Summit Declaration' (G20 Summit, Toronto 2010).

61   Ibid para 20.

creation of new FSB thematic and country peer review processes.[62] The remaining pillar concerns further expansion of SIFI regulation, with a particular focus on developing a regime for resolving the failure of a SIFI without further increasing moral hazard or national government liabilities as lender of last resort. Instructing the FSB to develop concrete policy recommendations on these matters, the G20 reiterates the need for 'more intensive supervision' and welcomes the development of transnational 'supervisory colleges' for SIFI institutions.[63]

By contrast with Toronto, the Seoul summit in November 2010 identified consumer protection as part of a category of financial-sector reforms that required more work and policy development.[64] However, there is still no connection between the emerging financial stability model of consumer protection and the G20's initiatives on financial inclusion and access to finance for the poorest, as the leaders continue to associate the latter exclusively with their development programme rather than with financial stability. To develop the new financial stability model of consumer protection beyond its earlier aspirational commitments, the Seoul summit instructed global policy-makers, specifically the

---

62   Ibid Annex II, paras 33–36.

63   Ibid Annex 2, paras 18–19. The Basel Committee on Banking Standards defines supervisory colleges as 'multilateral working groups of relevant supervisors that are formed for the collective purpose of enhancing effective consolidated supervision of an international banking group on an ongoing basis' (2010) 'Good Practice Principles on Supervisory Colleges', Basel, Bank for International Settlements. Informal supervisory colleges have existed for some time. Despite some notorious examples of failure of informal colleges such as Bank of Credit and Commerce International (BCCI), which was shut down by regulators on the discovery of systemic internal fraud, the crisis has sparked considerable interest among policy-makers in formalizing and extending supervisory college arrangements. Within the EU the role of supervisory colleges was recently strengthened under the CRD II amendments to the Capital Requirements Directive in Directive 2009/111/EC. In force since December 2010, these amendments require colleges of supervisors to be established to regulate banking groups that operate in multiple European countries: Article 33 of Directive 2009/111/EC, inserting article 131a into Directive 2006/48/EC. The amending directive also required the Committee of European Banking Supervisors to develop guidelines for the 'operational functioning of supervisory colleges'. These were published in June 2010 and are available at: <http://www.eba.europa.eu/Supervisory-Colleges/Publications/CEBS-guidelines-for-the-operational-functioning-of.aspx>. For general analysis of the role of supervisory colleges, see Duncan Alford, 'Supervisory Colleges: The Global Financial Crisis and Improving International Supervisory Coordination' (2010) 24 Emory Int'l L Rev. 57; Rolf Weber, 'Multilayered Governance in International Financial Regulation and Supervision' (2010) 13(3) Journal of International Economic Law 683.

64   Other aspects of financial stability that were similarly regarded as warranting more attention are the regulatory tools and policy frameworks of 'macro-prudential' regulation, the distinct financial stability and regulatory reform needs of emerging market and developing economies, regulation and oversight of shadow banking and commodity derivatives markets' and 'generally improving financial market integrity and efficiency': G20, 'The G20 Seoul Summit Leaders' Declaration' (G20 Summit, Seoul 2010).

OECD and the FSB, 'to explore, and report back by the next summit, on options to advance consumer finance protection'.[65] Tellingly, the G20 spelt out its view of the appropriate means of advancing consumer finance protection, these being neoliberalism's conventional consumer market remedies of 'informed choice that includes disclosure, transparency and education; protection from fraud, abuse and errors; and recourse and advocacy'.[66] The policy development instructions were amplified at the February 2011 meeting of G20 finance ministers and central bank governors, which, at the request of the French G20 presidency, asked the FSB and OECD to supplement the options paper with draft 'common principles' of financial consumer protection.[67]

The Cannes summit of 2011 was held in the shadow of the euro crisis and growing austerity in many rich countries. Unable to agree on a response to the economic turmoil in Europe, this summit did little to enhance the credibility of the G20's claims to be the 'premier forum for international economic cooperation' and a site to 'generate the political agreement necessary to tackle the challenges of global economic interdependence'.[68] With respect to the financial-sector reform programme, however, there was some common ground. In the G20's most explicit statement to date about consumer protection, the leaders agreed that 'integration of financial consumer protection policies into regulatory and supervisory frameworks contributes to strengthening financial stability'.[69] They also endorsed the reports they had received on stocktaking and options to advance financial consumer protection and on proposed high-level principles.[70] More specifically, the leaders undertook 'to pursue the full application of these principles in our jurisdictions' and also to monitor their progress on implementing the new measures at future G20 summits.[71]

The financial stability model of financial consumer protection: options and principles

The OECD and FSB split up the policy development work assigned to them by the G20 leaders, with the OECD taking on the task of formulating 'high-level' consumer protection principles and the FSB investigating existing institutional

---

65   Ibid.

66   Ibid.

67   Finance Ministers and Central Bank Governors of the G20, 'Communiqué', 18–19 February 2011, available at <http://www.g20.org/Documents2011/02/COMMUNI QUE-G20_MGM%20_18-19_February_2011.pdf>, para 6.

68   G20,'Cannes Summit Final Declaration: Building our Common Future: Renewed Collective Action for the Benefit of All' (G20 Summit, Cannes 2011) para 91.

69   Ibid para 33.

70   Financial Stability Board, 'Consumer Finance Protection with Particular Focus on Credit' (Financial Stability Board 2011); OECD, 'G20 High-Level Principles on Financial Consumer Protection' (OECD 2011).

71   G20, 'Cannes Summit Final Declaration' (n 67).

arrangements for financial consumer protection across the G20 and examining options for their further development.[72] Defining its scope quite narrowly, the FSB focused its work on consumer credit regulation, including residential mortgages, leaving stocktaking and policy research on other important consumer finance products, including insurance, current accounts and savings products, for the future.[73] Options were researched by surveying regulators and policy-makers in FSB member states and through discussions with international organizations, such as the Network of Financial Consumer Regulators (FinCoNet) and the World Bank Global Program on Consumer Protection and Financial Literacy, about their financial consumer protection initiatives.[74] There was some consultation with consumer groups about key issues, best practices and the role of international coordination, and the same groups were consulted on a preliminary draft.[75]

The FSB reported on the take-up of particular consumer protection standards, such as responsible lending, disclosure guidelines, product intervention, and complaints and dispute resolution as well as on the institutional arrangements for delivering financial consumer protection across the G20. Although the FSB found 'numerous national and international initiatives' to strengthen financial consumer protection in different countries,[76] it also observed considerable variation in institutional arrangements and in their capacity to protect consumers. Financial regulators and supervisors in several G20 jurisdictions lacked knowledge and expertise in the field of consumer protection, few had a specific consumer protection mandate and they seldom seemed to interact professionally with consumer market regulators or representatives of financial consumers. Conversely, consumer market regulators who possessed the requisite knowledge and skills to respond to unfair and exploitative practices that harm consumer interests would typically play only a small role in monitoring and supervising consumer finance markets in many G20 countries.

In terms of substantive consumer protection measures, the FSB found that norms such as responsible lending and product feature disclosure are widely adopted, while other standards such as product benchmarks, suitability indicators and disclosure of incentive compensation schemes used by firms in retail markets are found more rarely.[77] On the basis of these findings the FSB recommended more

---

72   Financial Stability Board, 'Consumer Finance Protection' (n 69).
73   Ibid.
74   Ibid.
75   Ibid.
76   Ibid 19.
77   Thus, the report notes at p. 2 that: 'Consumer protection authorities use a broad range of regulatory and supervisory tools, which generally include promoting responsible lending practices and providing disclosure guidelines. More work could be done to ensure consumer protection authorities are equipped with the necessary supervisory tools while at the same time ensuring that sufficient information is being provided to consumers. Some areas where more work might be needed are: (i) establishing indicators of unsuitable product features; (ii) aligning and disclosing incentive compensation arrangements; and

research into the less common regulatory instruments as well as further work to improve the institutional arrangements for financial consumer protection, focusing in particular on the mandates, accountability, authority and capabilities, tools and resources of supervisors and regulators.[78] To help close the gap between financial supervisors and consumer protection authorities in the many jurisdictions where these functions are separated, the FSB report recommends the empowering of an international organization of consumer protection regulators to provide leadership and expertise on global financial consumer protection measures. This organization should have 'a clear mandate and adequate capacity [to] help maintain the international momentum on consumer protection; strengthen the connection with domestic developments; facilitate engagement with consumer advocacy groups and other stakeholders; and steer the work in a productive direction'.[79] The FSB also indicated that the new organization should serve as 'a global platform for consumer protection authorities to exchange views on experiences as well as lessons learnt from the crisis' and, as such, 'help to strengthen consumer protection polices across the FSB membership and beyond'.[80]

The high-level principles developed by the OECD are framed by its well-established neoliberal perspective that views the expansion of consumer financial markets as an aspect of generating economic growth.[81] This perspective sees consumer protection primarily in terms of strengthening confidence and trust in financial markets, so that consumers will buy more financial products and make wiser purchasing decisions; and it advocates the integration of consumer protection regulation with financial literacy and financial inclusion policies that also aim to expand consumption of personal finance products. Responding to a crisis that was triggered and exacerbated by overexpansion of consumer credit, the OECD adapted this perspective to the G20's concerns about the destabilizing effects of firms' market-expanding practices in consumer financial markets. This adaptation is reflected in an approach that continues the OECD's preference for market-enabling regulation in the form of information-based consumer rights and remedies but takes some account of the institutional context of consumer finance markets and the organizational cultures of the firms that populate them. Thus, the ten high-level principles combine elements of the neoliberal model of consumer protection that the OECD and World Bank were engaged in internationalizing as the crisis struck, with provisions about the context, culture and environment of financial consumer markets.

Principle 1 of the 'Legal, Regulatory and Supervisory Framework' of financial consumer markets, for example, requires national authorities to embed financial

---

(iii) evaluating the benefits of offering consumers and providers with benchmarks for financial products that can be used safely by a wide variety of unsophisticated users.'

78   Ibid.
79   Ibid 19.
80   Ibid.
81   OECD, 'G20 High-Level Principles on Financial Consumer Protection' (n 69).

consumer protection in the legal, regulatory and supervisory framework of financial markets, and Principle 2 requires them to designate oversight bodies with explicit responsibility for financial consumer protection and 'the necessary authority to fulfil these mandates'.[82] These principles respond to the FSB's findings about fragmentation of regulatory authority for financial consumer protection in countries where the financial regulator has no consumer protection objectives or powers and the consumer protection bodies lack the mandate, expertise or resources to regulate consumer finance markets effectively.

Principles 3 and 6 respond to a crucial element of consumer finance markets – and a contributor to the instability of the US consumer finance markets: the predatory orientation of financial firms towards their customers. Principle 3 sets out an 'equitable, honest, and fair treatment' standard, applicable to all stages of firms' dealings with consumers.[83] This OECD principle resembles the norms of the Treating Customers Fairly standard developed by the UK's Financial Services Authority (FSA) in requiring fair treatment of customers to become 'integral ... [to] the good governance and corporate culture of all financial services providers and authorised agents'.[84] Further responsibilization of financial services providers forms the core of Principle 6, which requires financial firms 'to have as an objective, to work in the best interest of their customers and be responsible for upholding financial consumer protection ... [And] also be responsible and accountable for the actions of their authorised agents.'[85] To comply with this responsible business conduct, standard firms will have to demonstrate that they have assessed the capabilities, situations and needs of potential customers before agreeing to provide financial products and services. The explanatory text on this standard also sets out norms about staff qualifications, training and remuneration structures, and provides direction on how firms should manage conflicts of interest with customers. This responsible business conduct principle thus inserts a regulatory standard of consumer-regarding decision-making into the business model and organization of the financial firm, challenging the firm's traditional autonomy over its services, products and operations.[86]

The remaining principles set out standards that are familiar from consumer finance policy discussions before the crash. Principles on disclosure (4), financial education (5), complaints handling and redress (9) and the promotion of competitive

---

82   Ibid 5.

83   Ibid.

84   Ibid. The FSA's Treating Customers Fairly standard is discussed below.

85   OECD, 'G20 High-Level Principles on Financial Consumer Protection' (n 69).

86   For elaboration of this point in the context of the TCF model adopted by the UK's Financial Services Authority see Toni Williams, 'Open the Box: An Exploration of the Financial Services Authority's Model of Fairness in Consumer Financial Transactions' in James Devenney, Mel Kenny and Lorna Fox O'Mahony (eds), *Unconscionability in European Private Financial Transactions: Protecting the Vulnerable* (Cambridge University Press 2009).

markets (10) reproduce the pre-crisis model discussed above. Taken together with Principle 7, which concerns protecting consumer assets against fraud and misuse, and Principle 8 on data protection, these regulatory standards purport to foster consumer confidence and enhance their capacities in aid of the neoliberal model of expansion and discipline in markets for consumer financial products and services.

This continuity with familiar strands of established neoliberal ideology and practice may give impetus to financial consumer protection reform in G20 countries; and the FSB's proposal to establish an international organization of financial consumer protection regulators may facilitate research and policy discussion on addressing problems in consumer finance markets. G20 members may employ peer pressure to foster change if they follow through on their undertaking to monitor each other's progress on implementation of the financial consumer protection principles at future summits. Implementation of the principles by G20 members alone would ostensibly cover much of the global economy, including many countries with large consumer finance markets populated by giant firms.[87]

Institutionalization of the G20/OECD principles through regulatory reform, therefore, may be attainable, although even this change is by no means guaranteed given the variations in capacity and expertise reported in the FSB options document and the differences in political environments and regulatory resources across the G20 membership. Just as significant as formal implementation of the principles, however, is the question of whether, once institutionalized, the G20's model of consumer protection is likely to further the G20's goal of financial stability and protection of financial consumers. A preliminary answer to this question may be found by studying recent experience in jurisdictions which, by the time the crisis struck, already had in place the main elements of the financial consumer protection model that the G20 has endorsed.

---

87 Statistics reported on the G20 web page indicate that the G20 members account for 'almost 90% of global GDP; 80% of international global-trade; 64% of the world's population; and 84% of all fossil fuel emissions', <http://www.g20.org/index.php/en/numeralia>, citing <http://www.principalglobalindicators.org/default.aspx>. It is interesting to note also that the high-level principles are published by the OECD, which counts among its 34-country membership several that do not belong to the G20. The principles may not carry the same weight formally among the OECD (non-G20) membership as those that emanate from an OECD-led policy-making initiative, but it is plausible to think that the role of the OECD in their development, together with the size of the financial consumer markets in the G20/OECD countries that have committed to adopting them may lend itself to large-scale adoption of the principles. On the other hand, studies of the consequences of declarations made at the G20 summits indicate that these international commitments may not materialize in domestic policy changes. See George Von Furstenberg and Joseph Daniels, "Economic Summit Declarations, 1975–1989: Examining the Written Record of International Cooperation' (1992) Princeton Studies in International Finance 72; John Kirton and Zaria Shaw, *G20 Accountability Report on Domestic Financial Regulation* (G20 2010).

4 Regulating payment protection insurance

Payment protection insurance, also known as consumer credit insurance (hereafter PPI/CCI), is a financial product that 'insures a debtor's capacity to make repayments under a credit contract'.[88] Unlike other types of consumer insurance, PPI/CCI products are not individually underwritten according to the risks posed by a particular consumer's circumstances, nor are they usually sought out by consumers. Instead, the insurance is sold by the provider, usually alongside the credit product that it collateralizes, on more or less the same terms to all eligible customers.

Intuitively, the product may seem to be a rational response to the growth of mass selling of instalment credit in which loans are advanced essentially on the security of the debtor's future income. Designed to protect creditors when that security fails, PPI/CCI appears to reduce economic aspects of the consumer's vulnerability to systemic and biographical risk – unemployment, injury and illness – that impair the capacity to repay debt. According to neoclassical economic theory that reduction in risk should make it easier for consumers to obtain credit and on better terms than otherwise would be available, and, in a competitive market populated by price-taking firms and active, comparison-shopping, product-switching individuals, the cost of the insurance premiums should not exceed the benefits consumers obtain from the products.

In practice, however, the contracts that constitute PPI/CCI markets are typically structured to deliver little benefit to consumers, who seldom claim successfully;[89] to thwart consumers' attempts to compare or switch; and to secure extremely high profits for PPI/CCI providers. From 2002 to 2006, for example, the peak years of PPI sales in the UK, the PPI premium revenue of the 12 largest distributors was estimated at some £18 billion.[90]

Whereas the marketing of PPI/CCI may represent the insurance as a safety-net, ancillary to the credit sale which is the main purpose of the transaction, the product's role within the firm's business model may be quite the reverse, with

---

88   Australian Securities and Investments Commission, *Consumer Credit Insurance: A Review of Sales Practices by Authorised Deposit-taking Institutions* (ASIC 2011).

89   The claims ratio on PPI products is notoriously low. The UK's Competition Commission reported that only about 11–28 per cent of premium income is returned to customers in claims: Competition Commission, *Market Investigation into Payment Protection Insurance* (Competition Commission 2009). The recent report of the Australian Securities and Investments Commission (ASIC) similarly estimates low net loss ratios on CCI in the order of 18 per cent in 2008, 22 per cent in 2009 and 34 per cent in 2010: Australian Securities and Investments Commission, *Consumer Credit Insurance* (n 85).

90   Another study referenced in the Competition Commission report, *Market Investigation into Payment Protection Insurance* (n 86) estimates the PPI premium revenue for 2002–2006 at £24.6 billion: ibid, table 2.4 citing Mintel, *Creditor Insurance Report* (Mintel 2007).

the loan serving as a 'loss leader' for the sale of PPI.[91] Findings in the UK's Competition Commission's report on the PPI market, for example, indicate that the 'profit margins that PPI distributors earn on the underlying credit product are far lower than those earned on PPI … Credit sales therefore have a proportionately lower impact on profits than the loss of a PPI sale.'[92]

Regulators in the UK and Australia have tackled PPI/CCI by using powers that incorporate core elements of the OECD/G20 model of financial consumer protection. Principles 1 and 2 are met because designated financial market regulators in both jurisdictions are charged with advancing aspects of financial consumer protection. Both countries have embraced the neoliberal idealizing of the competitive market that is reflected in Principle 10 and both have the institutional capacity to investigate financial consumer markets that do not appear to be competitive. Furthermore, Australia and the UK are among the earliest adopters of the regulatory project of upskilling consumers through financial literacy education as per Principle 5[93] and each has a financial ombudsman service that satisfies Principle 9. Extensive disclosure of product characteristics, risks and costs, as envisaged by Principle 4, is well established in the two regulatory systems, as are cooling-off periods and prohibitions on tied sales of PPI/CCI.

Each country also has tried to strengthen PPI regulation beyond these basic norms. Australia provides for statutory rebates of CCI premiums on termination of a credit contract and, more generally, has legislated a price ceiling on commission for CCI sales of 20 per cent of the premium.[94] Regulatory action in the UK's PPI market was based on a Treating Customers Fairly model that sought to responsibilize the management of financial firms in ways that are reflected in the OECD/G20's high-level Principles 3 and 6. In neither Australia nor the UK, however, has the regulation of PPI/CCI prevented firms from exploiting financial consumers at and beyond the point of sale.

---

91 Financial Services Authority, *The Financial Conduct Authority: Approach to Regulation* (FSA 2011) para 33.

92 Competition Commission, *Market Investigation into Payment Protection Insurance* (n 86) appendix 3.7.

93 Australia established a task force to develop a national strategy on financial literacy in 2004: The Consumer and Financial Literacy Task Force and Australian Government: The Treasury, 'The National Strategy for Consumer and Financial Literacy: Terms of Reference' (Australian Government 2004) <http://cfltaskforce.treasury.gov.au/content/terms.asp?NavID=2> accessed 8 November 2005. The UK's FSA also became active on financial literacy education in the middle of the last decade: Williams 'Empowerment of Whom and for What?' (n 18). The Financial Services Act 2010 c.28, s.2 transferred responsibility for overseeing the development and implementation of financial literacy education away from the FSA to the Consumer Financial Education Body, which is now the Money Advice Service.

94 The price control was s 135 of the Uniform Consumer Credit Code, which is now s 145 of the National Consumer Credit Protection Act. The statutory rebate is s 148 of the National Consumer Credit Protection Act.

PPI/CCI is a product that is sold rather than bought in the sense that providers actively market it to consumers whose focus is on obtaining credit rather than the ancillary insurance against unpleasant contingencies. This process of active marketing is a site of significant problems of deception, unfairness and high-pressure sales tactics. PPI/CCI markets are notable for the persistence of exploitative sales practices after regulators have identified problems and implemented rule changes that are intended to stop them. Australian authorities, for example, conducted reviews of the consumer credit insurance market in 1991 and 1998,[95] which highlighted the nature and scale of aggressive and misleading sales practices, before implementing regulatory changes to curtail such practices. Information on the regulatory expectations about CCI marketing and sales, and the reasons for those expectations, therefore, has been available to financial firms in Australia for more than 20 years. Nevertheless, a recent study by the Australian Securities and Investments Commission (ASIC), a regulator of CCI sales practices, found ample evidence of non-compliance with even the simplest regulatory requirements among its sample of 15 regulated firms.[96]

For instance, with respect to the basic question of whether consumers understand that the sale of CCI is optional and not part of the credit transaction, the ASIC study found that about half the firms in its sample had devised sales scripts that did not specifically indicate the optional nature of CCI or failed to clearly separate the sale of insurance from the credit transaction.[97] Four firms used scripts that contained ambiguous verbs such as 'activate', 'enrol' or 'process', rather than 'purchase' or 'buy', to confirm a CCI sale, and nine of the 15 firms used scripts that did not clearly verify the consumer's consent to the sale. The study also found that most of the 15 firms tolerated or encouraged high-pressure telesales, with 11 training staff on 'tips' for overcoming consumer resistance to the sale of CCI[98] and only four firms instructing their staff to end the sales conversation when consumers indicated that they did not want to buy the insurance. Moreover, one in five firms (3/15) sold CCI without using any script at all, exacerbating the risk of telesales staff giving misleading or deceptive information and advice and precluding review of compliance.[99]

---

95   Australia Trade Practices Commission, *The Market for Consumer Credit Insurance: A Study of Competition, Efficiency and the Welfare of Consumers*, (ATPC 1991); Australian Competition and Consumer Commission, *Consumer Credit Insurance Review: Final Report*, (ACCC 1998).

96   Australian Securities and Investments Commission, 'Consumer Credit Insurance' (n 85).

97   The specific finding as summarized by ASIC is that the scripts of 8/15 firms failed to state that sales staff's intention to sell insurance or to ask the consumer permission to discuss the sale of insurance and 7/15 failed to indicate that CCI was optional: ibid.

98   Ibid 24, para 91.

99   Ibid 5–6, para 17.

The study found also that scripted disclosure about product characteristics and cost was often misleading, deceptive or confusing. With respect to eligibility criteria, for example, the sales scripts of two out of three firms (10/15) did not disclose the information required by the regulation, but simply referred to the product disclosure statement. Many consumers would not see this statement before they had committed the sale as the study found that half the firms (6/12) engaged in CCI telesales did not mail the disclosure statement until consumers had agreed to purchase the product on the phone.[100] Thus, the ASIC found high rates of CCI claims denial in the region of one-third of claims (30 per cent) at seven firms and one firm reporting a denial rate of 47 per cent for one of its CCI products.[101]

Cases and regulatory enforcement actions in the UK show that similar problems occurred there, with consumers being led to believe that the purchase of PPI was compulsory, or at least that its purchase would significantly improve their chances of obtaining credit, and PPI pricing being opaque and sometimes predatory.[102] Regulators also found evidence of distributors not only selling PPI products without clearly pointing out the cost or the exclusions, and sometimes without obtaining the consumer's consent, but also of consumers being sold PPI they did not want and policies that had no value to them either because they did not meet the eligibility criteria or because they already had better or cheaper coverage from other sources.[103]

---

100   Ibid paras 122, 118.

101   Ibid para 13.

102   During the period of its TCF initiative on PPI sales, the FSA took action against 24 firms for PPI sales misconduct, imposing fines ranging from £28,000 to £7 million; for examples see the sources cited below. PPI disputes were also taken to the Financial Ombudsman Service and to the UK county and superior courts. While the FOS consistently found the conduct of PPI providers to be unfair, its reports do not contain much detail about the selling processes. Reported cases in the county courts and high court, by contrast, often do describe the PPI selling process in some detail. It is striking to compare the creditor-friendly interpretations of the sales processes in the high court with the more critical readings that are found in the county courts, the FOS summaries and the FSA decisions. For examples of county court decisions see *Yates and Lorenzelli v Nemo Personal Finance*, 14 May 2010, Manchester County Court, Case no 9HG00904; *Smith & Smith v Black Horse Ltd*, 10 March 2010, Chester County Court, Claim no 9CH04096, *Ian Wollerton v Black Horse Ltd*, 26 March 2010, Leicester County Court, Case no 9NN02070. For an illustration of the high court's approach, see *Harrison v Black Horse Ltd* [2010] EWHC 3152 QB, upheld by the Court of Appeal [2011] EWCA 1128 CA.

103   For examples of the problems that it found, see the decision notices against GE Capital Bank, 30 January 2007, Liverpool Victoria Banking Services, 29 July 2008 (fined £840,000) <http://www.fsa.gov.uk/library/communication/pr/2008/083.shtml>; HFC Bank, 16 January 2008 (fined £1,085,000) <http://www.fsa.gov.uk/library/communication/pr/2008/004.shtml>; Alliance and Leicester plc, 6 October 2008 (fined £7 million) <http://www.fsa.gov.uk/pages/library/communication/pr/2008/115.shtml>; and Egg banking plc, 10 December 2008 (fined £721,000) <http://www.fsa.gov.uk/pages/library/communication/pr/2008/149.shtml>.

That the same dishonest and unfair sales practices have become embedded in the distinct consumer finance markets of Australia, the UK and other jurisdictions that have investigated PPI/CCI[104] is consistent with the notion that neoliberalism enables the large transnational financial firms in PPI/CCI markets to constitute the prevailing norms and practices of the markets around the world in which they operate. The size and capacity for dominance of these firms may also account for the findings of the UK's regulator, the FSA, that the organizational 'cultures' and business models of financial firms were almost impervious to their initiatives to responsibilize retail distributors of PPI through their Treating Customers Fairly (TCF) model. TCF requires firms to be able to demonstrate compliance with three FSA conduct-of-business principles. These principles are to: 'pay due regard to the interests of [their] customers and treat them fairly'; 'pay due regard to the information needs of [their] clients and communicate information to them in a way which is clear, fair and not misleading'; and 'take reasonable care to organise and control [their] affairs responsibly and effectively, with adequate risk management systems'.[105]

During the development of the model, the FSA envisaged that firms would embed TCF into management activities – including leadership, strategic planning and decision-making, management controls, and staff recruitment, training and monitoring – and that managers would then diffuse TCF norms throughout the working practices of their organizations. Acculturation to TCF would then be demonstrable through the firm's ability to achieve the FSA's TCF-compliant outcomes. Thus, a firm that had fully adopted the model ought to be able to show that: the fair treatment of customers is integral to its corporate culture; its products are designed to meet consumer needs and perform in accordance with any expectations that the firm had created; its marketing and selling practices are targeted appropriately and incorporate clear, suitable information disclosure 'before, during and after the point of sale'; and it provides suitable advice tailored to a consumers circumstances. Beyond the point of sale, the FSA expected a TCF-compliant firm to be able to demonstrate that it does not unreasonably impede consumer switching, claiming or complaining.[106]

PPI was the primary consumer finance product market to which the FSA applied the TCF model. After assuming jurisdiction over insurance products in January 2005, the regulator took several measures to secure compliance with the TCF

---

104   Consumer Credit Union and Centre for Economic Justice, *Credit Insurance: The $2 Billion A Year Rip-Off* (Centre for Economic Justice 1998); Peet Nienaber, *A Report by the Panel of Enquiry on Consumer Credit Insurance in South Africa* (Life Offices' Association of South Africa and the South African Insurance Association 2008).

105   Principles 6, 7 and 3 respectively. The development of the TCF models is analysed in more detail in Williams, 'Open the Box' (n 83); Ramsay and Williams, 'The Crash that Launched a Thousand Fixes' (n 10).

106   Financial Services Authority, *Treating Customers Fairly – Towards Fair Outcomes for Consumers* (FSA 2006) 60.

in the PPI market. These measures included: testing PPI sales practices through thematic reviews and mystery shopping exercises; integrating review of PPI sales into its supervision of individual financial firms, which enabled FSA supervisors to conduct file reviews of sales records and recordings; taking enforcement actions that resulted in fines ranging from £28,000 imposed on a car dealer to £7 million imposed on a large firm with a substantial PPI business,[107] and directing firms to remove from the market a PPI product that was highly profitable for them and particularly bad value for financial consumers.[108] Despite these regulatory activities, the adverse findings of a Competition Commission investigation into the working of the PPI market, a substantial volume of complaints and persistent bad publicity, banks and other financial firms continued to sell PPI in ways that were highly detrimental to financial consumers. In this, the firms may have been somewhat encouraged by the UK high court, which repeatedly interpreted consumer credit legislation in ways that supported exploitative sales practices – an interpretation that the Court of Appeal endorsed in 2011.[109]

In 2009, at the instigation of the Financial Ombudsman Service (FOS), which had become concerned about the volume of PPI-related complaints it was receiving, the FSA began to focus on firms' handling of PPI complaints and redress. Finding a significant discrepancy between financial firms' practices of rejecting most PPI complaints (60 per cent) and the FOS record of upholding 'the vast majority' of complaints (89 per cent in 2009), the FSA developed complaints-handling and fair redress norms that required firms to review their files, assess their past business conduct and then contact and compensate customers whose product purchases had been tainted by deceptive and misleading sales practices.[110] The development of these norms was fiercely contested by financial firms and then unsuccessfully challenged in court by the banks' trade association, the British Bankers Association (BBA) and a finance company.[111]

The BBA's main attack on the complaints and redress policy argued that the FSA's high-level principles on which the policy – and its entire TCF model – is based do not impose obligations on financial firms. Absent an obligation on firms to comply with the principles, there would be no lawful basis for the FSA to require them to answer complaints and provide redress for breach of the principles. The judge comprehensively rejected this argument, characterizing the 'true role of the principles' as 'the overarching framework for regulation ... always in place to be

---

107 See sources referenced at n 100.

108 Dear CEO letter, 24 February 2009, available at <http://www.fsa.gov.uk/library/communication/pr/2009/031.shtml>.

109 *Harrison v. Black Horse* (n 99).

110 Policy Statement 10/12 'The Assessment and Redress of Payment Protection Insurance Complaints', available at <http://www.fsa.gov.uk/pages/library/policy/policy/2010/10_12.shtml>.

111 *R (on the application of) British Bankers Association v The Financial Services Authority & The Financial Ombudsman Service*, [2011] EWHC 999 (Admin).

the fundamental provision which would always govern the actions of firms ...
The Principles are best understood as the ever present substrata ... The Principles
always have to be complied with.'[112]

The BBA's decision not to appeal removed the last impediment to the
implementation of the FSA's scheme to redress PPI mis-selling. The full extent
of materialized consumer detriment is as yet unknown, but, according to monthly
data reported as part of the FSA scheme, the largest financial firms paid out more
than £3 billion in redress from January 2011 to February 2012, and these sums do
not include claims activated by the mandatory customer contact exercise, which
started to be rolled out on a large scale in March 2012.[113] Other useful data points
on the likely scale of redress can be found in the amounts that major banks have
set aside to cover their liabilities: Lloyds, a large bank that was rescued by the
UK government in 2008/09, has taken a charge on earnings of £3.6 billion for
its expected PPI liabilities.[114] Barclays bank recently increased its provision for
PPI redress from £1 billion to £1.3 billion, and RBS has set aside £1.2 billion to
date.[115]

5 Conclusion

In light of the case study findings, it seems doubtful that the G20's financial
stability model of consumer protection has the capacity substantially to protect
financial consumers from predatory and exploitative practices of financial firms,
even in rich countries with well-resourced regulators. Most of the elements of
this model existed in Australia and the UK by the time the crisis struck, and the
regulators in these jurisdictions have, over the years, provided financial firms with
plenty of information, rules, guidance and evidence about the nature and extent
of the problems with their PPI/CCI business models and retail market conduct.
Between them, the Australian and UK regulators tried rules, principles, incentives
and deterrents, sanctions, publicity, education and 'best-practice' models to
regulate the conduct of PPI/CCI sales, seemingly with little effect, at least in terms
of modifying firms' behaviour. While the UK regulators' achievements in securing

---

112   Paras 160–161.

113   The FSA collects data from 24 firms who accounted for 96 per cent of all PPI
complaints received in 2011.

114   News stories in February 2012 reported that Lloyds also was to reclaim £1.5
million in bonuses paid to senior management in office during the PPI mis-selling),
see, for example, 'Lloyds Bank Claws Back £1.5 Million Bonuses from Directors'
Guardian (London, Monday 20 February 2012) available at <http://www.guardian.co.uk/
business/2012/feb/20/lloyds-bank-reclaims-bonuses>.

115   <http://moneyfacts.co.uk/news/mortgages/rbs-adds-another-125m-to-its-ppi-
provision040512/>.

redress for consumers, which by August 2012 had exceeded £6 billion,[116] should not overlooked, that such redress is necessary perhaps indicates the limitations of its regulatory model. Thus, the FSA's own assessment of its work on PPI sales is that 'overall, its response to the mis-selling of PPI should have been stronger. Stronger action sooner could have limited the growth of the problem.'[117]

Reflecting on its five-year struggle to modify the behaviour of PPI retailers, the FSA identified the 'cultural challenges' it encountered in its attempt to change how firms conduct PPI sales. More generally, the FSA described the capacities and powers that a consumer financial market regulator needs if it is 'to prevent the crystallisation of large-scale risks and widespread consumer detriment'.[118] In its view, effective regulation of consumer financial markets requires a more activist approach than the neoliberal G20/OECD model seems to imagine in terms of proactive identification of problems as they begin to materialize in consumer markets, plus a willingness to intervene early and the capacity to take robust action against an individual firm or more widely if necessary.[119]

Work has started in the UK on a more proactive regulatory model, the elements of which include systematic research and analysis to identify at an early stage what the FSA terms 'retail conduct risks' – that is, the products, business models and market practices of financial firms that are potentially detrimental to consumers,[120] and empowerment of the regulator to intervene in firms' processes for developing and marketing consumer finance products. Such intervention may range from early scrutiny of a firm's decisions during the product design phase, through requiring firms to withdraw or amend misleading financial promotions, to removing detrimental and dangerous products from the market.[121] The model builds on the FSA's Treating Customers Fairly initiative, but relies less heavily on meta-regulation through the compliance and management systems of financial firms, favouring instead an emphasis on fair outcomes that a regulator can monitor.[122]

---

116   Monthly updates to these data are available at: http://www.fsa.gov.uk/consumer information/product_news/insurance/payment_protection_insurance_/latest/monthly-ppi-payouts.

117   Financial Services Authority, *The Financial Conduct Authority: Approach to Regulation* (FSA 2011) para 5.16.

118   Ibid.

119   Ibid.

120   Financial Services Authority, *Retail Conduct Risk Outlook 2011*(FSA 2011); Financial Services Authority, *Retail Conduct Risk Outlook 2012* (FSA 2012).

121   S 137C Financial Services Bill; HL Bill 25 2012–2013, available at <http://services.parliament.uk/bills/2012-13/financialservices/documents.html>. The product intervention powers are discussed in Financial Services Authority, *The Financial Conduct Authority: Approach to Regulation* (FSA 2011).

122   Ibid. See also 'Financial Conduct Authority: A New Regulatory Approach', speech by Margaret Cole, interim managing director of the conduct business unit, 28 June 2011, available at <http://www.fsa.gov.uk/library/communication/speeches/2011/0628_mc.shtml>.

Proactive regulatory supervision is to be intensified further through closer scrutiny of individual firms and more systematic surveillance of trends, themes and developments in consumer financial markets; and the new financial regulatory model continues the FSA's work on 'credible deterrence' through enforcement action based on 'disgorgement, discipline and deterrence'.[123] It remains to be seen how much of this aspirational proactivity will become institutionalized in regulatory practice. Nonetheless, it is interesting to observe that an experienced consumer financial market regulator perceives that effective protection of financial consumers requires the activation of more regulatory expertise, more intensive surveillance and closer scrutiny of firms and consumer finance markets than the G20 model envisages.

If the consumer protection principles of the financial stability model appear to offer little succour to financial consumers, do other aspects of the G20's work on strengthening the financial sector provide support for financial consumer protection? One avenue that may be worth further investigation is the emerging international regulatory scheme for supervising systemically important financial institutions (SIFIs), those 'financial institutions whose distress or disorderly failure, because of their size, complexity and systemic interconnectedness, would cause significant disruption to the wider financial system and economic activity'.[124] The recent focus on SIFI regulation to improve financial stability responds to the 'too-big-to-fail' problem that they present. Recognizing the moral hazard attendant on the risk-taking of such firms, the new SIFI regulation regimes impose more intensive, intrusive and coordinated supervision on the decision-making of SIFI firms in order to stop them taking excessive risks. Although global finance policy-makers have not identified consumer financial markets as a priority area for SIFI regulation, consumer advocates might question whether there is any reason why the new regimes of 'intensive and effective supervision' of SIFIs through transnational supervisory colleges should not extend also to their conduct in financial consumer markets.[125]

---

123   Ibid; Financial Services Authority, *Policy Statement PS 10/4, 'Enforcement Financial Penalties'* (FSA 2010) <http://www.fsa.gov.uk/library/communication/pr/2010/036.shtml>.

124   Financial Stability Board, *Policy Measures to Address Systemically Important Financial Institutions* para 3 (FSB 2011). This publication also lists 29 global SIFIs that are subject to the new international standards for enhanced loss absorption, resolution planning and supervision.

125   As noted above (n 62), supervisory colleges are working groups of supervisors from different jurisdictions and product lines who collaborate on the regulatory supervision of international financial groups in order to facilitate group-wide cross-border supervision and maintain continuous and comprehensive supervision: Basel Committee on Banking Supervision, *Good Practice Principles on Supervisory Colleges* (Basel Committee on Banking Supervision 2010). In April 2008 the Financial Stability Forum (now the Financial Stability Board – FSB) published *Enhancing Market and Institutional Resilience*, which recommended that a supervisory college be established for each of the largest global

It would appear that extending the SIFI regulation model to consumer financial markets could potentially strengthen implementation of the financial stability model of financial consumer protection through at least two avenues. First, the transnational supervisory colleges may provide a means for sharing regulatory experience about the conduct of giant firms in local financial consumer markets, which in turn might enable regulators in different jurisdictions to act in concert against products and conduct that are detrimental to consumers' interests. Second, the inclusion of financial consumer protection within the remit of supervisory college might provide an incentive and an opportunity for financial regulators to improve their expertise in the field of financial consumer protection. Given the neoliberal core of the financial stability model, however, the question of whether and to what extent financial consumers may benefit from its more effective implementation in the SIFI regulation scheme requires careful investigation.

---

financial institutions as a means of improving information exchange and cooperation between authorities. This recommendation was taken up by the G20 at the November 2008 summit, which supported the creation of supervisory colleges for all major cross-border financial institutions.

Chapter 3

Access to, and Exclusion of, European Consumers from Financial Markets after the Global Financial Crisis

Hans-W. Micklitz[1]

> We need to democratize finance and bring the advantages enjoyed by the clients
> of Wall Street to the customers of Wal-Mart ... Democratizing finance means
> effectively solving the problem of gratuitous economic inequality.
>
> R. Shiller, 2003[2]

1 Introduction

The quote from Shiller condenses what has been the overall credo of the financial service sector and for all those who believed in it. Easy access to cheap money for everybody – this was the promise the financial sector conveyed to all consumers worldwide, in line with the promises Bill Clinton made in his election campaign that every US citizen has a 'right' to his or her privately owned home. Social and financial inclusion – to bring in the language of the EU[3] – is the automatic result of the release of market powers. The 2007/2008 global financial crisis tells a different story, and it is far from being over. Much has been written on the reasons behind the crisis, at the global as well as at the European level, on the

---

1   This chapter is part of the ERC research project on European Regulatory Private Law; see <http://blogs.eui.eu/erc-erpl/>. I would like to thank Guido Comparato, Norbert Reich, Antonio Marcacci, Thomas Roethe, Klaus Tuori, Annika Wolf for their critical and most helpful comments. Responsibility is mine.

2   Robert Shiller, *The New Financial Order: Risk in the 21st Century* (Princeton University Press 2003) 5–6. Shiller maintains his own website, <http://www.newfinancialorder.com/>, cited by Joseph Vogel, *Das Gespenst des Kapitals* (Diaphenes 2010) 111–112: 'Wir müssen die Finanzwelt demokratisieren und die Vorteile der Kundschaft von Wallstreet zu den Verbrauchern von Walmart bringen ... Die Demokratisierung des Finanzwesens bedeutet eine wirksame Lösung des Problems willkürlicher ökonomischer Ungleichheit.'

3   Guido Comparato, 'Europe's Steps towards a Financially Inclusive Private Law' H-W Micklitz and Y Svetiev (eds), *A Self-sufficient European Private Law – A Viable Concept?* (EUI–ERPL Working Paper 1 2013). To be published as an EUI Working Paper within the ERC project on European Regulatory Private Law.

effects of the sub-prime financing, which yielded the euro crisis.[4] This chapter builds on the analysis of others who have focused on the much broader picture behind the global crisis, and brings it down to the world of the consumer who had concluded a consumer credit agreement for whatever purpose and who is now faced with the potential impact of the global crisis on his debts. I use the term 'credit agreement' as being understood to cover mortgages. Currently, attention in the media and academic writings is currently largely focused on state default in the eurozone, on the pros and cons of allowing banks to go bankrupt (if at all), investment banks, saving banks, and the necessary safeguard measures the international community has to take to rescue both the financial system and the euro. In such a dramatic and frightening scenario, the consumer debtor is still all too often simply overlooked. If considered at all, the consumers are portrayed as citizens who are withdrawing their money from the bank because they no longer trust even state-owned institutions (Spain) or who are demonstrating in the streets against the state (Greece), or who form part of Blockupy, the bottom-up initiative against the power of banks.

The promises of salvation (*Heilsversprechen*) in financial economics *à la* Shiller had reduced the consumer to a magical and competent average statistical heuristic figure, which allowed the financial sector to penetrate the consumers' lifeworld (Habermas) and submit it to its own logic of efficiency.[5] The consumer in whom I am interested is living in a real world; he or she is not merely a heuristic figure. Rising interest rates jeopardize not only his or her standard of living, but all too often his or her existence in the pure sense. Enshrined in the hard fall back to reality is the much deeper question of whether financial mathematical economics can escape economic history. Vogel writes in his book *Das Gespenst des Kapitals* (*The Ghost of Capital*) which has not yet been translated):[6]

> Allerdings kann man kaum glauben, dass sich das soziale Gewebe mit der Einpflanzung neoliberaler Systemideen tatsächlich durchwalten läßt. Viel eher sollte man daran erinnern, dass Gesellschaften fortlaufend Verschleiß und Verlust, Ausschuss und Dysfunktionen produzieren, dass sie von Köchern, Ermüdungen und Tümpeln der Unproduktivität durchsetzt sind ... *Wirtschaftsgeschichte*

---

4   Fritz W Scharpf, *Monetary Union, Fiscal Crisis and the Preemption of Democracy* (LEQS Paper no 36, 2011); Paul De Grouve, *The Governance of a Fragile Euro-Zone* (CEPS No. 346, May 2011); Poul Kjaer, Gunther Teubner and Alberto Febbrajo (eds), *The Financial Crisis in Constitutional Perspective: The Dark Side of Function Differentiation* (Hart 2011).

5   Gary Becker laid the ground in *Der ökonomische Ansatz zur Erklärung menschlichen Verhaltens* (Mohr 1982) and then spelt out the impact of what has later been called financialization of the lifeworld; see his *A Treatise on the Family* (Harvard University Press 1993).

6   Vogel, *Das Gespenst des Kapitals* (n 2).

selbst appelliert an ein feineres Differenzierungsvermögen und erweist sich als Verzweifelungsgebiet ökonomischer Theorie. (Emphasis added)

In English:

> However, one can barely believe that the social tissue could be effectively pervaded by the implementation of neoliberal conceptions. Instead, one should be cognizant of the fact that societies continuously produce wastage and damage, trash and malfunctions, that they are infiltrated by quivers, fatigue and puddles of unproductiveness ... *Economic history itself calls for a subtle faculty of differentiation and turns out to be a field of desperation for economic theory.* (Emphasis added)[7]

From here one might easily enter into a discourse on the theoretical premise on which financial economics has been built, on the underlying equilibrium theorem, on the conflation of economic models and societal reality,[8] on the effects of an economy where speculation has become a normal enterprise even if for skilled private investors, on the relationship between risk and danger[9] and so forth. Economic history as a *Verzweifelungsgebiet* – as a field of desperation for financial economics – raises the question of whether and to what extent 'reality' and 'history' fit into a concept of the financial market, which remains distinct from the market of commodities. This chapter, however, has a much more modest objective. It starts with a bottom-up perspective, trying to get to grips with the potential impact of the global crisis on consumers who are over-indebted or even insolvent. It does not claim to be economic history, but is at least based on economic reality, which forms an integral part of economic history. In short, the chapter deals with the socially and financially excluded. Whilst these categories of exclusion might be kept distinct, they are often strongly interrelated.

---

7   Translated by Conor Talbot, third-year PhD researcher at the EUI.

8   Critical on this is Hyman Minsky, *Financial Instability Revisited: The Economics of Disaster*, prepared for the Steering Committee for the Fundamental Reappraisal of the Discount Mechanisms appointed by the Board of Governors for the Federal Reserve System (Federal Reserve System 1978); Benoit Mandelbrot, Richard Hudson and Helmut Reuter (trans), *Fraktale Finanzen, Märkte zwischen Risiko, Rendite und Ruin* (Piper Verlag 2009); George Soros has most recently attacked the foundations of economic theory in 'Remarks at the Festival of Economics' 2 June 2012) http://www.georgesoros.com/interviews-speeches/entry/remarks_at_the_festival_of_economics_trento_italy/>.

9   For such a distinction in the field of product safety, see Hans-W Micklitz, Thomas Roethe and Stephen Weatherill (eds), *Federalism and Responsibility: A Study on Product Safety Law and Practice in the European Community* (Graham & Trotmann 1994). Whether and to what extent product safety regulation can contribute to getting to grips with risks associated with financial markets ranks high on the agenda since the explicit recognition of 'systemic risks'.

2 Three scenarios

From a European perspective, three scenarios must be kept distinct as they affect consumers in very different ways: the inbound European perspective versus the outbound perspective; those EU member states that have introduced the euro versus those who have not; and, last but not least, the distinction between the currently strong EU member states and the currently weaker ones – that is, those who are experiencing economic difficulties.[10]

Consumers in the EU are still fortunate if they are living in economically strong countries or in one of those countries which seems to have coped with the impact of the global crisis, such as Austria and Germany which have not (yet) been the subject of attention of rating agencies and the international media.[11] There are certainly a number of member states for which the overall expectation seems to be that they will be able to overcome current difficulties and steer their ships back to quieter waters. France belongs to this category as do the UK and Ireland, where consumer credit interest rates are much higher than in the eurozone.[12] All of these countries have in common consumers who have committed to credit obligations but who are not *particularly* affected by the global crisis.[13] They may be experiencing all sorts of payment difficulties, but these are not directly related to the current economic crisis. A disclaimer, however, is needed. If consumers have concluded credit contracts on the basis of variable interest rates, they may be confronted with a certain volatility as the interest rates they pay depend on Libor and Euribor – that is, on the rates the banks are charging for interbank loans. In

---

10   There are differences between the North and the South in Europe. In southern Europe (with the exception of Spain) cheap credit ideology did not really take root easily, although the crisis is still affecting those countries hard. The link between easy credit and the crisis is probably different in Europe and the US. In fact, one might feel tempted to argue that whereas in the US private debt has turned into public debt, in Europe the exact opposite is happening, and public debt is being turned into private debt, especially among the PIIGS (Portugal, Ireland, Italy, Greece and Spain). For overall statistics of consumer credit in Europe, see <http://ecri.be/new/system/files/Info_ECRI-StatisticalPackage2011. pdf; http://aei.pitt.edu/9434/2/9434.pdf>.

11   Times are changing. On 23 July 2012 S&P confirmed the AAA rating of Germany, whereas Moody's has described future prospects on 'negative'.

12   Although it must be recalled that France and the UK are among the countries with the highest public debt in Europe, which has raised concern on the part of the rating agencies.

13   We do not have clear-cut statistics here. For Germany, see the graphics in <http:// de.statista.com/statistik/daten/studie/150565/umfrage/privatinsolvenzen-in-deutschland- seit-2000>, which show an *increasing number* of private insolvencies in the last decade (with a peak in 2010). This same year also witnessed the peak of individual insolvencies in England and Wales; see the graphics in 'The Insolvency Service', *Statistics Release: Insolvencies In The Fourth Quarter 2011* (BIS 2012) 6, available at <http://www.insol- europe.org/download/file_/6518>.

the following I will call this scenario the *normal* case and, correspondingly, the consumer involved the *normal* consumer.

The second scenario addresses consumers living in one of the eurozone member states that are in trouble. We immediately think of Greek and Spanish consumers, and to some extent Italian consumers also belong to this risk category.[14] In these countries consumers cannot escape the deep difficulties that their national banking sector is facing. Interest rates, though still held down by the European safety shield, have risen considerably. This rise, it is true, primarily affects the banks, which might have to refinance themselves at higher interest rates than those received from their consumer debtors. *Pacta sunt servanda* protects consumers against any direct effect of a price increase. However, should they need to restructure (change) or refinance (replace) their debts, they will have to pay higher interest rates, too. Looking beyond individual consumers, an adjustment of the interest rates consumers are currently paying to those asked for by the financial market may be postponed for the duration of the consumer credit contract, but, in the long run, the gap between low consumer interest rates and higher refinancing market interest rates exacerbates the already shaky stability of the national banking sector.[15] The bankruptcy of his or her bank would not necessarily mean that the consumer would be deprived of his or her debts. Member states tend to avoid the bankruptcy of banks, although whether this will be the case in Greece is hard to predict. A much more realistic approach than speculating on the future of consumer creditors is to consider the repercussions of the austerity policy imposed by the so-called troika – the International Monetary Fund (IMF), the European Central Bank (ECB) and the European Commission – on the national labour market. Unemployment rates in Spain and Greece have risen dramatically, and there is a clear and empirically proven correlation between the loss of one's job and the risk of insolvency.[16] Consumers living in countries such as Spain and

---

14   The reasons are different. Spanish sovereign debt is in trouble because of a deadlocking banking system,. too many securitized mortgages in the last 15 years, too much debt on banks' balance sheets, the credit crunch and general shrinking of consumption. The Spanish state may not have enough revenue to bail everyone out. Italian banks are in trouble because they have too much Italian sovereign debt which is currently evaluated as it was before Italy joined the euro (higher interest rates on Italian debt, lower capital tier for banks, less money banks can lend consumers [businesses and households], the credit crunch and general shrinking of consumption).

15   I am aware that it is difficult to speak of national banking sectors and national banks tied to the national economy. For the sake of the argument I leave it like this.

16   Nik Huls, Udo Reifner and Thierry Bourgoinie, *Overindebtedness of Consumers in the EC Member States: Facts and the Search for Solution* (Kluwer 1994); Gianni Betti, Neil Dourmashkin, Mariacristina Rossi, Vijay Verma and Ya Ping Yin, *Study of the Problem of Consumer Indebtedness: Statistical Aspects*, Contract no B5-1000/00/000197, Final Report (Commission of European Union 2001); William Whitford, Johanna Niemi-Kiesilainen and Iain Ramsay (eds), *Consumer Bankruptcy in Global Perspective* (Hart 2003), Johanna Niemi, Iain Ramsay and William Whitford (eds), *Consumer Credit, Debt & Bankruptcy.*

Greece – I will call them 'consumers at risk' – have to face a double challenge: a highly probable increase in interest rates and the risk of losing their jobs.[17]

There is a third category of consumers who are already facing the effects of the global crisis to considerable degree: these I call 'affected consumers'. These are consumers living within the EU in countries that do not belong to the eurozone, such as Hungary,[18] or live outside the EU in countries where consumer credit is bound to the euro, either because the contract itself is in euros or the value of the national currency is bound to the euro, such as Iceland. The Hungarian and Icelandic banks have built safety measures, such as price indexation clauses,[19] into consumer credit contracts in order to secure the risk that the national currency might lose value in relation to the euro. This means that the consumer is not the one who may benefit from the value gap between the euro and the national currency as price indexation clauses are legal in these countries. Information given to consumers is often misleading in that it does not disclose the impact of price indexation clauses on the capital of the consumer credit.[20] Loans may be calculated in such a way

---

Comparative and International Perspective (Hart 2009); Robert Anderson, Hans Dubois, Anne Koark, Gotz Lechner, Iain Ramsay, Thomas Roethe and Hans-W Micklitz (eds), *Consumer Bankruptcy in Europe. Different Paths for Debtors and Creditors* (EUI Working Paper Law 2011).

17   In Spain, in 2011, there was a general (both individual and business) 25 per cent increase in insolvencies and 221 consumer insolvencies; see <http://www.insol-europe.org/download/file_/6314>. Statistics in France only concern business insolvencies. Amazingly enough, the situation differs in Ireland. Maria Gerhardt, 'Consumer Bankruptcy Regimes in the US and Europe: Further Effects and Implications of the Crisis' (CEPS Working Document no 318, July 2009) summarizes the development as follows: 'Consumer bankruptcy procedures are seldom used in Ireland, as can be seen from the low number of actual adjudications: in 2007, only 5 persons were declared bankrupt, 10 were discharged from their debt, and those numbers have remained rather stable in recent years. This is surprising indeed since Ireland has been experiencing a strong housing bubble with mortgage volumes having increased steadily from 20% of GDP (1998) to 65% (2007), and slightly decreasing again to 62% of GDP in 2008. The multiplication of outstanding debt has so far not led to more bankruptcy cases … Even though Irish insolvency legislation clearly gives priority to creditors' rights and represents a heavy burden to bankrupts, the requirements are painful enough to encourage debtors and creditors to find other solutions for recovery. Renegotiation plays an important role, and is actually strongly recommended in the official IBF code of conduct.'

18   See <http://pesterlloyd.net/2011_20/20kreditnot/20kreditnot.html>.

19   Icelandic law permitted mortgages denominated in foreign currencies but prohibited mortgages in Icelandic krónas (ISK) linked to the fluctuation of foreign currencies: Act No 38/2001.

20   The figures refer to Iceland. I would like to thank Professor Mendez Pinedo, University of Iceland and visiting scholar at the EUI in autumn 2011 for this valuable information. For more details, see M Elivria Mendez-Pinedo, *Overview of European Consumer Credit Law: Protection of Consumers with Foreign Currency Mortgages in the Aftermath of the Icelandic Crisis* (University of Iceland 2010).

that their real costs for the consumer are hidden behind a veil of complexity.[21] Consumers think that price indexation affects the interest rates, not the capital. Instead, the principal amount of the loan increases geometrically over time by adding compound interest and interest to the interest. A 30-year loan with 5 per cent annual interest in 7 per cent annual inflation then ends up not as a loan with 12 per cent interest, as implied by the initial numbers, but as a non-indexed loan at a 22 per cent annual interest rate.[22] The consequences of this keep the national Icelandic courts busy. At the time of writing, the Surpeme Court of Iceland has held that non-indexed interest rates should replace foreign-currency indexation in the case of car loans. However, the Court had not yet decided whether the same holds true for housing loans.[23]

---

21   Other examples are contracts on certificates or structural instruments like CDOs.

22   Ibid.

23   On 27 May 2012 I received the following information from Professor Mendez Pinedo who is personally concerned and involved in litigation:

'My husband and I won a second case before the Supreme Court where the illegality of the loans was confirmed for consumers (and probably for companies) through contract law. It also declared that there was a partial violation of the Constitution (expropriation of economic rights of consumers cannot be done through an ordinary law). This is case 600/2011 which made the front page of the news for a whole week due to its impact on the financial sector. The Supreme Court also reversed its jurisprudence and made a distinction between *ex nunc* and *ex tunc* effects of the first ruling declaring illegality of these loans which had to be considered to be given and paid in ISK. So it determined in our case that initial interest had to be applied until February 2011 and from then the interest of the Icelandic Central Bank would take over. This means a second recalculation of these loans but this time to the benefit of all consumers.

Unfortunately the financial sector argues now that the ruling is too unclear to recalculate loans in a general way and a group composed of financial sector, debtors' ombudsman, consumer's spokesman is determining how to proceed. Probably they will take some extra cases to the courts to clarify some pending issues. We have requested the enforcement of the Supreme Court's ruling but the Resolution Committee of the failed bank has not replied to us. They make time hoping there will be a reverse of jurisprudence. We are trapped. But now the failed bank owes us a significant amount of money.

The complaint sent to the ESA resulted in the ESA declaring they had no competence to act in this field (property rights, contract law and ECHR). Now they have sent a formal letter to Iceland saying that the prohibition of foreign-indexed loans is contrary to the EEA Agreement so that Iceland cannot be an exception, foreign loans must be allowed. They misunderstand Icelandic legislation. Pure foreign loans have always been allowed, what is prohibited is indexation of ISK loans to foreign currency or indexes.

As for the loans linked to the inflation (*verðtrygging*) which represent 90% of all house loans: These are still legal and for the Government it is very difficult to adopt a horizontal debt restructuring solution. Iceland is working on the incorporation of the most recent directive on consumer credit 2008/48. In Iceland, as in Scandinavia, all loans are treated the same. Residential property or house loans have been given the same protection as consumer loans. The newest law has to be adopted before the summer but it still proposes to allow

This scenarios of the normal consumer, the consumer at risk and the affected consumer will accompany us throughout this chapter. This will highlight the fact that the global crisis adds another layer to the set of reasons for consumer over-indebtedness and insolvency – a layer in which the global financial crisis bears a human face. In section 2 I will first provide an account of the new financial economics that enabled the 'easy access to consumer credit ideology' and then try to explain why consumers who engaged in credit obligations to finance their house purchases beyond all boundaries nevertheless felt safe and protected by the dynamics of the global market. Section 3 is devoted to the particular role the EU has been playing in the construction of the new global ideology on access to consumer credit. This leads to a discussion on financial inclusion/exclusion, through the various efforts made by the EU to provide the concept of union with a social outlook, despite limited competences and despite the prime responsibility still remaining with the member states. All in all, it will be demonstrated that the EU followed the American approach. In the final section I will discuss to what extent Europe could and should play a more active role as a counterpart to the still dominant liberal market financial economics.

3 The global ideology of easy access to consumer credit

At the outset I have to make a statement, which is central to my reading of the reasons behind the global financial crisis as well as the search for an appropriate solution. I do not understand the consumer as a mere victim of the global crisis.[24] Consumers worldwide benefited from cheap and easily accessible credit, particularly in the EU since the introduction of the euro which is the starting-point and the focus of my interest. It has been amply demonstrated that the interest rates in Europe before the introduction of the euro in 1999/2002 and after the economic crisis in 2007/2008 strongly correlate.[25] Leaving aside the dramatic scenario in Greece and, to some extent, in Spain, consumers in Europe had to pay higher or lower different interest rates depending on the strength of their national economy. During the prosperous years between 2001 and 2007 the interest rates in all eurozone countries have approximated to each other and have led to a nearly equivalent level of interest rates, meaning that Greek and the Spanish consumers paid more or less the same interest rates as their French, German or Italian counterparts. Economists are arguing that the crisis has brought back the differences in national economies.

---

this price-indexation of the capital and interest on interest practices although it increases the information requirements for consumers.'

24   See Greta R Krippner, *Capitalizing on Crisis: The Political Origins of the Rise of Finance* (Harvard University Press 2011).

25   Scharpf, 'Monetary Union, Fiscal Crisis and the Preemption of Democracy' (n 4); De Grauwe, 'The Governance of a Fragile Euro-Zone' (n 4).

My point is that all consumers in the EU benefited for a couple of years from what Shiller so forcefully calls the democratization of the financial markets. For some years – more precisely between 2001 and 2008 – the European financial market seemed to provide evidence of the democratizing effect of cheap money. The American counterpart was the loans granted to low-income consumers who financed their houses on the expectation that higher selling prices would secure the risk against over-indebtedness resulting from 100 per cent or even over 100 per cent financed properties. In the US the Clinton and Bush administrations had forcefully promoted the idea that cheap credit might serve as a substitute for social policy.[26] It might be interesting to consider whether and to what extent there is a parallel here to the situation in Albania where high-ranking politicians actively participated and promoted pyramid schemes which led to the collapse of the Albanian economy and society.[27] This brings to the fore the question as to whether financial derivatives could and should be regarded as a form of gambling. However, I will not pursue this strain of argument any further.[28] In Europe, cheap money for the poorer members of the EU – particularly the consumers in southern Europe – fulfilled a similar social policy function.

In a way, the 'promises of salvation' seemed to have materialized. Looking back, one might raise all sorts of questions, which could be merged into one: how was it that an overall climate emerged over time, culminating in the early twenty-first century, in which nobody – not the states, the banks or consumers – ever asked how all these debts could or would(?) be repaid, not individually but by society as a whole? Certainly, nobody ever openly undermined *pacta sunt servanda*, although there were rumours that the former Citigroup was operating its credit business for small loans (up to a couple of thousands of euros) on an 80/20 logic – that is, if 80 per cent of the debtors are prepared to repay their loans,[29] this quota suffices to guarantee the bank the desired profit margin. Publicly, the mechanism of debt collection was not put into question.

A tentative answer is to draw a distinction between capital and interest. Inspired by Vogel,[30] my tentative hypothesis is that during the high days of the stock market

---

26   J Gunnar Trumbell, *Consumer Credit in Postwar America and France: The Political Construction of Economic Interest* (CUP forthcoming).

27   Christopher Jarvis, 'The Rise and Fall of Pyramid Schemes in Albania', 99/98 *IMF Working Paper* (IMF 1999) at <http://www.imf.org/external/pubs/ft/wp/1999/wp9998.pdf> accessed 27 May 2012; Roberto Morozza della Rocca, 'Socio-cultural Aspects of the Albanian Crisis' (1998) 33 The International Spectator 69. In the broader context, see World Bank, *Albania beyond the Crisis: A Strategy for Recovery and Growth*, Report No. 18658-ALB, 7 December (World Bank, 1998).

28   Vogel, *Das Gespenst des Kapitals* (n 2) 103 argues that financial mathematics have lifted the precarious resemblance of financial derivatives and gambling.

29   Statement made at the Journalisten workshop organized by the Schufa on 12–13 October 2004, Germany (the author participated in the meeting).

30   Vogel, *Das Gespenst des Kapitals* (n 2) Chapter 3, 'Zeit des Kapitals' ('Time of Capital'), 53; and Chapter 4, 'Idylle des Marktes II' ('Idyll of the Market II'), 83.

hype, when capital seemed to be available *ad infinitum* as long as the future risks of repayment could be secured via financial derivatives, when consumer debts did not show up in the balance sheets of the borrowing bank, but have themselves become a source of profit through securitization, creditors were satisfied as long as they could count on the payment of interest and left the question of when and how the capital could or would(?) be paid back, by the wayside. Arguably, these psychological and sociological considerations can be grounded in economic theory through what has been termed 'financialization'[31] which is meant to cover the economic and the societal transformation process that has been triggered by the reshaping of the financial market and the financial system.

The first step in this process was the decision of the Western nation-states in 1973 to lift the Bretton Woods agreement and to allocate monetary policy to the market.[32] The former concept of politically determined *stable currency exchange rates*, as agreed in 1944 at Bretton Woods was replaced by the *expectation of a stable system* of currency exchange rates. The second step constituted the 'invention' of financial derivatives, an independent form of money (capital), separate from both the market of commodities (*Gütermarkt*) and the currency in circulation. The so-called Black–Scholes differential equation had been developed in 1973 and was both the break-even point and the formula that underscored Friedman's credo on 'The Need for Futures Markets in Currencies'.[33] In the early 1970s financial derivatives hardly existed, whereas today they are the largest global market by far. If money – that is. capital – can be 'produced' through financial derivatives, independent from the currency in circulation, if borrowing has become a risk-free enterprise through securitization and debt-making being an additional source of money-making, then the distinction between the capital bound in the credit (debt) and the interest rates – secured via financial derivatives – seems to fall apart.[34]

---

31   There is no commonly agreed definition of what financialization means. I use the term in the meaning given to it by Gerald Epstein (ed), *Financialization and the World Economy* (Edward Elgar Publishing 2005). See his statement: 'By *financialization*, we mean the increasing importance of financial markets, financial motives and financial actors in the operations of the economy. This is but one of many different meanings that scholars ascribe to this relatively new term. The origins of the term are obscure, though it is being used with increasing frequency because of its obvious heightened relevance in modern capitalist economies. Indeed, in the last few months, a new international network has sprung up to study financialization': <http://www.peri.umass.edu/341/> accessed 24 May 2012. In German it cannot be equated with *Finanzkapital* (Rudolf Hilferding); *Finanzialisierung*, bears a more positive or a more negative connotation, depending on the context.

32   See Barry Eichengreen (ed), *Global Imbalances and the Lessons from Bretton Woods* (MIT Press 2007).

33   Milton Friedman, 'The Need for Futures Markets in Currencies' in *The Futures Market in Foreign Currencies* (International Monetary Market of the Chicago Mercantile Exchange 1973) 6–12.

34   In more technical language: financial derivatives multiply, thus create, money by securitizing (that is, insuring) debts. Thus derivatives, on the one hand, create money but,

What is much harder to grasp is the impact of the then 'idyll of the financial market' on consumer debts and, more particularly, on the ethics of 'guilt' (*Schuld*) and 'debts' (*Schulden*). Since the rise of capitalism rise in the late nineteenth century, the relationship between capitalism and religion has been subject to controversy.[35] The financial market economy, condensed in Schiller's wording, has revitalized Benjamin's famous words: 'Kapitalismus als verschuldender Kultus' ('Capitalism as indebting cult'). Capitalism – this is Benjamin's major message – does not know expiation; capitalism tries to involve the whole world in a state of indebtedness. This is what financial capitalism in the last 30 years managed to achieve – and the process continued after 2008.[36]

Following Benjamin, it is possible to argue that 'guilt' is deprived of its ethical dimension; there is no longer an ethical obligation to repay debt. 'Guilt' has turned into 'debt' as the normal state of affairs in a capitalist economy/society. The relationship between the state of emergency (*Ausnahmezustand*) and the normal state of affairs (*Normalzustand*) has turned upside down. From such a perspective, member states with a low rate of indebted consumers seem to be underdeveloped. Statistical comparisons serve to open up new markets for the financial sector. Consumers are enticed by potential opportunities.[37] The promised land, in which capital and interest rates are disconnected, loosened the ties between guilt and debts even further, thereby undermining the ethics of credit transactions. Let me put the potential effects in the form of a question: are consumers relieved of the obligation to repay their debts – if not legally, then morally – and, if so, what are the consequences thereof, ethically and legally?

Current developments in Greece might constitute a lesson for the capitalist economy and society as a whole. A political party gained the support of 20 per cent of Greek citizens with the slogan 'We want to keep the euro but we do not want to repay our debts'.[38] Enshrined in this message is the uncoupling of capital

---

on the other hand, dim the risks enshrined in the creation of money.

35 Wolfgang Palaver, 'Kapitalismus als Religion' (2001) Quart Nr. 3+4, 18; see also Karl Marx, *Fetischcharakter der Ware*, Georg Simmel, *Psychologie des Gelds*, Max Weber, *Protestantische Ethik*, Walter Benjamin, *Kapitalismus als Religion* (Fragment 1921).

36 For a critical account, see Christopher Kobrak and Mira Wilkins, 'The 2008 Crisis in an Economic History Perspective: Looking at the Twentieth Century' (2011) 53(2) Business History 175; in defence, see Robert Shiller, *Finance and the Good Society* (Princeton University Press 2012), where he suggests that it is possible to tame capitalism by its own means, in a response to the Occupy movement.

37 This is a standard argument which consumer advocates also bring forward. Udo Reifner had already stated in his PhD thesis written in 1979, 'Alternatives Wirtschaftsrecht am Beispiel der Verbraucherverschuldung, Luchterhand', that consumer credit may serve as a necessary source of income, particularly for those who do not have the resources to pay for larger investments in cash.

38 Interview given by the leader of the party when visiting Berlin in May 2012.

and interest.[39] In fact, nobody seriously knows how Greece could ever settle its enormous debts. This does not exclude the fact that Greece is ready to pay interest, at least within limits and at least as long as the interest rates are 'affordable' in that they no longer increase the total amount of the public debt. One may interpret such a claim as a form of redemption of the promise[40] given to the Greek people when Greece joined the European Monetary Union (EMU). If the member states, the IMF and the ECB give way to such a claim, they may indirectly execute the promise, turning promise into a contract, thereby strengthening the people's belief that debt and guilt, and capital and interest, can be kept distinct.

However, a major shift would then have occurred, in that the original risk inherent in that distinction, which had been proffered by the securitization mechanisms, would be delegated from the private financial sector to the public sector – the nation-state, the EU and the international community. This has already happened in part, but the belief that Greece has to repay its debts remains. If the Greek people manage to redeem the promise, the private financial sector would be relieved of the debts it had collected due to the failed securitization mechanism. The guilt–debt interplay would then also work to the benefit of the banking sector itself. The states (the European Union and the Community of the States in the IMF) would become the guarantor of the promise originally delivered by the financial sector. The final moral and economic addressee of the vanishing distinction between capital and interest, between guilt and debt, would be the state. The state appears as the ultimate institution against which Greek citizens will direct their expectations – state monopoly capitalism is back on the agenda, but nobody discusses the current development in the terms that dominated the discussion in the aftermath of the 1968 revolution in France.

Even if such a scenario came about, it is hard to imagine that the Greek state would relieve Greek consumers of their personal debts. In Iceland, consumer organizations lobbied hard to lift the effects of the indexation clauses, but managed to achieve only half-hearted success by adjusting the interest rates, with the help of the Supreme Court.[41] They remain bound to their consumer credit contracts, and they will have to repay the capital. From a bottom-up reality-bound perspective, the result is ambiguous: as citizens, consumers might learn that the state is ready to save the bank to cover the risk of securitization. The maintenance of the financial system as a public good in a capitalist market/society prevails over the logic of bank bankruptcy, thereby stabilizing private profit-making expectations. On

---

39   A more technical explanation: on the one hand, securitization creates money out of debt (and the interests therein) and derivatives – fuelled up by securitization – create money out of capital. On the other hand, securitization proffers the promise to free access to capital thus hinting at the possibility of disentangling the bond that links interests to capital (or guilt to a deed).

40   Promise should not be conflated with contract. A promise is not even self-binding, at least not in the marketing of derivatives.

41   See Mendez-Pinedo, *Overview of European Consumer Credit Law* (n 20).

the other side of the story are the broken promises: the financial sector cannot honour the representations made to consumers – the financial world has not been democratized. Economic imbalance and social injustice via the stock market hype was suspended, but not overcome. Inequalities remain in place. The result of social injustice and economic imbalance is social and financial exclusion. My threefold scenario is an attempt to capture the reality (contract) of all those who suffer from the broken promises.

In this context, the hard landing into over-indebtedness yields a painful process of societal 'resocialization', one in which the consumer debtors have to understand that the distinction between capital and interest, between guilt and debt, still exists.[42] For the consumers concerned, over-indebtedness means social and economic suffering. They have to atone for having relied on false promises – in economic terms, for having spent too much money, indeed so much that they are no longer in a position to repay their debts. This scenario comes close to the commonly agreed definition of over-indebtedness, which, setting aside differences in legislation and legal culture, runs like this: 'the result of an imbalance between the consumer's expenditure (included the reimbursement of capital borrowed and interest) and the consumer's income, which leads to defaulting payments. This situation may be temporary or longer term.'[43]

From a strictly *legal* contractual perspective, financial economics have not changed responsibilities in the underlying dynamics of bilateral contracts. There was a huge gap between the 'promises of salvation' promoted through advertising and, to some extent, through politics (Clinton and Bush), on the one hand, and the hard black-letter reality of consumer contract law drafting and conclusion, on the other. Worldwide consumer credit law left the responsibility and the obligation of the consumer unaffected, only timidly inserting elements of what is widely discussed as 'responsible lending'[44] – a matter I will return to later when discussing future regulatory design. It is notable that, at the level of day-to-day practice, the rhetoric of democratization, easy access to credit for all and 'total inclusion' did not, at that time, find a legal contractual expression that allowed consumers to execute their promises or, at the very least, ask for adjustment in case the idyll of the financial market were to fail – that is, in the event that the expectations of

---

42   See Thomas Roethe, *Verbraucherverschuldung junger Menschen – Gesellschaftliche Ursachen, insbesondere die Bedeutung eines gesellschaftlichen Wertewandels* (German Ministry for Agriculture, Nutrition and Consumer Protection 2004), in which Roethe discusses to what extent over-indebtedness and insolvency initiate a process by which the banking sector is *de facto* taking over the role and function of socializing the consumer – that is, teaching him or her the basics of money and debts in our context that the capital forms part of the debt and has to be repaid.

43   Betti, Dourmashkin, Rossi, Verma and Yin, *Study of the Problem of Consumer Indebtedness* (n 16) 113.

44   There is an enormous and steadily growing literature on this topic, mainly guided by the hope that this new regulatory device might lead to a concept of shared responsibilities; see http://www.responsiblelending.org/.

rising housing prices, on which the whole credit construction in the US was built, would collapse. Quite to the contrary, Icelandic, Spanish and American consumers tell endless stories about how vigorously the banks collected their capital, evicting consumers from their homes under court orders.[45] The contingency risk remained with the consumer alone.

There was an undercurrent, easily recognizable, which stood in stark contrast to the creed of easy and democratic access for all. Since 2002 I have participated in this process as a member of the scientific committee of the Schufa,[46] which is by far the largest German credit bureau, organized in the form of a private limited company. Quite independent from the stock market hype and the ambitious promises enshrined in it, the steadily increasing numbers of over-indebted consumers have triggered concern in the banks, politicians and consumer organizations, at the national as well as European level.[47] A growing number of studies on over-indebtedness and on consumer insolvency provide ample evidence for this development. There is division over the reasons for over-indebtedness and insolvency. Consumer organizations have promoted objective reasons such as unemployment and divorce. The banking sector has accepted these external factors but has strongly insisted on subjective individual responsibility, sometimes even going as far as discussing subjective psychological factors that might explain why some consumers are more inclined than others to engage in behaviour leading to over-indebtedness.[48] The legislature by and large followed the individual responsibility mantra promoted by the banking sector and relied on information as the basic tool for educating consumers and making them fit for the market. In this way, the legal information paradigm is inherently linked to financial literacy programmes. There are only a few countries in the EU where objective factors provide a legal argument, enshrined in the doctrine of social *force majeure*.[49] Attempts in countries like Germany to implant such logic through reference to the

---

45   See the report in German tv ARD, *Verzockt und Verklagt, die Guten Geschäfte der Deutschen Bank* (21 May 2012) <http://www.ardmediathek.de/das-erste/reportage-dokumentation/verzockt-und-verklagt-die-guten-geschaefte-der-deutschen?document Id=10592810>. However, in the US, unlike in Germany for example, non-recourse financing was the rule. The decisive parameter was speculation on steadily rising housing prices. Private assets were set aside.

46   See http://www.schufa.de/de/>.

47   Comparato, 'Europe's Steps towards a Financially Inclusive Private Law' (n 3) gives a reconstruction of these activities.

48   See the Schufa study *GFK-Umfrage zu Schuldenneigung und Zahlungswissen* (2003) <http://www.schufa-kredit-kompass.de/de/analysen_/ueberschuldungsforschung/gfk_umfrage.jsp>; Gunter Zimmermann, *Wege in die Überschuldung und ihre Ursachen* (2004) <http://www.schufa-kredit-kompass.de/de/analysen_/ueberschuldungsforschung/wege_in_ueberschuldung.jsp>.

49   See, in particular, Thomas Wilhelmsson, *Social Contract Law and European Integration* (Aldershot 1995).

doctrine of good faith and *bonos mores*, as set down in the German Civil Code, have failed.[50]

In sum, consumer credit legislation was not well prepared for the new challenges triggered by the 'promises of salvation'. The new ideology of financial economics, the colourful world of 'we now all get rich at no risk' or 'there is a decent standard of living even for the poor', stayed at the level of politics and/or sales promotion. Seen through the lens of consumer credit legislation, and through the eyes of banking lawyers and the majority of politicians, the potential consumer default in the aftermath of the crisis appears as just another variant of the self-responsible consumer who participated in the stock market hype without taking precautionary measures – in short, new wine in old bottles.

The *normal consumer* in countries such as Austria, Germany, France and the UK has not yet felt the impact of the global crisis due to the relatively stable economy in those states, which recovered quickly after the crash of the stock markets as a result of the bankruptcy of Lehman Brothers. The *consumers at risk* in countries like Greece and Spain are typically those who suffer most from rather underdeveloped social and legal support systems. Becoming unemployed does not constitute any justification for stopping the debt collection process. Support systems, which could smooth down the impact of over-indebtedness on the individual consumer, exist, but it is hard to say to what extent they are able to cope with the consumer issues that have arisen in light of such massive problems.[51] These countries have introduced consumer insolvency legislation, though in the case of Greece as late as 2010.[52] Many more concrete and hard legal facts may be reported from Iceland where consumers are fighting hard against price-indexation clauses. Here, there is a concrete European private-law dimension. Iceland as a member of the European Economic Area (EEA) has implemented not only the consumer credit directive 2008/48/EC, but also the unfair contract terms directive 93/13. The former does not apply to mortgages, which is subject to a recent EU proposal now pending in the legislature.[53] The above-mentioned Icelandic law that

---

50   OLG Stuttgart NJW 1988, 833; Thomas Wilhelmsson, 'Social Force Majeure – A New Concept in Nordic Consumer Law' (1990) 13 JCP 1.

51   <http://www.sfz.uni-mainz.de/1898.php>. This overview points out that: in Greece, debt advice is provided free of charge by a consumer association, EKPIZO; in Ireland it is provided by the Money Advice and Budgeting Service; in Hungary's bigger cities since 1994 it is provided in cooperation between the Népjóléti Képzési Központ (Institute for Education) and a Dutch company for social services PLAN – Praktijk dynamic assistance bv.

52   For a general overview, see Gerhardt, 'Consumer Bankruptcy Regimes in the US and Europe' (n 17); Signe Viimsalu, 'The Over-indebtedness Regulatory System in the Light of the Changing Economic Landscape' (2010) XVII Juridica International 217, 222, available at <http://www.juridicainternational.eu/public/pdf/ji_2010_1_217.pdf>. With regard to Greece's law 3869/2010, see <http://greeklawdigest.gr/topics/insolvency-bankruptcy/item/78-law-3869-2010-arrangement-of-debts-of-over-draft-individuals>.

53   COM (2011) 142 endg.

legalized price-indexation clauses goes back to *Trummer and Mayer*,[54] in which the ECJ held that parties cannot be forced to express their security right in terms of the national Austrian currency (as it then was), as this deprives them from the right to free movement of capital. That is why the Icelandic parliament legalized contracts for home loans in a foreign currency secured by a property in Iceland with monthly instalments payable in that currency. What is prohibited under Icelandic law is to contract for loans denominated in Icelandic krónas where no real exchange of foreign currency takes place between lender and borrower, and link the payment of both the capital and the interest to the fluctuation of the foreign currencies. Annex 2(l) of the indicated list of directive 93/13/EC prohibits price indexation clauses subject to the fulfilment of two conditions.[55] No ECJ case law exists with regard to the *Trummer and Mayer* verdict. So what remains are 'broken promises', disappointed and desperate consumers and the lesson that the capital has to be repaid.

4 Europe's role and position in the 'easy access to consumer credit' saga

I will argue that the European Union, as it is now called, closely followed the mainstream ideology triggered in the US[56] and took appropriate measures to open up financial markets, thereby paving the way for financial derivatives, a precondition for easy and cheap access to consumer credit. Europe – here being understood as the EU – was all too ready to subscribe to the democratizing function of the new financial markets, though not with the same intensity and the degree of belief that could be reported from the US. In line with Whitman[57] I will present the hypothesis that the US triggered, but the EU promoted, transformation of the European capital market aimed at shifting the focus from European *producerism* to American *consumerism*, the consumer demand side to the producer supply side, or, in policy terms, from social to market regulation, from a long-standing stable policy to short-term welfare considerations. Consumerism fits nicely into the understanding of the EU as a market state, a concept developed elsewhere.

However, the EU has neither the competence nor sufficient political power of its own to directly implement the shift. The EU is not the US, and it is hard to imagine that the differences between them will be overcome despite the rising

---

54   C-222/97 [1999] ECR I-01661.

55   (l) Providing for the price of goods to be determined at the time of delivery or (2) allowing a seller of goods or supplier of services to increase their price without, in both cases, giving the consumer the corresponding right to cancel the contract if the final price is too high in relation to the price.

56   This is not to say that the EU had no choice. One might very well debate the differences between the US and the EU.

57   James Whitman, 'Consumerism versus Producerism, A Study in Comparative Law' (2007–2008) 117 Yale LJ 340.

importance and impact of the market state paradigm. Therefore, in the EU the shift to consumerism (consumer welfare), to market regulation, is accompanied by means of social regulation. Some go as far as arguing that there is a genuine European social model.[58] However, even if such a thing exists, it is of limited importance for the subject-matter of this chapter. The inclusion/exclusion paradigm nicely expresses the ambivalence of the EU approach to financial regulation. It is a 'yes-but' approach: the market should be opened for easy credit – the *consumerism* perspective – but it should be done in such a way that nobody will be excluded, and it is for the state (EU and/or member states) to take appropriate measures to protect consumers in this environment – the *producerism* perspective.[59] And if somebody is excluded, then there should be precautionary regulatory measures to reintegrate him or her – the *producerism* perspective. What makes the role of the EU so complex is that it has competence under the EU Treaty to open up the market – the means to initiate the shift to *consumerism* – but it has no or only limited competence to initiate social regulation, at least not to assure the reintegration of the formerly excluded. This needs to be developed in two steps. I will first look into the market opening process before I embark on social regulation.

Elsewhere I have presented my understanding of the EU as a blueprint of the transformation process,[60] one which can be caught by the notion of the *market state* so forcefully promoted and analysed by Bobbitt,[61] Patterson and Afilalo,[62] and Sassen[63] to name just a few of the most eminent writers. I place the emergence of the market state towards the end of the twentieth century, when global economies started to integrate and give way to a more diffuse, interleaved set of market states whose ethos focused on the preservation of the market and the maximization of opportunity, rather than top-down welfare entitlements. Europe's expansion into market-state regulatory territory coincided with this timetable. The market state paradigm pushes the EU towards *consumerism* and challenges the welfare state variant of *producerism*.

---

58   Dragana Damjonovic and Bruno de Witte, 'Welfare Integration through EU Law: The Overall Picture in the Light of the Lisbon Treaty' in Ulla Neergard, Ruth Nielsen and Lynne Roseberry (eds), *Integrating Welfare Functions into EU Law: From Rome to Lisbon* (DJOF Publishing 2009) 5.

59   See the discussion on Whitman, 'Consumerism versus Producerism' (n 57) in Chapter 1 of this book.

60   Hans-W Micklitz and Dennis Patterson, 'From the Nation State to the Market: The Evolution of EU Private Law as Regulation of the Economy beyond the Boundaries of the European Union' in Bart van Vooren, Steven Blockmans and Jan Wouters (eds), *The Legal Dimension of Global Governance: What Role for the EU?* (OUP 2012).

61   Philip Bobbitt, *The Shield of Achilles: War, Peace and the Course of History* (Knopf 2002).

62   Dennis Patterson and Ari Afilalo (eds), *The New Global Trading Order* (CUP 2008).

63   Saskia Sassen, *Territory, Authority, Rights: From Medieval to Global Assemblages* (Princeton University Press 2006).

This is not the place to tell the full story of the EU transformation process. However, we might need to recapitulate the major steps in that transformation. Seen through the EU lens, the adoption of the Single European Act (SEA) in 1986 constituted the most visible break-even point, which paved the way for EU's successful regulatory programme to complete the 'internal market'. The SEA constituted a turning-point in the history of the European integration process. The building of the 'internal market' was tied to the realization of minimum social standards to the benefit of consumers, although less so of workers. Reconstructed into Whitman's categories,[64] the 'internal market' programme tried to combine the old *producerism* with the new trend towards *consumerism*, being promoted through Carter,[65] and later through Reagan and Thatcher. The next step was less visible and turned out to be even more ground-breaking: the adoption of the Maastricht Treaty in 1991, which established the European and Monetary Union to be realized in 1999/2002. The Maastricht Treaty changed the (ordo-liberal) Economic Constitution of Europe, which had underpinned the European integration process in the first 30 years, thereby relying on a distinction between EU market competencies and member states' social competencies.[66] The Maastricht Treaty did not establish minimum standards for the protection of workers; instead, it deprived the member states of the most powerful tool for combating economic equalities, mainly between the North and South, by devaluing their national currencies – the exit option, a major blow to producerism. A common European currency is certainly not a precondition for the establishment of a European financial market, independent from the market of commodities. But a common European currency helped to shape the financial European market after its US and UK counterparts. Nearly 30 years after the end of Bretton Woods, Europe joined the world economy with a new currency, which competed from then on with the US dollar. This we may call the European turn to *consumerism*.

In the establishment of the new financial market the EU initially played the role of a catalyst. Over time, however, the EU gained political influence and turned out be the driving force behind transforming the requirements of international financial economics into a legal framework for a European financial market. The International Organization of Securities Commissions (IOSCO) became the key player behind the curtain. Marcacci gives the following account:[67]

> Currently, IOSCO has 115 ordinary members (most of them are public financial market regulators), eleven associate members (like regulators non dealing with

---

64   Whitman, 'Consumerism versus Producerism' (n 57).

65   1980 Depository Institutions Deregulation and Monetary Control Act.

66   Christian Joerges, 'A Renaissance of the European Economic Constitution' in Ulla Neergard, Ruth Nielsen and Lynn Roseberry (eds), *Integrating Welfare Functions into EU Law: From Rome to Lisbon* (DJOF Publishing 2009) 29.

67   Antonio Marcacci, 'The EU and IOSCO: An Ever Closer Union?' (EUI–ERC Working Paper, forthcoming). The following analysis of the EU's role in paving the way for securitization is based on this paper.

regulated capital markets), and seventy-five affiliate members (usually stock and futures exchanges or dealers associations) from all around the world.[68] It covers more than ninety-five percent of the world's securities and futures markets,[69] and it is not only the key global institution producing international standards for financial regulation,[70] but it also has wider global responsibilities by being one of the three members of the Joint Forum of international financial regulators, alongside the Basel Committee on Banking Supervision and the International Association of Insurance Supervisors, established in 1996.

What matters in our context is that IOSCO paved the way for the transformation of the financial markets, in what was later been termed the securitization of debts via financial derivatives. Here was where it was decided to transform mortgages into tradable financial products.[71] There was some resistance, but this did not stop the process.[72]

The way in which IOSCO works as an international organization is the perfect example of how the international impact on nation-states operates, how nation-states have to transform into market states, responding to the needs of the market and how producerism in the EU is affected and substantially challenged. It is a non-body; it has no clear institutional and legal status. The decisive criterion for membership is expertise generated in national agencies. Consultation takes place in a closed-shop system, to which the financial sector has access, but not consumers or their representatives. The rules agreed upon are not legally binding, but they have made their way into the legal financial systems of the member states. The EU is an affiliate member only; this means that it is not even on an equal footing with the member states. However, Marcacci has amply demonstrated the EU's growing political influence in IOSCO, independent of the EU's shaky competences in external financial relations.

The impact of the new global financial system, as agreed upon within IOSCU, and its underpinning market-state ideology on the EU is well documented in two pieces of EU legislation that, read together, provide a deeper insight into

---

68   See <https://www.iosco.org/lists/index.cfm?section=general>.

69   See <https://www.iosco.org/about/index.cfm?section=background>.

70   Chris Brummer, 'Post-American Securities Regulation' (2010) 98 California Law Review 327.

71   This is a 1993 resolution: <http://www.iosco.org/library/resolutions/pdf/IOSCO RES10.pdf>. This is a 1996 resolution: <http://www.iosco.org/library/resolutions/pdf/IOSCORES13.pdf>. This is a 2006 resolution: <http://www.iosco.org/library/resolutions/pdf/IOSCORES25.pdf>.

72   OLG Frankfurt (Frankfurt Court of Appeal), 25.5 (2004) 8 U 84/04; (2004) NJW 3266; for a deeper analysis on the personal charachter of a debt, see K-W Knops, *Die Personalität des Schuldverhältnisses: Eine Untersuchung über die Vertragspartnerwahlfreiheit, ihre theoretischen und rechtstatsächlichen Grundlagen und ihre Erosion in der neueren Entwicklung des Zivilrechts und des Umwandlungsrechts* (Mohr Siebeck 2012).

the European variant of the intermingling of producerism and consumerism, or perhaps the 'third way' that Europe is seeking. I will now discuss the so-called MIFID Directive 2004/39/EC[73] and the Consumer Credit Directive 2008/48/EC in light of the producerism–consumerism paradigm. My hypothesis is that both directives, read together, may and should be understood as documenting the shift to consumerism as the dominating feature, despite the consumer protection rhetoric, which seems to point towards the maintenance of the producerism perspective. It is here where the divide between EU consumerism and national producerism can be pinned down, a distinction to which I will return.

The so-called MIFID Directive 2004/39, adopted shortly before the ten new member states officially joined the EU, translated the international agreement requirements for an independent global financial market into a European legal framework.[74] The focus of the legislative debate lay on the development and implementation of appropriate implementation mechanisms, which would allow for a speedy adaptation of the former financial market regulation to the changing international environment through the adoption of appropriate market access rules and the integration of the competent national regulators. Looking at the predecessor Directive 93/22, the more consumer retail investor-oriented approach of the MIFID springs to mind and seems to strengthen old-fashioned European producerism. Indeed, the MIFID introduces the distinction between a 'professional' and 'a retail client' (who can be equated with the consumer within the meaning of the consumer credit directive).[75] The MIFID strengthened the role of the national financial supervisory authorities, focusing on prudential supervision, though cautiously triggering market surveillance.[76] The key consumer protection device

---

73   [2004] OJL 145, 30.4, 1.

74   International Organization of Securities Commissions, 'Objectives and Principles of Securities Regulation' (IOSCO 2010); , International Organization of Securities Commissions, 'Principles for Ongoing Disclosure and Material Development Reporting by Listed Entities' (IOSCO 2002). International Organization of Securities Commissions, 'Client Asset Protection' (IOSCO 1996). These documents were incorporated into MIFID (and other pieces of EU legislation) and they stress the importance of disclosure as a cure-all solution: IOSCO Technical Committee, 'Public Document No 16, International Equity Offers: Changes in Regulation since April 1990' (IOSCO September 1991); IOSCO Technical Committee, 'Public Document No 38, International Equity Offers: Changes in Regulation Since April 1992' (IOSCO October 1994); IOSCO, 'IOSCO Resolution No 44: Resolution on IASC Standards' (IOSCO May 2000); IOSCO Technical Committee, 'IOSCO Public Document No 141: General Principles Regarding Disclosure of Management's Discussion and Analysis of Financial Condition and Results of Operations' (IOSCO February 2003).

75   See Christian Armbruster, 'Kapitalanleger als Verbraucher' (ZIP 2006) <http://zip-online.de/2d4ad60deb95a8e5a34777931df240af>, 406.

76   See Jurgen Kessler, Hans-W Micklitz and Norbert Reich (eds), *Institutionelle Finanzmarktaufsicht und Verbraucherschutz: Eine rechtsvergleichende Untersuchung der Regelungssysteme in Deutschland, Italien, Schweden, dem Vereinigten Königreich und der Europäischen Gemeinschaft* (Nomos 2010).

is information.[77] The MIFID imposed a dense set of mandatory, fully harmonized information and some loose consultation rules on the investment service providers, which are further elaborated in the level 2 directives and regulations. These weak regulatory devices do not reintroduce producerism. The focus on consumerism slipped under the radar of public scrutiny. The European financial market system stood side-by-side with the American market system, allowing for easy access to cheap money. It seems that the Spanish property bubble comes nearest to the US sub-prime crisis. However, contrary to the US where the banks disclosed all the hidden risks directly after the Lehman Brothers bankruptcy, the Spanish banks apply a salami technique similar to that of Greece. The information is made public in portions, and the public remains uncertain as to whether the newest figures are the last ones or whether there is more to come.[78]

The second piece of EU legislation is Directive 2008/48/EC, meant to establish a European consumer credit market. The Directorate-General for Health and Consumers (DG–SANCO) had worked for more than ten years on the revision of the original Directive 87/102.[79] The legislative history is telling in that the European Commission (EC) initially defended a more social model, relatively close to producerism, whereas the European Parliament (EP) pushed for a more consumerist approach, advocating a mere information-based model. The stumbling-block in the debate, not so much between the EC and EP, but between the Community organs and the member states, was the full harmonization principle, in line with the Consumer Strategy 2002–2006.[80] The revised directive is regarded as a milestone in the new European consumer policy enforced in the aftermath of the Lisbon Strategy 2000.[81] The consumer shall 'reap the full benefits

---

77   More generally on the role of the private investor, see Michael Chlistalla, Uwe Schweickert and Roland Wittner, 'Markets in Financial Instruments Directive: The Way Forward in European Securities Market Integration?' (2006) available at <http://ssrn.com/abstract=964492 or http://dx.doi.org/10.2139/ssrn.964492>; Niamh Moloney, 'Building a Retail Investment Culture through Law: The 2004 Markets in Financial Instruments Directive' (2005) 6 European Business Organization Law Review 341–421.

78   See Spiegel online 'Spanische Krisenbank braucht weitere 19 Milliarden Euro' (25 May 2012) <http://www.spiegel.de/wirtschaft/unternehmen/sparkasse-bankia-braucht-von-spanien-19-milliarden-euro-hilfen-a-835382.html>; *Financial Times Deutschland*, 'Bankia-Rettung kommt Spanien immer teurer' (25 May 2012) <http://www.ftd.de/unternehmen/finanzdienstleister/:spanische-sparkasse-bankia-rettung-kommt-spanien-immer-teurer/70041955.html> accessed 25 May 2012.

79   Peter Rott, 'Consumer Credit' in Hans-W Micklitz, Peter Rott and Norbert Reich, *Understanding EU Consumer Law* (Intersentia 2009) 177.

80   [2002] OJC 137, 8.6, 2.

81   European Parliament, 'Lisbon European Council 23 and 24 March 2000: Presidency Conclusions <http://www.europarl.europa.eu/summits/lis1_en.htm> which is currently under revision, COM (2009), 647/3 Provisional – Consultation on the Future '2020' Strategy.

of the internal market'. Whether the directive contains the appropriate tools for setting up an internal market for consumer credit is, however, highly doubtful.[82]

Contrary to the debate around the MIFID, the focus of European consumer credit legislation on market state consumerism did not remain unnoticed. Member states, academics and consumer organizations argued that easy access to cheap credit cannot be regarded as a substitute for an urgently needed social dimension that takes the risks and the consequences for credit consumers into account. This is the starting signal to look into countermovements in EU regulation, the aspects of a European legal framework that stayed focused on those who might not have access, or might have had too easy access to credit, as well as to look at the consequences of over-indebtedness, if not insolvency – in short, the maintenance of producerism during the first decade of the twenty-first century.

5 Countermovements in the EU legal order against the ideology of easy access to consumer credit

As usual in the EU there is no clear-cut picture on the social–producerism perspective. Any such perspective needs to be gleaned from the few existing rules that have to be collected together, principles in the various EU treaties, fundamental rights, protocols to the treaties, secondary Community law and, last but not least, policy recommendations. Arguably, the European legal order provides ground rules in a strange combination of broad constitutional principles concretized in strong policy recommendations on financial inclusion/exclusion and over-indebtedness, on the one hand, and a few hard rules in secondary community law, on the other. Therefore, the degree to which the consumer might benefit from producerism, from social welfare, ultimately depends very much on the standards set in the member states.[83] I will start from a top-down perspective, from the Treaty downwards to policy recommendations.

There is an amazing temporal coincidence between the adoption of the Lisbon Treaty and the global financial crisis. Despite the subterranean cracks in the 'financial market idyll', resulting from uncertainties in the American housing markets as early as 2007, the political discussions on the Lisbon Treaty took place without taking notice of the ground-breaking change in the architecture of the global financial markets. The path-dependency of the drafters, at whatever level, is astonishing. This holds true even with regard to the transformation of nation-states into market states, a process that precedes the financial collapse by nearly 20 years.

---

82   Peter Rott, *Broad Economic Analysis of the Impact of the Proposed Directive on Consumer Credit* (EP Policy Department Economic and Social Policy 2007) <http://www.europarl.europa.eu/comparl/imco/studies/0704_consumercredit_en.pdf>.

83   Sven Steinmö, *The Evolution of the Modern States: Sweden, Japan and the United States* (CUP 2010).

This would have required an open political discussion of the social dimension of the new European legal architecture.

Nevertheless, under French pressure the outlook of the Economic Constitution changed. The formula introduced into Article 3 lit g) of the Treaty of Rome in 1957 on the guarantee of undistorted competition was replaced by non-economic objectives in Article 2 of the Treaty of the European Union (TEU Treaty of Lisbon):

> The Union is founded on the values of respect of human dignity, freedom, democracy, equality, the rule of law and the respect of human rights, including the rights of persons belonging to minorities. These values are common to the Member States in a society in which pluralism, non-discrimination, tolerance, justice, solidarity and equality between women and men prevail.

The economic objectives have been transferred to TUE Article 3(3):

> The Union shall establish an internal market. It shall work for the sustainable development of Europe based on balanced economic growth and price stability, a highly competitive *social* market economy, aiming at full employment and social progress, and a high level of protection and improvement of the quality of the environment. It shall promote scientific and technological advance. (Emphasis added)

The old Art. 3 lit g) has been deported to Protocol 27. The more social outlook of the European Union, not least in combination with the Charter of Fundamental Rights has raised much debate, particularly in France but also in Germany, on the feasibility of a genuine European model.[84]

The Charter is more concrete. Consumer protection is referred to as a principle: Article 36 provides that Union policies shall have a high level of consumer protection and Article 47 grants the consumer the right to effective legal protection. Provided that financial services can be regarded as universal services, which I argue they should,[85] then Article 36, combined with Protocol 14, comes into play.[86]

---

84   See Special issue RIDE 4/2011, 'La constitution économique revisé'; Joerges, 'A Renaissance of the European Economic Constitution' (n 66).

85   Hans-W Micklitz, 'Universal Services: Nucleus for a Social European Private Law?' in Marise Cremona (ed), *Market Integration and Public Services in the European Union* (OUP 2011).

86   Article 1: 'The shared values of the Union in respect of services of general economic interests within the meaning of Article 16 EC Treaty include in particular: the essential role and the wide discretion of national, regional and local authorities in providing, commissioning and organising services of general economic interests as closely as possible to the needs of the users; the diversity between the various services of general economic interest and the differences in the needs and preferences of users that may result from different geographical, social or cultural situations; a high level of quality, safety and affordability, equal treatment and the promotion of universal access and of user rights.'

In investment services, the debate over whether access should be restricted has just started, mainly in the aftermath of the sub-prime crisis. The debate is led by DG Market. The concept of 'responsible investment' does not arise. It remains to be seen whether the envisaged revision of the MIFID will draw a parallel. In consumer credit transactions, the extremely controversial debate turns around the concept and importance of 'responsible lending'.[87] Are creditors obliged, and should they be obliged, to provide advice to consumers on whether the envisaged credit fits their needs, perhaps risking the consumer withdrawing the application?[88] The rule in question (Article 8) is drafted as an information requirement which renders the constitutional uploading difficult. A more outspoken rule on responsible lending is foreseen in the proposal on mortgage credits. However, it is by no means clear whether it will survive the legislative procedure.[89]

There is quite some potential in the combination of individual rights with the principles of the Treaty and the Charter of Fundamental Rights. Loic Azoulai[90] has convincingly shown that the logic of *Viking*[91] and *Laval*[92] can be turned upside down. Private parties, insofar as they are recipients of market freedoms, may very well become addresses of social rights, too. Economic freedoms may be bound to the limits of social rights. The key question is: who are the private parties who could become recipients of economic freedoms? So far the ECJ has only extended the horizontal direct effect to private collective entities. One might wonder, however, whether and to what extent the case law could be extended

---

87   Iain Ramsay, 'From Truth in Lending to Responsible Lending' in Geraint Howells, Andre Janssen and Reiner Schulze (eds), *A Challenge for Party Autonomy and Transactional Fairness* (Ashgate Publishing 2005) 47; Udo Reifner, 'Verantwortungsvolle Kreditvergabe im Europäischen Recht' in Luc Thévenoz and Norbert Reich, *Droit de la consommation Konsumentenrecht* (Nomos 2006), 383; Peter Rott, '"Responsible Lending": Vorsorge statt Nachsorge?' in Gundula Maria Peer (ed), *Die soziale Dimension des Zivilrechts: Zivilrecht zwischen Liberalismus und sozialer Verantwortung, Jahrbuch Junger Zivilrechtswissenschaftler* (Sellier 2003) 173. See also the European Coalition on Responsible Lending website <http://www.verantwortliche-kreditvergabe.net/>; Udo Reifner, 'European Coalition for Responsible Credit: Principles of Responsible Credit' in Christian Twigg-Flesner, Deborah Parry, Geraint Howells and Annette Nordhausen (eds), *The Yearbook of Consumer Law 2008* (Ashgate 2007) 419.

88   For Switzerland's tough policy, see Anja Böhnlein, U Portmann and Hans-W Micklitz, 'Rechtsvergleichende Schlussfolgerungen' in G. Pirker, Georg Kathrein, Franz Mohr and Beate Pirker-Hörmann (eds), *Verschuldung: Individuelle und sozialstaatliche Verantwortung* (vol 37, Lexis Nexis 2008) 113, 197.

89   See Article 14 COM (2011) 142 final and the very supportive Opinion of the European Economic and Social Committee, 29 October 2011.

90   Loic Azoulai, 'The Court of Justice and the Social Market Economy: The Emergence of an Ideal and the Conditions for its Realization' (2008) 45 CMLR 133.

91   Judgment, 11 December 2007, Case 438/05, *The International Transport Workers' Federation and The Finnish Seamen's Union* [2007] ECR I-10779.

92   Judgment, 18 December 2007, Case 341/05, *Laval and Partners* [2007] ECR I-11767.

to the area of universal services, where secondary Community law requires the member states to nominate one supplier of last resort who provides access to the public services and where a parallel can be drawn to financial services. *Viking* and *Laval* might pave the way for imposing social rights on private parties, an issue very well known in international economic law.[93] In such a light, the notion of responsible lending, combined with the constitutional principles, may gain importance as a constitutional concept. The poor record of the EU legislature is somewhat compensated by the perspectives it offers for the judiciary. However, so far this is mere intellectual speculation; there are no cases pending.

At the lower end of the community measures appear the declarations and recommendations on financial inclusion/exclusion. As Comparato has shown,[94] it took the EU until 2007 to recognize explicitly the link between social and financial exclusion/inclusion.[95] Concrete measures are not envisaged. If anything, the EC is strongly advocating financial literacy as a solution to financial exclusion. This remains very much within the consumerism perspective and provides little help to the socially and financially excluded, at least in the short run. Over time the European Commission has become more focused on over-indebted and insolvent consumers. Since 1994 the EC has financed a number of statistical studies on over-indebtedness. Comparato concludes:

> As a consequence of this involvement [of the European Ministers of Justice], a Group of Specialists on Seeking Legal Solutions to Debt Problems (CJ-S-DEBT) was appointed and entrusted to prepare a draft Recommendation. On this basis, Recommendation (2007)8 of the Committee of Ministers to member states on legal solutions of debt problems was issued. This recommendation explicitly refers to over-indebtedness as a cause of social exclusion that has to be mainly prevented and whose consequences have to be alleviated by the member states.[96]

The just adopted Consumer Agenda calls for 'a snapshot of the situation and list(ing) the best practices in force'.[97]

The result is modest, to say the least. European law does not really care about the socially and financially excluded. At the European level, consumerism prevails over producerism. There are no requirements against which the national rules on financial inclusion/exclusion could be measured, perhaps with the exception

---

93   Alien Tort Act (multinational corporations as addressees of human rights); see, from the vast literature, Gralf-Peter Calliess and Peer Zumbansen, *Rough Consensus and Running Code: A Theory of Transnational Private Law* (Hart 2011).

94   Comparato, 'Europe's Steps towards a Financially Inclusive Private Law' (fn 3).

95   COM (2005) 629, as identified by the European Parliament.

96   Comparato, 'Europe's Steps towards a Financially Inclusive Private Law' (fn 3).

97   The full title is *A European Consumer Agenda: Boosting Confidence and Growth* (COM 2012) 325 final, under 4.4 financial services.

of constitutional rights, fundament rights and soft-law recommendations. Even worse, there is no European civil society, which would allow for bringing together those consumers who are the potential or real victims of the global financial crisis. There is not even a common financial European market that would spread the risk of failure equally among consumers, independent of their nationality. The European consumer organization, BEUC, is stuck at the European policy level. The bankruptcy of Lehman Brothers triggered litigation in a number of member states.[98] Private investors tried to seek compensation from the banks that marketed the toxic papers, claiming a lack of information and/or appropriate advice. Others have sued the national supervisory authorities, blaming them for insufficient supervision of the market to the detriment of private investors. Both strains of litigation must be read in conjunction with the disappointment over broken promises, and both bear a genuine European dimension. The first addresses the question as to whether and to what extent advertising measures on the 'promised land of the new financial economics' impact private law obligations. The second turns on state liability under the MIFID Directive, which has already been subject of an ECJ case, though in a different context.

Overall, the claimants have not even tried to exploit the relevant aspects of European law, in the first case, Directive 2005/29/EC on unfair commercial practices,[99] and the MIFID Directive 2004/39 in its twofold objective: protection of the market and investors.[100] The producerist potential of the European legal order remained untouched, as did consideration as to how far it could potentially reaches and whether it would really improve the situation of the consumers at risk or affected consumers.[101] None of the national consumer organizations took a European-wide initiative. BEUC would have liked to do so, but met resistance from national organizations and suffers from a lack of resources anyway. Even worse, the European legal order bars BEUC as the sole competent European actor to launch an action in the court. BEUC has no legal standing, either under EU or national law. There is no European counterpart to the American class action to mobilize the law collectively and seek compensation for financial losses. At the 'last resort' avenue of judicial protection, consumers in the EU remain prisoners

---

98   Caterina Ghelli Luserna di Rorà, 'Investor Protection after the Lehmann Brothers Case' (EUI LLM thesis 2011); Sebastian Capek, *Der Anlegerschutz in Deutschland: Welche Rechte haben geschädigte Anleger von Lehman Brothers Zertifikaten?* (Diplomica Verlag 2010).

99   See Hans-W Micklitz and N Reich, *AGB-Recht und UWG – (endlich) ein Ende des Kstchendenkens nach Perenic'ova und Invitel?* (Europäische Zeitschrift für Wirtschafts- und Steuerrecht 2012) 257.

100   See Kessler, Micklitz and Reich, *Institutionelle Finanzmarktaufsicht und Verbraucherschutz* (n 76).

101   The Heiniger saga does not trigger much hope. However, Icelandic consumers and consumer activists are seeking support in the European legal order to strike down price-indexation clauses; see Mendez-Pinedo, *Overview of European Consumer Credit Law* (n 20).

in their national legal boxes – separated from each other and individualized. The resocialization process triggered via the crisis is a lonely process. It does not take place in the public eye.

6 What can Europe do to redesign the level of protection for consumers? An outlook

Each crisis is an opportunity. The deeper the crisis, the broader the opportunities to rethink financial market design. Taking a genuinely European, realistic and pragmatic perspective, I will outline what I would like. First and foremost, this means taking as given the divide between the consumerist European market state and the producerist national welfare states with all their differences. It is hard to imagine that the EU will adopt regulatory measures to overcome social and financial exclusion, either through an upgrading of responsible investment and responsible lending or through the introduction of a European scheme on consumer insolvency backed by debt and advice centres along the lines of Chapter 11 bankruptcy, but for consumers rather than companies,[102] let alone all the other instruments on the 'wish-lists' of consumer advocates, such as class actions which, in the US, counterbalance the weaknesses of market regulation via public agencies. Maybe directly after the collapse of Lehman Brothers and the stock market crash, there was some preparedness to take the consumer–investor dimension in the post-crisis financial architecture more seriously, but these inclinations faded away, first with the quick recovery of economies and then with the dominance of state defaults. Getting to grips with socially and financially excluded consumers in the future will depend more than ever on member states' willingness and capacities.

However, I am wondering why the EU could not play a similar political role in the area of financial services to the one it plays in the promotion of human rights[103] and environmental protection in its external relations. In the last couple of years the ECJ has strengthened the position of the EC and the EU in defending higher human rights and higher environmental standards against international pressure, in particular from the US. It suffices to recall the *Kadi* judgment[104] and the judgment in *Air Transport Association of America* on emissions trading.[105] With some

---

102   There is a long-standing and still ongoing discussion in the US as to whether Chapter 11 on Business Reorganizations should be extended to consumer bankruptcies; see Sally S Neel, 'Chapter 11 Business Reorganizations: How BAPCAP Changes Chapter 11 Cases for Individuals' (American Law Institute/American Bar Association Continuing Legal Education ALI-ABA Course of Study 28–29 April, 2011).

103   Marise Cremona and Bruno de Witte (eds), *EU Foreign Relations La: Constitutional Fundamentals* (Hart 2008).

104   ECJ C-402/05P and C-415/05 P [2008] ECR I-6351.

105   ECJ, 21 December 2011, Case C-366/10 *American Airlines Association v Secretary of State for Energy and Climate Change* (K) nyr.

imagination, one might even read the *Kadi* logic into the *TNT* judgment,[106] in which the ECJ strongly argued that international commercial law rules must be 'equivalent' to the EU rules, thereby 'defending' higher liability standards within Europe.

Along this line of argument I would like to propose three measures aimed at strengthening a more investor–creditor-oriented financial architecture for Europe, which could set a benchmark beyond the internal market. They build on the regulatory parallel between product safety and financial products regulation.[107] In product safety, as in human rights and environmental protection, the EU has played an ever more important role worldwide. Drawing a parallel between dangerous consumer products and toxic financial products would fit into the image the EU has given itself in the international arena. A European contribution could be built on three pillars:[108]

1. A directive or regulation shaped along the line of the product safety directive 2001/95, which is currently under revision to include services. I have laid down my arguments for this elsewhere, so I refrain from going into details here. The idea is to oblige all those who bring financial products on to the market to take systemic risks into consideration.[109]
2. A prior approval procedure for particularly dangerous financial products. In the aftermath of the crisis, the banking sector, at least in Europe, started to discuss how to rank financial products according to the degree of risks they produce for the market and for investors. These attempts quickly faded away because politicians failed to show any preparedness to get to grips with the product regulation of financial services. However, ranking provides the answer.
3. A shift from prudential supervision to market surveillance – a process which, in Europe, started with the adoption of the MIFID, but never led in practice to substantial changes. Again, product safety regulation could serve as a blueprint, particularly in combination with Regulations 765 and 768/2008[110] on market surveillance.

---

106   4 May 2010, Case C-533/08 *TNT v AXA* [2010] ECR I-nyr at 49.

107   Elizabeth Warren, Issue 5, Summer 2007, 'Unsafe at Any Rate' (2007) 8(5) Democracy <http://www.democracyjournal.org/5/6528.php>.

108   In the same vein, Sol Picciotto, 'Dis-embedding and Regulation: The Paradox of International Finance' in Christian Joerges and Joseph Falke (eds), *Karl Polanyi, Globalisation and the Potential of Law in Transnational Markets* (Hart 2011), 157.

109   Hans-W Micklitz, 'Herd Behaviour and Third Party Impact as a Legal Concept – On Tulips, Pyramid Games and Asset-backed Securities' in Stefan Grundmann, Florian Mößlein and Karl Riesenhuber (eds), *Contract Governance: Dimensions in Law and Interdisciplinary Research* (OUP forthcoming).

110   OJL 218, 13.8.2008, 30 setting out the requirements for accreditation and market surveillance relating to the marketing of products and repealing Regulation (EEC) No 339/93.

It is beyond the scope of this chapter to develop such a concept in detail. However, it would be consistent with the EU's regulatory approach, in which the emphasis has always been on market access. A general clause and a prior approval procedure could be incorporated into such a scenario. Over time the European legislature had to accept, first in product safety, then in services of general economic interests and now in financial services, that a European enforcement structure is needed as a counterpart to European open access rules, particularly when surveillance is exercised not only to guarantee the workability of the market, but also to take care of the interests of private investors who may then to a certain limit hold the financial authorities accountable for non-action or insufficient action. From a US perspective, such a scenario may signal a return to European producerism. However, it is unrealistic to assume that the EU will adopt a US-style class action mechanism in the field of financial markets. There is only a timid European civil society that is ready to engage in collective actions to hold the private investors responsible. With the exception of the Netherlands,[111] member states do not allow for forum shopping and are not ready to establish a European platform for collective, if not class, actions.

---

111   Franziska Weber and Willem H van Boom, 'Dutch Treat: The Dutch Collective Settlement of Mass Damage Act (WCAM 2005)' (2011) 1 Contratto e impresa/Europa 69; Andreas Mom, *Kollektiver Rechtsschutz in den Niederlanden* (Mohr Siebeck 2011).

PART III
Current Responses

Chapter 4

Culture or Politics? Models of Consumer Credit Regulation in France and the UK

Iain Ramsay

Credit is like cholesterol. There is good and bad.

Christine Lagarde[1]

Britain is a sort of United States within easy reach of Europe, but without the attraction of the frontier.[2]

1 Introduction

The Great Recession[3] has stimulated reappraisal of credit regulation and analysis of the relationship of household credit to changes in capitalism over recent decades, when household finance became a large share of bank profits.[4] Consumer credit may be a substitute for redistribution,[5] a supplement for stagnant wages,[6] with housing bubbles funded by easy mortgage credit providing a form of demand-side Keynesianism to substitute for government investment.[7] Christine Lagarde's comment above suggests that countries should adopt institutional structures for regulation which encourage the 'right' rather than the 'wrong' type of credit, recognizing that institutions matter in shaping access to markets and individuals' exposure to, or protection from, risk. Governments have rarely left credit 'to the market' since credit is often an instrument of economic and social policy, and is central to housing policy.

---

1   See <http://www2.economie.gouv.fr/protection-du-consommateur/index-credit-consommation.html> accessed 19 June 2012.

2   Rosa-Maria Gelpi and François Julien-Labruyere, *The History of Consumer Credit Doctrines and Practices* (Palgrave Macmillan 2000) 133.

3   See IMF, 'Dealing with Household Debt' in *World Economic Outlook: Growth Resuming Dangers Remain* (IMF 2012) 89–124.

4   Paulo Dos Santos, 'On the Content of Banking in Contemporary Capitalism' (2009) 17 Historical Materialism 170.

5   Raghuram Rajan, *Fault Lines: How Hidden Fractures Still Threaten the World Economy* (Princeton University Press 2010).

6   Aldo Barba and Massimo Pivetti, 'Rising Household Debt: Its Causes and Macroeconomic Implications – A Long Period Analysis' (2009) 33 Cambridge Journal of Economics 113.

7   Colin Crouch, *The Strange Non-Death of Neoliberalism* (Polity 2011).

This chapter focuses on the ground rules for consumer credit in France and the UK. This might appear to be a narrow and Eurocentric focus. However, these countries represent distinct approaches to consumer and mortgage credit within both the EU and other high-income countries. Before the Great Recession, France appeared to the casual observer as an exception to the dominance of neoliberalism associated with US and UK economic models.[8] The recent international success of French author Stéphane Hessel's *Indignez-vous*, which upholds a French 'social model', seems emblematic of a 'French alternative'. France and the UK therefore provide sites for understanding the significance and consequences of distinct approaches to not only consumer finance, but also the role of the state in exposing its citizens to, and protecting them from, market risks.

Several differences exist in the ground rules of credit markets in the two countries. Interest rate ceilings on consumer and mortgage credit exist in France but not in the UK. French policy-makers and consumer groups regard ceilings as a protection for consumers from the dangers of high-cost credit, over-indebtedness and potential social exclusion.[9] In contrast, UK policy-makers and consumer groups generally regard ceilings as creating financial exclusion and increasing illegal lending. Second, distinct credit reporting regimes operate in France and the UK. Positive credit reporting and private credit reference agencies exist in the UK, whereas negative reporting, managed by the Bank of France, operates in France. Third, until the mid-2000s home equity lending was not possible in France, so homes could not operate as a piggy-bank for consumer credit withdrawal, and home mortgage lending practices differ between the two countries. Fourth, there are higher supply-side barriers to entry for consumer credit lenders in France than in the UK. Finally, French higher courts are more likely to 'moralize the market' than English courts.

Perhaps as a consequence of these policies, a substantially lower level of consumer and mortgage credit has existed in France, compared with the UK and the US. In 2008 the ratio of household debt to gross disposable income was 95 per cent in France and 175 per cent in the UK,[10] and France's level of consumer credit was half that of the UK. In 2009 the home ownership rate in France was 63.3 per cent compared with 69 per cent in the UK.

The institutional differences outlined above may represent distinct collective understandings of the role of consumer credit in the economy – a democratic social choice in France for greater protection from the market rather than a UK emphasis on consumer choice.[11] This distinction is sometimes collapsed into the argument

---

8   For a full discussion, see Monica Prasad, 'Why is France so French? Culture Institutions, and Neo Liberalism, 1974–81' (2005) 111 American Journal of Sociology 357.

9   See the discussion in Iain Ramsay, '"To Heap Distress upon Distress?" Comparative Reflections on Interest Rate Ceilings' (2010) 60 University of Toronto LJ 707.

10   Athling Management, *Pour un développement responsable du crédit renouvelable*, Report for the Comité Consultatif du Secteur Financier (Athling Management, 2008).

11   '[T]he French tradition ... protects the consumer against himself' and 'the majority of French society is distrustful of credit': Claude Taffin and Bernard Vorms, *Elargir l'accès*

that cultural differences exist between these countries in their approach to credit – that France has distinct historical traditions which result in a distrust of credit and neoliberal models of the role of credit in the economy. While culture underlines the importance of historical tradition, I reject the idea of culture as the dominant explanation for the differences in ground rules between the two countries.[12] Neoliberal ideas have been influential in both countries, and the explanation for the distinct trajectories lies rather in political economy and the role of political interest groups, including state interests as well as elements of path-dependency and contingency.

Section 2 sketches the distinct historical trajectories of the UK and France in regulating household credit and the role of political interest groups, and ideas in that trajectory. Section 3 focuses on central distinctions in the institutional frameworks: the role of credit information systems, interest-rate ceilings, mortgage financing, and private-law ground rules. Section 4 draws together themes from this discussion and discusses the potential distributional consequences of the differences. Section 5 sets this discussion within the contemporary politics of developing a European approach to credit markets and over-indebtedness. There is no 'European model' of credit regulation but a contemporary conflict between interest groups, including state and EU actors, that appeals to distinct ideas about the role of credit markets in facilitating choice and creating risks for consumers. The French–English comparison is relevant to the European debate in its demonstration of the limits of empiricism in settling these conflicts, the unconvincing nature of arguments based on 'national traditions' or culture, and the consequent need to understand the political economy of the influence of transnational interest groups and ideas at the European level.

2 Explaining the distinct trajectories

France

Post-Second World War governments in France and the UK controlled the overall levels of consumer credit so that it did not crowd out investment in production and reconstruction. Terms control – requiring minimum deposits and limiting repayment periods – existed in both countries. Consumer credit was primarily associated with retailers and specialized finance companies which provided credit mainly to working-class consumers, with the mainstream banks playing little role

---

au crédit au logement des emprunteurs atypiques (2007) <http://www.anil.org/fileadmin/ ANIL/Etudes/2007/acces_credit_emprunteurs_atypiques.pdf>. Others perceive 'an entirely different culture of money and borrowing and debt': John Lanchester, *Whoops! Why Everyone Owes Everyone and No One Can Pay* (Penguin 2010).

12 See the discussion in Prasad, 'Why is France So French?' (n 8) 374–381.

until the 1970s and the increasing *bancarisation* of the population.[13] Consumer credit was regressive in the UK. More affluent consumers could write off mortgage interest: in 1969 a small minority of consumers could access overdrafts at 9 per cent while the average hire-purchase interest rate was 28 per cent.[14] Both countries differed from the US where a large growth of mortgage and consumer credit in the post-war era supported a 'consumer's republic'[15] where access to credit was increasingly regarded as a right and was subsequently linked to the civil rights movement. At the end of the 1960s UK and French levels of consumer credit relative to disposable income were one-third of those in the US and Canada, and in 1970 the UK was the least unequal society in Europe and France the most unequal.[16]

Policy-making in France and the UK reflected the influence of different groups. In France, labour and family groups were influential within the consumer movement, and labour representatives on the Economic and Social Council on Credit distrusted credit, viewing it as an erosion of working-class buying power and as an aspect of labour exploitation.[17] Jean Baudrillard reflected this sentiment in 1970, characterizing credit as a 'disciplinary process' that 'extorted' savings.[18] Price controls were a central part of economic regulation in post-war France so that modernized interest-rate ceilings, introduced in 1966 and updated in 1989, were a natural form of regulation. Transactional control of consumer credit was introduced by the Loi Scrivener of 1978, inspired partly by the English Consumer Credit Act of 1974, which focuses on pre-contractual informational obligations and cooling-off periods. An important French addition in 1984 was the strict regulation of *crédit gratuit* – offers of 'free' credit.[19]

Consumer credit increased significantly during the 1980s when the Mitterand government, in a neoliberal turn, deregulated financial services only three years after nationalizing the banks. However, the financial crisis of the late 1980s resulted in a brake on credit, and the introduction of a series of consumer protection measures in 1989, including updating the form of interest-rate ceilings, the introduction of over-indebtedness commissions and registration on a *fichier negatif* for individuals applying to the Commission. There has been a continuing increase during the 1990s

---

13   For the development in France, see Jeanne Lazarus, *L'épreuve de l'argent. Banques, banquiers, clients* (Calmann-Lévy 2012).

14   See Avner Offner, *The Challenge of Affluence* (OUP 2006) 189.

15   See Elizabeth Cohen, *A Consumers' Republic* (Knopf 2003); and Gunnar Trumbull, *Consumer Credit in Postwar America and France: The Political Construction of Economic Interest* (CUP in press 2012).

16   As measured by the Gini co-efficient. See Prasad, 'Why is France so French?' (n 8) Table 2, 362.

17   See the discussion in Alain Chatriot, 'Protéger le consommateur contre lui-même: La régulation du crédit à la consommation' (2006) Vingtième Siècle Revue d'Histoire 95.

18   Jean Baudrillard, 'Consumer Society' in *Jean Baudrillard: Selected Writings* (ed. Mark Poster, Stanford UP 2001) 49.

19   See now L. 311–27 of the Consumer Code.

and 2000s of over-indebtedness as measured by those using the state-financed over-indebtedness commissions that dominate the treatment of over-indebtedness in France. Reforms to the over-indebtedness regime in 1995, 2003 and 2010 have created a publicly financed personal insolvency system.

During the early 2000s the French conservative government promoted consumer credit as a method of economic growth, to kick-start a sluggish economy.[20] The 'Anglo-Saxon' model of using credit to drive the economy seemed attractive, and the argument was aired that the French population were *under-indebted*.[21] This may also have reflected French banks' interest in the highly profitable household finance market. The Châtel reforms in 2005 had somewhat modified the strict regulation on offers of *crédit gratuit.* This regulation had been justified in 1984 as consumer protection to protect individuals against impulsive purchases. However, banks and smaller retailers viewed offers of *crédit gratuit* as unfair competition by large retailers and department stores and had criticized the practice. There was, to paraphrase Whitman, an underlying 'producerist' theme to this consumer protection.[22] In 2006, two further measures to stimulate growth through credit were the *hypothèque rechargeable* that permitted the possibility of using a mortgage for equity release, and reverse mortgages (*le prêt viager hypothécaire*). Some economists attacked the role of interest-rate ceilings as leading to credit exclusion.[23]

The credit crisis has tempered enthusiasm for the 'Anglo-Saxon' model, and there is continuing concern about the increasing number of applications to the over-indebtedness commissions. Christine Lagarde, in introducing the 2010 reforms to implement the 2008 EU Consumer Credit Directive indicated that the objective was 'to protect consumers without discouraging consumer credit'.[24] Consumer credit was a useful method of budgeting for both small and large purchases and contributed to maintaining economic growth during a period of crisis. There is a mild tendency to describe problems in consumer credit practices, such as *crédit renouvelable* (see below) as being of 'Anglo-Saxon' origin, although *crédit renouvelable* differs from the model of the all-purpose credit card.

The French banking system is relatively concentrated, and the large network of branches and tax benefits for the mutual banks that dominate retail banking create barriers to foreign entrants. The EU has initiated antitrust actions against

---

20 Isabelle Rey-Lefebvre, 'La croissance par l'emprunt?' *Le Monde* (12 January 2004); Catherine Maussion, 'Faut il s'endetter plus?' *Libération* (13 June 2007).

21 Joel Bourdin, *Accès des ménages au crédit en France* (Senate 2006).

22 James Whitman, 'Consumerism versus Producerism: An Essay in Comparative Law' (2008) 117 Yale LJ 340. See also Christian Gavalda, 'Un frein à l'extension du crédit gratuit' (1984) D Chronique 181.

23 See, for example, André Babeau, *La Demande des Ménages en Matière de Crédit à la Consommation et les Ajustements Nécessaires pour y Répondre* (BIPE 2006).

24 Assemblée Nationale, first sitting, Discussion d'un projet de loi adoptée par le Sénat (24 March 2010).

French financial practices that limit foreign entry or competition[25] in the payment card market. Significant controls exist on supply-side entry in terms of minimum capital requirements and a prospective lender must be authorized by the Autorité de Controle Prudential (ACP),[26] the new financial regulatory agency modelled partly on the UK's Financial Services Authority (FSA).

Banks in France have historically focused on relationship lending, relying on opportunities to cross-sell other products, such as insurance, with high barriers to switching. Contemporary policies, as in the UK, propose to reduce these barriers and make bank charges more transparent. A contrast is often drawn between England and France in terms of the variety and depth of the English credit and mortgage market, sometimes attributed to the absence of interest-rate ceilings, positive credit information and less competition in the French market.

Consumer credit in France consists of personal loans, overdrafts and the *crédit renouvelable* that grew out of financing of retail credit,[27] offering general lines of credit to established clients of retailers and mail-order companies. It is a central form of French working-class credit. These forms of credit are partly a consequence of institutional history. Trumbull notes that the electronic payment system established by the French *carte bleu* system of 'credit cards' was structured only for debit payments: the English practice of carrying a balance on the card was not possible. *Crédit renouvelable* is not dissimilar to a continuing line of credit with fixed levels of repayment. It is possible to borrow small amounts of money that are advertised to assist consumers to pay for items such as unexpected car repairs. Le Compte Accessio operated by Cofidis, for example, offers consumer loans of €400 for this purpose. Repayment is staggered over a year or longer (*express, rapide, confort*) unlike the Anglo-Saxon payday loan which is a short-term repayment. As an individual pays down the €400, the balance is available for other credit use. Because the initial repayment period is longer than a payday loan, the interest rate does not exceed the usury rate. When the usury laws were amended in 1989, this was recognized as a distinct category with rates higher than a personal loan.

This form of credit evokes similar controversies to credit card debt in the UK. *Crédit renouvelable* is popular because of its convenience and speed and the freedom it provides to a consumer from the necessity of facing a bank employee who might apply 'bourgeois' norms and wish to know the reason for the loan.[28]

---

25   See, for example. Résumé de la décision de la Commission du 17 octobre 2008 relative à une procédure d'application de l'article 81 du traité CE (Affaire COMP/D1/38.606) [notifiée sous le numéro C(2007) 5060 final]. Journal officiel no C 183 du 05/08/2009). 0012–0012.

26   Ordonnance no 2010-76 du 21 janvier 2010 portant fusion des autorités d'agrément et de contrôle de la banque et de l'assurance.

27   See the discussion in Helen Ducourant, 'Le crédit revolving: un succès populaire ou l'invention de l'endetté permanent?' (2009) 76 Sociétés Contemporaines 41, 46.

28   Pauline Jauneau and Christine Olm, *Les conditions d'accès aux services bancaires des ménages vivant sous le seuil de pauvreté* (CREDOC 2010) <http://www.banque-

Some low-income households have no alternative to this form of credit.[29] Critics describe it as leading to a 'spiral of over-indebtedness' and cite statistics indicating that 80 per cent of over-indebtedness files contain a *crédit renouvelable*. The Loi Lagarde of 2010 now requires minimum capital repayments, limits on the length of contracts and a requirement that retailers offering *crédit renouvelable* also offer a personal loan with fixed repayments for purchases over a certain amount.[30]

The municipal pawnshop, the '*crédit municipal*', that grew out of the state pawnshop, the *mont-de-piêté*, caters to the 'sub-sub-prime' consumer. Two-thirds of users of these shops are women, and the great majority are immigrants; the loans requested range from €100 to €2,000. Consolidation loans as a form of credit repair also exist in France – the so-called *rachats de credit* – but the ceilings on loans secured on real estate prevent the existence of the so-called tertiary second-mortgage market (as in the UK), which charges high rates of interest.

The UK: Crowther to the Coalition

A key document in the UK was the Crowther Report in 1971,[31] chaired by the mercurial Geoffrey Crowther, former editor of *The Economist*. The Report legitimated and promoted consumer credit within 'a competitive environment which will ... offer every incentive for innovation and experiment'. It distanced consumer credit from its seedy association with moneylending, the Moneylenders Acts 1900–1927 or paying on the 'never-never', the colloquial term for hire purchase that was the predominant form of working-class credit. The Committee argued that consumer credit could be as productive a form of credit as credit directed towards business investment, marshalling a battery of economic arguments for its generally beneficial role in the economy and the need to liberate the credit market from historically complex regulation which seemed to be based on a model of credit as a 'dangerous business'.[32] The Committee's proposals were intended to make the consumer market attractive to the high-street banks, which until then had been involved in credit through their finance company subsidiaries. Consumer confidence in the increased use of credit was a primary goal of regulation, but the Committee was concerned that it 'did not bend too far in its efforts to protect the consumer because in certain situations the creditor was equally in need of

---

france.fr/ccsf/fr/telechar/publications/rapport_credoc_etude_conditions_acces_services_bancaires_pauvrete.pdf>.

29   Ibid.

30   See L311-8-1, 311–16, 311–17 and the discussion in Jean Calais-Auloy and Henri Temple, *Droit de la Consommation* (8th edn, Dalloz, 2010) paras 361-1–361-4.

31   Gordon Borrie, in 'The Credit Society: Its Benefits and Burdens' (1986) Journal of Business Law 181, refers to Crowther as establishing the 'post-war orthodoxy on consumer credit'.

32   Lord Loreburn, describing moneylending in *Kirkwood v Gadd* [1910] AC 422.

protection'.[33] Crowther drew on US and Canadian experience, countries whose debt relative to personal income levels were then almost three times those of the UK.[34] Criticism by the DTI of its neglect of European sources elicited the comment that 'Britain appears to be on the way to the US and Canadian position as far as the economics of consumer credit goes, rather than the European one.'[35]

The Committee concluded that 'it is possible for the individual to use too little as well as too much'[36] credit and its starting-point was that 'the state should interfere as little as possible with the consumer's freedom to use his knowledge of the consumer credit market to the best of his ability and according to his judgment of what constitutes his best interests'.[37] Abolition of terms control – which required minimum deposits and maximum repayment periods as part of macro-economic policy to restrain demand, dampen inflation and induce manufacturers to focus on the export market – was recommended.

The Committee's recommendations were supported by the Consumers Association, the middle-class consumer group that had campaigned strongly for truth in lending, but did not support interest-rate ceilings as a method of consumer protection.[38] The credit industry 'warmly welcomed' the findings of the Committee.[39] Labour groups contributed little to the Crowther Committee, and the Labour party failed to develop a coherent consumer policy until the development of New Labour in the mid-1990s.[40]

---

33   Minutes of the Crowther Committee 18 September 1969, CCC 69(11) BT 250/49 National Archives BT 250/12.

34   Ibid Table 3.5, 123.

35   Letter from N H Nail (Secretary to Committee) to Hyde (DTI) 21 April 1971, National Archives BT 250/5.

36   *Consumer Credit: Report of the Crowther Committee* (Cmnd 4596, HMSO 1971) para 3.2.6.

37   Ibid para 3.9.1.

38   See the Consumers Association's submission to the Crowther Committee: 'Maximum rates were dangerous because they could lead to a clustering of all rates close to the maximum. In certain cases it might be right to say that there should be an upper limit and perhaps the Credit Commissioner ... could be given reserve power to impose such a limit': CCC. (69) 9th meeting, Section B, Oral Evidence Consumers' Association (National Archives BT 250/123). The Citizens Advice Bureau, in their evidence, noted that '[i]t was suggested that it might be possible to control instalment charges but it was agreed that this was not a good idea as any legally enforced maximum would probably become the standard rate': Oral Evidence, National Citizens Advice Bureau Council to Crowther Committee CCC (69) 6th Meeting, Section A, para 22. (National Archives, BT 250/49).In 1980 the National Consumer Council, assessing the development of the consumer credit market, commented that 'any traditional mistrust of credit as such which may have inclined people towards its close regulation must be dissociated from a practical concern about genuine risks of abuse, exploitation or harmful confusion': National Consumer Council, *Consumers and Credit* (NCC 1980) 19.

39   *The Times* (21 November 1971).

40   Although it did establish the National Consumer Council in 1974. See the discussion in Matthew Hilton, *Consumerism in 20th Century Britain* (CUP, 2003) 295.

The Crowther recommendations embodied in the Consumer Credit Act 1974 would not be fully implemented until the early 1980s, a period that coincided with Thatcherite deregulation and the macro-economic use of credit as a method of stimulating the economy. However, the Report did provide intellectual scaffolding for the 1980s deregulation when a major rise in consumer and housing credit was triggered by the abolition of the Bank of England corset on lending, mortgage market deregulation that effectively ended the interest-rate cartel operated by the building societies, and abolition of terms control. The entry of the banks into housing finance and the sale of council housing led to a substantial rise in household credit. Social grants to low-income consumers were abolished in 1988 to be replaced by interest-free loans from the new social fund. The crash of 1989 resulted in substantial increases in mortgage foreclosures and bankruptcies. Temporary measures were enacted to control the level of foreclosures, but the general approach of the Conservative government during the 1990s was against protection for consumers from credit market risks, with most reform focusing on the possibility of deregulation. The main reform document of 1994 was titled *Consumer Credit Deregulation*.[41] From the late 1990s financial exclusion became a significant topic, sometimes attributed to the increased use of automatic credit-scoring techniques, which also contributed to the growth of the sub-prime lending regime.

Crowther's ideological influence is evident in the most recent statement of the Coalition government.[42]

> [W]e want all consumers to be empowered to make better choices for themselves. Consumers should be free to borrow if that is what they decide is in their best interest. It is not for the government to pass judgement on whether a particular product is good or bad but, in line with the Coalition principles of freedom, fairness and responsibility, we want to provide consumers with the tools they need to make informed decisions … [W]e want to ensure there is a safe and fair regulatory framework for both credit and personal insolvency. These frameworks must protect vulnerable consumers, particularly those at risk of falling into or those already in financial difficulty, and drive rogue companies out of the market.

But the Great Recession has also resulted in more focus in the UK on *ex ante* controls on credit to prevent 'toxic products' being marketed. The chief executive of the new Financial Conduct Authority that will regulate consumer finance has stated that:

---

41   OFT, *Consumer Credit Deregulation* (OFT 1994).

42   HM Treasury and Department of Business Innovation and Skills, *Consumer Credit and Personal Insolvency Review: Formal Response* (2011) 3. Available at <http://www.bis. gov.uk/assets/biscore/consumer-issues/docs/c/11-1341-consumer-credit-and-insolvency-response-on-credit>.

We need ... a new approach to getting the right outcomes for consumers ... The regulatory model had failed. The standard orthodoxy was that ... people make rational decisions when given sufficient information: that market are self-correcting and that if you oversee the distribution channels – the right products get to the right people. All three orthodoxies failed.[43]

Greater *ex ante* intervention earlier in the product chain is proposed in a number of documents, and the new Financial Conduct Authority (FCA) will have the power to suspend the supply of dangerous financial products. Introducing the second reading of the Financial Services Bill in the House of Lords the government states:

The Bill will also establish the Financial Conduct Authority as a focused conduct-of-business regulator. The Bill is good news for consumers of financial services. The FCA will be proactive in securing better outcomes for consumers, with a new competition objective and a new power to ban or impose requirements on products that could cause consumer detriment, enabling the FCA to intervene earlier, before there is evidence of widespread harm. This means that the FCA will be better equipped than the FSA to deal with mis-selling scandals, such as that of payment protection insurance.

The Bill enables responsibility for consumer credit regulation to be transferred from the Office of Fair Trading to the FCA. This transfer will ensure that the consumer credit market also benefits from the FCA's focused remit, proactive approach and wider powers. However, we are clear that securing effective competition in financial services markets will lead to better outcomes for consumers. That is why the FCA will have an objective to promote effective competition in the interests of consumers. It will also have a duty to seek competition-led solutions to conduct issues when pursuing its other operational objectives. For example, the FCA will consider barriers to entry, encouraging switching, increasing transparency and focusing more on the requirements for information of different consumers, including those who are vulnerable or marginalised.

We are confident that these reforms will make the UK a more attractive place in which to do business. They will help maintain the UK's position as the leading global financial services centre. A more stable and sustainable financial sector will undoubtedly be a more competitive one.[44]

I have included the full text of this statement because it illustrates the tension in contemporary UK debates between protection and choice, competition and regulation, with politicians seeming to talk out of both sides of their mouth at the same time. The emphasis in the 2011 Coalition statement differs in emphasis

---

43   Martin Wheatley, 'My Vision for the FCA' (2012) available at <http://www.fsa. gov.uk/library/communication/speeches/2012/0125-mw.shtml> accessed 3 July 2012.
44   Lord Sassoon, 2d Reading HL 11 June 2012 col 1150–1151.

from Lagarde's comment on consumer credit in France. English policy appears to be about choice, with protection for the 'vulnerable consumer'. French policy stresses consumer protection 'without discouraging consumer credit'. There is, however, a dissonance in the UK between Coalition documents emanating from the Department of Business, Innovation and Skills (DBIS) that emphasize consumer choice and those produced by the FSA, the expert agency that recognizes consumers' behavioural biases and the limits of relying on transactional control. The FSA proposals for responsible lending in mortgage sales include a blanket requirement of income verification, and greater caution in permitting phenomena such as interest-only mortgages, nudging the English system modestly towards the French model. The FSA estimated the impact of its mortgage affordability proposals on those who might most be affected – namely, first-time buyers, credit-impaired consumers, debt consolidators and the self-employed – concluding that the effects would be modest in terms of exclusion.[45] Consumer polls also indicate continuing reservations about the use of consumer credit in the UK, as they do in France. The outcome of current debates in the UK will depend partly on the relative power of political interests against a backdrop of institutional history where, at least since Crowther, the burden of proof is on those who propose restrictions on an individual's choice in the credit market.

Substantial path-dependency exists in UK consumer credit protection – with many modern forms of regulation, such as licensing, information disclosure and protections from repossession being modifications of protections from the 1930s. Crowther's novel extension of the connected lender principle[46] – whereby lenders may be held liable for defects in products financed – focused on problems associated with finance companies. Its unintended consequence has been the protection of primarily middle-class consumers purchasing goods on credit cards.

English documents recognize that the 'poor pay more' but often seem unable to offer any convincing solution beyond making 'the poor not poor'. The Crowther Committee thought that 'other things being equal, a poor man is likely to be a worse credit risk than a rich one'[47] and considered education, counselling for those in difficulties and self-help through credit unions based on the US model as a method of providing loans at a reasonable cost. It assumed a functioning welfare state in the background, and this affected its approach to interest-rate ceilings, a controversial topic within the Committee.[48] In the final version of the Report, the Committee proposed retention of the presumption in the Moneylenders Acts of unconscionability triggered by interest rates over 48 per cent, concluding that the needs of individuals who could only borrow for necessities at very high interest

---

45 See FSA, *Mortgage Market Intervention* (CP11/31).

46 For the origins of the doctrine see the US case of *Commercial Credit v Childs* (1940) 199 Ark 1073 137 SW2d 260.

47 *Consumer Credit: Report of the Crowther Committee* (n 36) para 3.6.6.

48 'We have found the question of statutory control of interest rates extremely difficult to resolve': ibid para 6.6.6.

rates should be met by social welfare services 'rather than by the granting of loans at enormous rates'.[49] The Consumer Credit Act 1974 did not, however, maintain the 48 per cent limit and introduced the relatively ineffectual 'extortionate credit bargain' standard, replaced in 2006 by the 'unfair credit relationships' standard. Unlike the Moneylenders Acts, the Consumer Credit Act permitted compound interest on loans.

Since the late 1990s public policy concerns have focused on credit card and bank charges, payment protection insurance, high-cost credit, problems associated with sub-prime credit, financial exclusion and the increasing problem of over-indebtedness.[50] There is a long history of high-cost working-class credit in the UK represented by moneylending, hire purchase, pawning, mail order and informal loan sharking.[51] Doorstep moneylending, payday loans and rent-to-own stores represent contemporary examples. The high APRs charged by these companies have generated a continuing debate over interest-rate ceilings as a method of protecting consumers. A consumer activist argues that the UK is 'the only wild west for payday lenders' and 'a crock of gold at the end of the rainbow for payday lenders who have been shut down all over the world and have been regulated'.[52] A campaign to introduce price controls on payday loans may succeed, but the government exhibits little enthusiasm for ceilings (see below). The solutions offered to the problems of the low-income consumer echo Crowther – more education, better information for providers and consumers, greater development of credit unions and other forms of mutual lending. *Plus ça change.* As Sean

---

49　Ibid.

50　It is not possible to list here all the inquiries, investigations, legislation and codes of practice that have appeared concerning consumer credit in the UK since the late 1990s. They include the Competition Commission investigation of Home Credit (2006), Store Credit Cards (2006) and Payment Protection Insurance (2008), the Treasury Select Committee investigation of credit cards (2003), the Consumer Credit Act 2006 (amending the 1974 Act) and its associated White Paper, *Fair, Clear and Competitive: The Consumer Credit Market in the 21st Century* (2003), the Treasury Report on Financial Inclusion (2004), and the various reports of the Task Force on Over-Indebtedness since 2000. The OFT was active in attacking penalty charges in credit cards that resulted in credit card providers reducing their late payment charge fees from £25 to £12 and challenging overdraft charges; see OFT, *Calculating Fair Default Charges in Credit Card Contracts* (OFT 2006). The FSA developed its Treating Customers Fairly initiative from 2005 (see Williams' discussion in Chapter 2 of this book). Since the financial crash and the Great Recession, initiatives include DBIS/HM Treasury, *A New Approach to Financial Regulation: Consultation on Reforming the Consumer Credit Regime* (2010); *A New Approach to Financial Regulation: Securing Stability, Protecting Consumers* (Cm 8268, 2012); The Financial Services and Markets Act 2010–2012; OFT, *Review of High Cost Credit* (OFT 1232, 2010).

51　Sean O'Connell, *Credit and Community: Working Class Debt in the UK since 1880* (OUP 2009).

52　Martin Lewis, quoted in DBIS Select Committee on Business Innovation and Skills, Fourteenth Report Session 2010–12 (2012) HC 1649.

O'Connell concludes, 'the evidence from our historical analysis suggests that cheap credit remains elusive for the depressingly large number of families who still have to manage on limited budgets'.[53] The problems associated with high-cost credit will not, however, disappear in a country where regressive forms of credit may substitute for adequate welfare provision.

3 Institutional variations in credit-market ground rules

Private-law credit ground rules

Consumer credit law is primarily statutory, but courts play an important interpretative role and regulation is inserted against the background understandings of private law and judicial interpretation. Katharina Pistor argues that coordinated systems of capitalism have a more 'socially conditioned private law' than common-law courts that focus on predictability and are less likely to 'moralize the market' than civil law courts.[54] The English appeal courts (high law) are certainly sensitive to the dangers of increased consumer protection affecting the availability of consumer credit and consumer choice[55] and demonstrate almost no willingness to police the price of credit unless a transaction is accompanied by some procedural unfairness. Judges routinely comment that although an interest rate appears high, 'that is what one might expect to pay in that market'.[56] They have also been cautious in exercising their power to write down contractual obligations.

France does not, however, fit neatly into Pistor's dichotomy. The Court of Cassation has imposed duties of responsible lending, through a duty to warn of potential risks on financial institutions dealing with ordinary borrowers.[57] It also shaped the law of over-indebtedness, describing it as a protection for the vulnerable – a form of *droit social* for the casualties of the credit society. No comparable common-law duty to warn exists in England, and the higher courts in England have treated consumer credit contracts as arm's-length contracts,

---

53   See O'Connell, *Credit and Community* (n 51) 291.

54   See Katharina Pistor, 'Legal Ground Rules in Coordinated and Liberal Market Economies' (2005) 30 ECGI – Law Working Paper.

55   See, for example. *Barclays Bank v O'Brien* [1994] 1 AC 180; *Royal Bank of Scotland plc v Etridge* [2001] UKHL 44. See further discussion in Iain Ramsay, 'Consumer Law, Distributive Justice and the Welfare State' (1995) 15 Oxford Journal of Legal Studies 177.

56   See, for example, Dyson J in *Broadwick Finance v Spenser* [2002] All ER (D) 274; *London North Securities v Meadows* [2005] EWCA Civ 956; *Robert Shaw v Nine Regions* [2009] EWHC 3514 (QB) where Evans J accepted that an APR of 119 per cent was fair since 'it was not high in comparison with lending in the subprime market generally, which is a high risk lending market'.

57   See the commentary in Stéphane Piedelièvre, 'La Réforme du crédit à la consommation' (2010) Recueil Dalloz.

with statutory regulation imposing responsible lending obligations treated as an exception, layered over a 'no duty to warn or disclose': the consumer credit transaction is not a contract of solidarity.[58] However, one should not overstate the differences. The frozen ideology in Article 1134 of the Civil Code – that a contract is a statute between the parties – has inhibited the willingness of French courts to alter contracts or write down contractual obligations. The English law of bankruptcy and over-indebtedness is more generous than that in France.

The English judicial approach is probably understood by politicians and civil servants in the UK. Political actors in the UK, faced with populist pressure to regulate the price of credit, delegate decision-making to courts, enacting open-textured standards as a method of addressing political gridlock, knowing that the courts are unlikely to control market prices. The unfair credit relationships test under the Consumer Credit Act 1974,[59] touted as an alternative to ceilings[60] is an example. Individuals do not succeed under these sections simply because they pay a high market price for credit. Individuals challenging the unfairness of contracts have been historically forced to frame a claim in terms of the failure of a credit grantor to meet statutory formalities.[61]

The extent to which judicial decisions shape the ground rules of credit markets is an empirical question. The willingness of financial institutions in the UK, as repeat players, to litigate issues until they receive a favourable outcome – for example, in relation to warnings to guarantors – does suggest that private-law rules do have some impact. The law of credit in the UK has been substantially shaped by test cases brought by the credit industry.[62] The law may also have an

---

58   See *Harrison v Black Horse* [2011] EWCA Civ 1128 (Court of Appeal Civil Division).

59   This is evidenced by the interpretation of the unfair relationships test in ss140A-D Consumer Credit Act 1974 (see cases at <http://www.oft.gov.uk/about-the-oft/legal-powers/legal/cca/CCA2006/unfair/unfair-business-practices/>) and the cautious approach to writing down debt under the very broad provisions of ss129–136 of the Act. See the test case *Southern and District Finance Plc v Barnes and another* [1995] CCLR 62; reported also in *The Times* (19 April 1995).

60   Thus, in introducing the unfair credit relationship test, the relevant government minister stated: 'I am very confident that the unfairness test and the ADR will work and that there will be no need for interest rate caps, but we will always keep that option open.' See UK, HC Parliamentary Debates, 6th ser, vol 434, col 1412 (9 June 2005) (Gerry Sutcliffe, Undersecretary of State, DTI).

61   See the discussion of upsurge in this form of litigation in Geraint Howells, 'The Consumer Credit Litigation Explosion' (2010) 126 LQR 617. This form of litigation also exists in France; see, for example, *Epoux X v Credit Foncier de France* Cass Civ 1e, 29 October 2002 Bull Civ No 1513; *Cofinoga Merignac SA v Sylvain Sachitanathan* [2004] ECR I-02157.

62   See the discussion of this role in Iain Ramsay, 'Consumer Credit Law, Distributive Justice and the Welfare State' (n 55).

expressive impact, and judicial pronouncements may affect public images of creditors, debtors and credit markets.

Public regulation is an important shaper of market practices in the UK and since the mid-2000s both the Office of Fair Trading (OFT) and the Financial Services Authority (FSA) have played active roles in regulating the market. Payment protection insurance (PPI) in unsecured credit is now moribund in the UK, unlike in France where it is a significant profit centre for financial institutions. The OFT[63] requires responsible lending practices by lenders throughout the credit transaction. The Financial Ombudsmen Service (FOS), through its power to develop norms of 'fair and reasonable' financial practices that may go beyond the law, affects the normative landscape. Scholars looking for the English 'law' of credit regulation must therefore go beyond court decisions to find the norms expected of credit grantors. There is a tension between the more consumer-friendly norms of the FOS and the generally market-liberal approach often adopted by the higher courts. Regulatory intensity, as measured by regulatory costs as a percentage of GDP and regulatory staff, is higher in the UK than in France or Germany.[64]

Credit bureaux and reference systems

International institutions, such as the World Bank, view credit bureaux and information-sharing by credit grantors as central to the development of credit markets.[65] Extensive information-sharing between creditors through centralized credit bureaux may achieve the following objectives: a reduction in bad debts through objective credit assessment and the creation of incentives for consumer repayment; increased competition by reducing the advantages of market incumbents; a widening of the availability of credit to higher-risk groups; and the provision of greater opportunities for consumer switching through a portable credit record.

Significant variations exist between countries in types of credit bureau (public agency, private for profit) and in the nature of information maintained by the agency. At first sight, France and the UK provide striking contrasts. France maintains a system of negative information administered by the central bank

---

63   Under s 25 of the Consumer Credit Act 1974. The guidance on the creditworthiness test is that of 'a borrower's ability to undertake a specific credit commitment, or specific additional credit commitment, in a sustainable manner, without the borrower incurring (further) financial difficulties and/or experiencing adverse consequences'.

64   Howell Jackson, 'Variation in the Intensity of Financial Regulation: Preliminary Evidence and Potential Implications' (2007) 24 Yale Journal on Regulation 253, 256.

65   See, for example, World Bank, *General Principles for Credit Reporting* (World Bank 2011); World Bank, *Doing Business* reports; Margaret Miller (ed), *Credit Reporting Systems and the International Economy* (MIT 2003), Federico Ferretti, *The Law and Consumer Credit Information in the European Community: The Regulation of Credit Information Systems* (Routledge-Cavendish 2008).

whereas in the UK credit reference agencies are private for-profit institutions that maintain both positive and negative information and market services to consumers and lenders. Several negative reporting systems exist in France. The FICP (fichier national des incidents de remboursement des crédits aux particuliers) is triggered either by an application to the over-indebtedness commission or by a period of default (for example, 60 days on revolving credit). The period of listing lasts five years. There is also the FCC (Fichier central des chèques) which lists individuals who have been subject to a prohibition on passing cheques (dating from 1955) and individuals whose credit cards have been withdrawn for abusive usage.[66] Although presence on the *fichier* will often mean a refusal of credit, consolidation loan companies providing *rachats de crédit* may still grant a loan to a person on the FICP.

The introduction of a *fichier positif* has been a recurring issue in France since the 1989 Loi Neiertz enacted the negative reporting system operated by the Bank of France.[67] The implementation of the EU directive on consumer credit that requires creditors to assess the creditworthiness of a borrower provided the latest stimulant. In 2010 the government established a committee to investigate the feasibility of a *fichier positif*. The report concluded that if such a register were introduced, it should be maintained by the Bank of France and include information on credit granted by credit institutions and micro-credit institutions, excluding overdrafts and short-term credits. This *fichier unique* would replace the FICP. Credit institutions would only be able to consult the *fichier* before granting credit: this would be compulsory. Individuals would be identified by their social security number.

This measure was opposed by some consumer groups, the French Banking Federation (Fédération Bancaire Française) and the national privacy regulator, the Commission Nationale de l'Informatique et des Libertés (CNIL). It was supported by retail financiers. The CNIL has been hostile to private credit bureaux and in 2007 refused Experian's request to establish a database, a decision upheld by the Conseil d'Etat.[68] A 2005 report by the CNIL concluded that the *fichier positif* might not reduce over-indebtedness since much over-indebtedness was caused by subsequent unforeseen events, such as illness or unemployment. It underlined the high costs of establishing a *fichier positif* and the potential intrusion on an individual's privacy. Information might be misused or its use extended beyond credit to insurers, landlords and employers. These costs outweighed the benefits

---

66   The review of the *fichiers* in 2008 indicates that in 2006 the FCC contained 1.8 million individuals, 0.66 million had credit cards withdrawn and 2.3 million individuals were on the FICP.

67   See the discussion in Commission Nationale de l'Informatique et des Libertés (CNIL), 'Les problèmes posés par les fichiers regroupant des informations sur la situation financière des individus au regard de la loi du 6 janvier 1978' (CNIL 2005).

68   See Conseil d'État, Section du Contentieux, jugement du 30 décembre 2009 (Experian/CNIL).

of preventing the small percentage of compulsive spenders. As for its role in promoting credit, the interaction of credit reference agencies and usury levels might lead to a reduction of interest for good risks but exclusion for others.

The introduction of a *fichier positif* remains on the French political agenda.[69] Distrust of credit bureaux might be traced to a conception of privacy as protection of individual dignity. Within this conception an individual may shield his or her financial affairs from market and commercial intrusion. Whitman argues that this conception of privacy underlies commercial credit reporting restrictions in France[70] and influenced the strong protections for privacy in the European Data Protection Directive. Undoubtedly this is a factor, although a recent poll indicates that some French consumers do appear to be in favour of positive credit reporting even if consumer groups are divided on this issue.[71] To these factors should be added the role of the banks. The French banks do not need a *fichier positif* since they already have sophisticated scoring information systems on their clients. A *fichier positif* could facilitate new entrants in credit-granting and greater foreign competition. As one commentator states, 'for the banks a *fichier positif* presents an enormous challenge: the risk of opening the gates of the Hexagon to foreign competition'.[72]

In contrast to France, in the UK three private providers dominate the credit reference industry that grew out of agencies servicing hire-purchase providers and moneylenders. These firms provide information to creditors as well as marketing a variety of credit risk services to credit grantors and landlords, and credit scores, reports and identity protection insurance to consumers. Statutory protection for data exists under the Data Protection Act 1998 which implemented the European Data Protection Directive in the UK. Much regulation of credit data in the UK is 'soft law' based on Principles of Reciprocity whose governing principle is that

---

69   See Rapport de la Commission des Affaires Economiques sur la proposition de loi tendant à prévenir le surendettement (no 4087) (Jean Dionis du Séjour) (13th Legislature) (2012); Sénat, *Rapport d'Information sur l'application de la loi portant réforme du crédit à la consommation* (Sénat, Session 2011–12 No 602) Mmes Muguette Dini and Anne-Marie Escoffier (19 June 2012). The most recent annual report of the French Banking Federation, *Fédération Bancaire Française Rapport d'Activité 2011* (FBF, 2012), opposes the introduction of the *fichier positif*.

70   James Whitman 'The Two Western Cultures of Privacy: Dignity versus Liberty' (2003–04) 113 Yale LJ 1190.

71   'Les trois quarts des Français surendettés sont pour la création d'un register des crédits' *Libération* (4 November 2011). The UNAF (a family and consumer group) is in favour, as is Crésus, a group working with the over-indebted. L'UFC Que Choisir (a middle-class consumer organization) is opposed. See *L'UFC – Que Choisir n'accorde toujours pas de crédit au fichier positif!* <http://www.quechoisir.org/argent-assurance/banque-credit/surendettement/communique-surendettement-l-ufc-que-choisir-n-accorde-toujours-pas-de-credit-au-fichier-positif> accessed 19 June 2012.

72   P Erb, 'Crédit: les lobbies font de la resistance: les Coulisses de l'Argent' *Mieux Vivre Votre Argent* (July 2011).

'data are shared only for the prevention of over-commitment, bad debt, fraud, and money-laundering, and to support debt recovery and debtor tracing, with the aim of promoting responsible lending'.[73] This soft approach to regulation of credit reference agencies in the UK may reflect a traditional UK preference for 'self-regulation'. It may also reflect the political influence of the industry.

UK policy-makers promote further information-sharing by creditors to expand consumer choice and manage risk. The Competition Commission, as a response to the perceived lack of competition in the low-income 'doorstep credit' market, introduced a requirement of data-sharing on high-cost lenders as a method of opening the market to new entrants and expanding consumer choice.[74] The OFT, in its review of high-cost credit, proposes that payday lenders and rent-to-own companies should make information available to credit reference agencies so that individuals with good payment records might graduate to more mainstream credit. The Coalition government in 2012 argues that 'additional data sharing could lead to better quality lending decisions to some extent ... and [it] wants to explore whether more high cost credit providers could provide information to credit reference agency databases'.[75]

Before the credit crunch, UK banks did not always share all information on their clients. Limits on data-sharing do exist because about 40 million accounts were opened before the banks introduced fair processing notices under the Data Protection Act 1998. The banks claim that both the duties of confidentiality and the requirements of affirmative consent prevent the sharing of positive information on these accounts and that it would be prohibitively costly to attempt to obtain the necessary consent.

The contrasting approaches to credit information policy in the UK and France may have allocative and distributional consequences for the consumer credit market. A burgeoning economic literature exists on the role of credit information and reporting systems.[76] The conventional economic wisdom on the value of credit reporting for creditors and debtors is that outlined at the beginning of this section. In practice, comprehensive credit reporting will probably result in an expansion of debt with higher levels of indebtedness and possibly higher numbers of defaulting debtors. In mature credit economies with pressures to maximize short-term profit, credit information may be used to maximize profits rather than minimize risk.

---

73 See 'Information Sharing, Principles of Reciprocity' (2008) <http://www.uk.experian.com/www/pages/downloads/compliance/porVersion30.pdf> accessed 19 June 2012.

74 Home Credit Market Investigation Order 2007 as amended by the Home Credit Market Variation Order 2011 available at <http://www.competition-commission.org.uk/our-work/directory-of-all-inquiries/home-credit> accessed 3 July 2012.

75 HM Treasury and DBIS, *Consumer Credit and Personal Insolvency Review* (n 42).

76 See, for example, Tullio Jappelli and Marco Pagano, 'The Role and Effects of Credit Information Sharing' in Giuseppe Bertola, Richard Disney and Charles Grant (eds), *The Economics of Consumer Credit* (MIT 2006).

This may mean targeting individuals who are highly profitable because they will yield high late payment and other fees.[77] There are also the potential increases in identity theft and concerns about privacy in a comprehensive reporting system. Within a system that includes both positive and negative information, individuals without a credit record are disadvantaged even if they are good credit risks. There is therefore pressure to build one's 'credit profile' by taking on more credit. Within the English system an individual who wishes to gain access to credit has little choice in whether to permit a creditor to make information available to a credit bureau. On the other hand, the absence of credit bureaux with positive information in France may reduce competition by limiting the possibility of the mass mailings of targeted credit offers that were common in the US and UK, and this might affect the overall level of credit demand.

Empirical uncertainties exist, therefore, as to the overall social value of positive versus negative information in credit information systems in mature credit economies. The expert group on credit histories in the EU concluded that 'given that economic literature offers contradictory (and often not definitive) views and that the European experience shows that both approaches can work effectively, the ECGH has not found a consensus on the need or not to recommend one or the other approach for cross-border exchanges'.[78] However, continuing pressure exists to develop extensive credit reporting. A European research centre, financed by the credit industry, has established a task force to assess how to apply the World Bank principles of credit reporting within the EU.[79] The private multinational credit reporting industry has a continuing interest in expansion. The example of France, where they are unable to operate, represents an important symbolic challenge to their continued growth.

Interest-rate ceilings

I have written elsewhere on interest-rate ceilings in France and the UK.[80] The distinct approaches by these countries represent institutional history, the influence of political interest groups and ideology. France had a tradition of price controls in the post-Second World War era, and modernizing usury laws in 1966 seemed a natural form of policy for regulating credit. It also reflected the views of labour representatives in the Conseil Economique who distrusted credit as a form of worker exploitation. The modest development of credit during this period by specialized finance companies and the absence of a strong interest by banks in consumer credit meant that the French financial sector did not oppose controls. The 1989 controls,

---

77 See Ronald Mann's 'sweatbox' theory of credit card lending. Ronald Mann, 'Bankruptcy Reform and the "Sweat Box" of Credit Card Debt' (2007) Univ Ill L Rev 375.

78 DG Internal Market, 'Report of the Expert Group on Credit Histories' (2009) 40.

79 See 'Ongoing CEPS/ECRI Task Force: Towards Better Use of Credit Reporting in Europe' <http://www.ecri.be/new/node/357> accessed 3 July 2012.

80 See Ramsay, '"To Heap Distress upon Distress?"' (n 9).

which made more complex distinctions in ceilings for different forms of credit, establishing them at one-third above the market average, represented the influence of both consumer and financial groups. The distinct category of revolving credit, linked to average market rates, permitted the increased ratcheting of rates for *crédit renouvelable* in order to expand the market to higher risks through the use of risk-based pricing, making possible the existence of a sub-prime market for personal borrowing.

The French ceilings are intended to exclude some consumers from obtaining credit; they will thus be protected from high-risk credit. Reliable data do not exist in France on the dimensions of financial exclusion and market distortion caused by ceilings and on the links between revolving credit and over-indebtedness. The study of working-class credit remains modest in France compared with the UK. The majority of French consumer groups support price controls, and the perception by political elites that public opinion would not favour abolition mean that there is unlikely to be change beyond the simplification of categories in the 2010 reforms.[81] This reform abolishes the separate category of *crédit renouvelable*, establishing a ceiling by reference solely to the amount of credit granted; this will exert a downward pressure on interest-rate ceilings. The only consumer group that dissents from the consensus on ceilings promotes the development of micro-credit, arguing that it is difficult to achieve this within existing ceilings. The question may be raised as to who represents those consumers currently excluded from the French credit system. Although lenders may support an easing of ceilings, there is probably little support among lenders for abolition that might permit greater competition from foreign institutions such as the English sub-prime lenders.

In the UK since the early 2000s there has been a continuing debate over the role of ceilings, with a number of campaigns proposing the introduction of ceilings on credit. The initial focus was on doorstep lending but is now on payday loans. The Labour government refused to introduce interest-rate ceilings in 2006, basing its decision primarily on a study by a consulting group which argued that the effects of ceilings in Germany and France were exclusionary and resulted in greater illegal lending.[82] The majority of consumer groups (Which?, Citizens Advice) also opposed ceilings, writing a collective letter of opposition to the House of Lords committee considering the bill. In response to continuing parliamentary pressures for price controls on payday loans, the Coalition government commissioned a further empirical study in 2011, perhaps as a method of deferring the necessity of making a decision. The dominant ideology of the relevant government department (DBIS) is against controls, fearing the effects on consumer choice. In its view,

---

81   See Athling Report (n 10).

82   This study and its methodology were criticized. See discussion in Ramsay, "'To Heap Distress upon Distress?'" (n 9) 716–717.

'there is a real risk that intervening in the market and introducing credit controls could reduce access to licensed credit for some consumers'.[83]

Mortgage lending

Mortgage lending is linked to housing policy and in both countries the state has promoted home ownership[84] through a variety of measures intended to facilitate this market and construct demand, such as the UK's 'right to buy' programme for council tenants. There is little evidence of cultural difference between the two countries in the desire for home ownership. Opinion polls indicate that the great majority of French individuals would like to own a home, and this is a Europe-wide tendency. Table 4.1 indicates housing tenure in several European countries in 2009 and the extent to which France is at the lower end of the homeownership spectrum.

Table 4.1   Housing tenure in selected European countries, 2009

	Tenant paying market price	Reduced price or free	Owner or with mortgage
France	19.7	17.3	63.0
UK	12.5	17.6	69.9
Germany	–	–	56.2
Netherlands	31.5	0.5	68.4
Sweden	29.8	0.5	69.5
Finland	10.4	15.4	74.5
Belgium	18.5	8.8	72.7
Austria	27.7	14.8	57.5

Source: Eurostat (Silc.).

During the 1970s a tension existed within French elites between a neoliberal approach to housing that primarily subsidized the potential house purchaser, and

---

83   HC Business, Innovation and Skills Committee, *Debt Management: Responses to the Committee's 14th Report of Session 2010–12* HC 301 (18 June 2012).

84   See the discussion in Waltraud Schelkle, 'A Crisis of What? Mortgage Credit Markets and the Social Policy of Promoting Homeownership in the United States and Europe' (2012) 40 Politics and Society 59; Anne Lafferre and David Le Blanc, 'Housing Policy: Low Income Households in France' in Richard Arnott and Daniel McMillen (eds), *A Companion to Urban Economics* (Blackwell 2007); Maurice Blanc, 'The Changing Role of the State in French Housing Policies: A Roll-Out Without Roll-Back?' (2004) 4(3) European Journal of Housing Policy 283. For English developments, see Mark Stephens, 'Mortgage Market Deregulation and its Consequences' (2007) 22 Housing Studies 201.

viewed home ownership as a bulwark against collectivism, and an approach that focused on building social housing.[85] The consequence of the increasing neoliberal turn from the mid-1970s onwards was the construction of many new homes in isolated suburbs. During the late 1980s significant numbers of these first-time buyers in the suburbs found themselves over-indebted, with the dream of home ownership transformed to a nightmare of debt tied to high fixed-interest loans. These lower-middle-class consumers were primary beneficiaries of the 1989 law on over-indebtedness which permitted the rescheduling of loan repayments.

In France, most mortgages are at a fixed rate without an initial low-rate period, and home equity is more constrained.[86] The introduction of the *hypothèque rechargeable* in 2006 was intended to encourage home equity lending but still restricts the extent of equity withdrawal and has been modestly used. The Lefebvre Report claims that a sub-prime mortgage market does not exist in France because of the financial institutions' approaches to risk which focus on the income and stability of the debtor, rather than the value of the property, and usury legislation.

The approach of French financial institutions to home lending may exclude borrowers who do not fit the 'standard profile' of individuals with secure, regular incomes[87] that constituted the classic profile of the ideal bank client who provided the possibility of relationship lending. A distinct characteristic of French home lending is the use of guarantees rather than a mortgage. More than 50 per cent of home credits include guarantees, viewed as an alternative to the conventional hypothec which is costly to take out because of notarial and administrative fees. The banks have created subsidiaries which guarantee the loan and charge a fee to borrowers (perhaps 1.5 per cent of the capital). In some cases, this may be a mutual organization that will repay the consumer a percentage of the fee on the payment of the loan. The use of guarantees may also lead to greater selectivity in lending. Bernard Vorms concludes that 'it is one thing to make sure that loans do not present intrinsic risks, it is another to only lend to the safest clients'.[88]

The default rate on mortgages in France is much lower than in the UK. However, in both countries repossession may be a long and difficult process. Since the deregulation of the UK mortgage market in the early 1980s, mortgage financing has been available to a wider range of 'non-standard' individuals and there was a proliferation of mortgage options (interest only, endowment, variable,

---

85   See the discussion in Pierre Bourdieu, *The Social Structures of the Economy* (Polity 2005).

86   See Frédéric Lefebvre, *Rapport d'information sur les emprunts immobiliers à taux variable* (Assemblée Nationale 2008).

87   See Cédric Houdré, 'L'endettement des ménages début 2004' (2007) Insée 1131– reporting data that indicate that those holding housing debt were generally couples with children holding stable incomes and earning more than the average wage.

88   Bernard Vorms, 'Après la crise des subprime, comment développer l'accession à la propriété?' (la vie des idées.fr 2008) <http://www.laviedesidees.fr/Apres-la-crise-des-subprime.html>.

initial low rate etc) that facilitated access to home ownership. From the late 1980s equity release provided access to credit for UK home owners in an economy of rising house prices.

The English housing market, which permitted more risky home ownership, emphasized the need for effective safety nets for individuals in an economy subject to periodic housing bubbles.[89] Housing arrears seem to be primarily related to macro-economic factors so that 'there is a large random element as to which home owners experience risk events such as redundancy'.[90] Insurance provides a safety net, but private insurance does not have a good reputation. Stephens has proposed a joint public–private insurance scheme which could form an alternative to the patchwork responses that currently exist.

The French system probably limits access to younger individuals, particularly those who are not in secure jobs, but given the relatively high entry barriers to home ownership there is less risk associated with it than in the UK. The credit crisis provoked a flurry of temporary measures by the UK government to protect those at risk of repossession, although the size of the sub-prime market in the UK is significantly lower than in the US. In the UK, housing repossessions have stabilized, partly because of a protocol on repossession that restricts its use to a last resort. The FSA has also closely scrutinized lenders' repossession procedures.[91] In France, the credit crisis had little effect, partly because of the *ex ante* controls on housing credit.

4 Summary

It is tempting to resort to generalizations in describing the UK and French approaches to consumer and housing credit, with the UK as the neoliberal little sister of the US, or, changing the metaphor, the neoliberal Trojan horse in Europe, with France reflecting a more cautious approach to credit embodied in greater state regulation and distrust of the market. The French approach might be explained by 'French exceptionalism', a hold-out against the increased global domination of a neoliberal capitalism of 'mindless consumerism' stoked by consumer credit and credit cards.

These are overly simple accounts. Ideas associated with neoliberalism have been influential in France since at least the late 1960s and, absent the crisis, would have been even more influential. One might describe the French approach as state-managed neoliberalism[92] with sporadic attempts to harness consumer credit as

---

89   Mark Stephens, *Tackling Housing Market Volatility in the UK* (Joseph Rowntree 2011) 58.

90   Ibid.

91   See FSA, Final Notice GMAC–RFC (2009) <http://www.fsa.gov.uk/pubs/final/gmac_rfc.pdf> accessed 12 June 2012.

92   See, for example, Vivian Schmidt, 'Putting the Political Back into Political Economy by Bringing the State Back in Yet Again' (2009) 61 World Politics 516. See also Prasad, 'Why is France so French? (n 8).

a vehicle of growth, but there are disagreements within the bureaucratic elites and social partners on the direction and extent of this neoliberalism. France has adapted pragmatically to issues such as over-indebtedness by making continual adjustments to the system of treatment. Excessive focus on the neoliberalism/ social market or consumer protection/consumer choice dichotomies obscures the role of government agencies, financial interests and consumer groups in the development of regulation. Strict regulation of credit advertising and the absence of a *fichier positif* partially represent the influence of financial producers as well as consumer protection motives.

Gunnar Trumbull traces the influence of labour and family groups in the French consumer movement, representing a coalition of the Left and Right that distrusted credit.[93] This established a status quo that placed a burden of proof on market liberalizers. In contemporary France the consensus on credit regulation recognizes the benefits as well as the costs, but the credit crisis tilted the balance towards the potential dangers of credit. In the UK, the Great Recession has called the neoliberal orthodoxy into question, stimulating sympathy among some regulators for a model of credit as a potentially dangerous product. This creates a political opportunity for change that is resisted by financial interests and those government bureaucrats schooled on neoclassical economic orthodoxies.

An element of path-dependency exists in credit regulation, for example, in the roles of interest-rate ceilings in France and credit licensing in the UK. Once a particular institutional pattern is introduced there is a status quo bias that acts as a barrier to change. During the 1990s the Conservative government failed to make substantial reductions in consumer credit regulation, including licensing, partly because industry had adjusted to working with it and consumer groups opposed the change.

The consumer protection/consumer choice dichotomy does not explain the difference in intensity of regulation between the two countries. For example, the mass mis-selling of payment protection insurance (PPI) has resulted in large numbers of public actions by the FSA, mass redress and the effective ending of PPI as a product. French financial institutions make large profits from a variety of transaction fees, including insurance which has a large market penetration in relation to credit cards and revolving credit. But there appears to be no major regulation in France of PPI beyond information disclosure. The focus and scope of regulation in different countries may depend, therefore, on the role of interest groups (and their construction of the consumer interest), ideology and contingency. Since PPI has existed for many decades, the difficult question is why it became a mass 'scandal' in the UK in the mid-2000s.

There are distributional issues concerning the structure of housing and consumer credit in the two countries. The French system of negative information-sharing and usury laws may result in some cross-subsidization among those who obtain credit. Negative information systems may make it more difficult to apply

---

93   See Trumbull, *Consumer Credit in Postwar America and France* (n 15).

models of risk-based pricing and exclude some consumers from access who might not be excluded under the UK system. In practice, however, French lenders have developed their own risk models, so that this effect may be reduced. The English system of positive information may result in exclusion for some consumers from prime lending markets, with these individuals being relegated to sub-prime status. The French system of ceilings may render the overall price of credit less transparent because of avoidance of usury through fees and insurance.

There remains the difficult question of explaining the substantial difference in levels of credit between the two countries. One might hypothesize that the greater limits on advertising (such as free credit) and the limits on marketing offers because of negative credit information systems may affect overall demand. The more restrictive mortgage market in France may also have a knock-on effect on consumer credit, since much consumer credit is associated with home ownership. Interest-rate ceilings may restructure the forms of credit but might have little impact on overall demand since the high-cost credit market is a tiny part of the market in both countries. Credit may be used more by individuals as a substitute for state welfare in the UK, where there is a higher risk of poverty, than in France. However, we need further studies of the distribution of credit use among the population and the extent to which credit substitutes for, or supplements, state support in the two countries. Finally, in France, the generous tax benefits for flexible savings accounts (*Livret A*) may result in their being used for financing purchases that would be made by credit in the UK.

5 Expanding the frame: European dimensions

The EU wishes to establish an integrated capital and credit market, but credit markets remain national. Distinct forms of capitalism and credit markets at different levels of development exist within the EU, along with differences in social welfare systems. The idea of the social market or a 'European social model' remains an unclear and contested concept,[94] notwithstanding the Lisbon Treaty's reference to a 'competitive social market economy'.

The influence of financial interests on EU financial services policy has been documented by ALTER-EU.[95] It concluded that the European Commission and its Internal Market Directorate General had been captured by financial interests, with expert committees dominated by finance interests. This suggests a neoliberal tendency in EU credit policy – a policy of 'consumerism' and market

---

94   Philine Ten Haar and Paul Copeland, 'What are the Future Prospects for the European Social Model? An Analysis of EU Equal Opportunities and Employment Policy' (2010) 16 European Law Journal 273.

95   ALTER-EU, 'A Captive Commission – The Role of the Financial Industry in Shaping EU Regulation' (2009) <http://www.alter-eu.org/documents/reports-studies/2009/11/05/captive-commission-financial-industry-shaping-eu-regulation> accessed 19 June 2012.

access, as argued by Hans Micklitz in Chapter 3 of this book. The period up until the Great Recession certainly demonstrates the power of financial interests. The introduction of the new consumer credit directive in 2002 by DG SANCO, the consumer protection directorate, took financial interests by surprise, since it adopted a protectionist Belgian model of 'responsible lending' that required a 'suitability of credit' approach by creditors, and included a requirement to consult credit databases. The UK and German governments opposed the directive. The UK, acting on behalf of its financial industry, wished to protect it from responsible lending obligations and facilitate its expansion into the green fields of the Central and Eastern European credit markets. Financial interests lobbied the Commission and European Parliament, and the European Parliament gutted the initial draft. Criticism was framed in terms of the impact of the EU proposals on consumer choice and access.[96] The ultimate political outcome – the 2008 directive – primarily standardizes information provision and provides a 14-day cooling-off period. Its modest and ambiguous 'responsible lending' provisions may have had some effect and may have stimulated changes in the UK. Its symbolic significance may provide a continuing reference-point for the improvement of credit practices. EU consumer groups provided limited support for the original Commission bill, arguing that it might reduce national protections, and they also opposed the idea of a centralized European credit bureau.

The economic crisis put the tendency to neoliberalism on pause and provided opportunities for a change in direction. DG Market (DG Internal Market and Services) dropped its proposals for speeding up foreclosure proceedings in Europe, and its mortgage-lending proposal includes slightly stronger responsible lending provisions than for unsecured credit, along with the monitoring of foreclosure rates.[97] The Commission notes the desirable effect of these measures in excluding certain borrowers from the market, protecting them from the risk of over-indebtedness. However, mortgage lender groups oppose its provisions,[98] and the ultimate outcome remains uncertain, particularly since the lead DG is DG Market, which has traditionally favoured extension of choice and regulation to facilitate market growth. This modest adoption of a consumer safety approach to credit may therefore be short-lived. Greater attempts are being made to include consumer representatives in community decision-making processes on financial

---

96   See European Parliament, 'Second Report on the Proposal for a European Parliament and Council Directive on the Harmonization of the Laws, Regulations and Administrative Provisions of the Member States Concerning Credit for Consumers' (2004) A5-0224 Final.

97   See European Commission, 'Proposal for a Directive of the European Parliament and of the Council on Credit Agreements Relating to Residential Property' COM (2011) 0142 Final Cod 2011/0062.

98   See for example, the position of European Mortgage Federation at <http://www.hypo.org/Content/default.asp?PageID=452> accessed 12 June 2012.

services,[99] but there is some division within consumer groups in the EU, with UK consumer groups being more willing to accept products regarded as dangerous by other groups.

The inclusion of consumer protection within the mandate of the European Banking Authority provides potential for increased networking and information-sharing between national governing authorities.[100] The Authority has a market surveillance role, can issue recommendations and guidelines, and has established a committee composed of national supervisory authorities to assess the effects of financial innovation on consumers, so that potentially harmful financial products may be identified. The Authority proposes to identify, analyse and 'address harmful financial innovations before their consumer-related ... risks materialise'.[101] Given the existence of systemic scandals in Europe – PPI in the UK, the Dexia affair in the Netherlands, real-estate investments in Germany – this could be a potentially valuable role. Dialogue may be initiated between different member states in the development of European norms, part of increased network governance within the EU.[102] It will also be a site for influence. Thus, the initial agenda of the committee seems strongly influenced by the FSA.

There is no consensus within the EU on the desirability of interest-rate ceilings,[103] or a pan-European credit reference agency, and differences exist between countries in their interpretation of privacy protections in the EU Data Protection Directive as applied to consumer credit.[104] Little EU 'hard law' exists on the social costs

---

99   See the Commission decision on setting up a Financial Services User Group, 2010/C 199/02.

100   Regulation (EC) No 1093/2010 of the European Parliament and of the Council of 24 November 2010, article 9.

101   EBA, *Financial Innovation and Consumer Protection* (2012). It will focus on 'Mortgages and Indebtedness, Payment Protection Insurance, Access to payment accounts, Complex savings products, Transparency and Comparability of Bank Account Fees, Bank account switching, re-hypothecation, and Contracts for difference (CfDs)'.

102   See the discussion of networks in Christine Poncibo, 'Networks to Enforce European Law: The Case of the Consumer Protection Cooperation Network' (2011) 35 Journal of Consumer Policy 175.

103   See EC Directorate General for Employment, Social Affairs and Equal Opportunities, *Towards a Common Operational European Definition of Over-Indebtedness* (EC 2008) 70: '... the debate around legislation setting interest rate ceilings tends to be emotive. On the one hand there is a strong moral argument for protecting consumers against excessive charges; on the other it can be argued that they distort markets and can contribute to financial exclusion. Both points of view have validity, but are almost impossible to reconcile'. See also DG Market, *Consultation on the Study of Interest Rate Restrictions* (2011) <http://ec.europa.eu/internal_market/consultations/2011/interest_rate_restrictions_en.htm>.

104   The Commission proposes a regulation on data protection to reduce this diversity of interpretation. See the proposals at <http://ec.europa.eu/justice/newsroom/data-protection/news/120125_en.htm>.

of credit and consumer over-indebtedness. The Open Method of Coordination, namely 'encouraging co-operation, promoting exchanges of information and best practices, promoting innovative approaches and evaluating experiences', has been adopted in this area. Some modest peer reviews – intended to facilitate the 'transfer of key components or policies or institutional arrangements'[105] – have been produced. The Council of Europe and academic reports have outlined general principles for the treatment of debts that include the concept of a swift discharge for the hopelessly indebted, repayment plans that do not last overly long (perhaps five years) and open access to insolvency procedures.[106]

6 Conclusion

The distinct French and English approaches to credit regulation demonstrate the influence of interest groups, ideology and some path-dependency. They do not represent English or French culture or 'national tradition'. Such an approach generally overstates the extent to which policy is hard-wired to a pre-existing menu and understates the conflicts and struggles between interest groups and ideologies within countries. Efforts to understand differences in regulation within Europe should focus on political economy rather than on cultural arguments that 'French or English civil society' opposes a measure or is distrustful of credit. Recognizing the 'made up' aspect of national culture should lead to greater focus on the interaction of interest groups and state agencies at both the national and regional level. The French/English comparison also highlights the empirical uncertainties and value judgements surrounding issues such as credit information-sharing and interest-rate ceilings – difficulties that are often papered over in international documents such as the World Bank's *Doing Business* reports which advocate universal principles for credit markets.

Public-choice literature suggests that diffuse groups such as consumers are unlikely to be successful in the market for regulation. James Q. Wilson modified

---

105   'The objective of the peer review programme is not competition or a ranking of policies. However, the reason why certain policies are successful in certain conditions can be replicated elsewhere, if appropriate care is taken in adapting them to different cultural, institutional and economic contexts ... Although success is a word to be used sparingly, the programme should indeed be looking for success stories, or at least inspiring stories': Hugues Feltese, EU DG Employment and Social Affairs Minutes, 'Amnesty of Debts: Amicable Agreement and Statutory Solution' <http://www.peer-review-social-inclusion. net>.

106   See, for example,. DR Korczak, EU Commission, *Towards a Common Operational European Definition of Over-Indebtedness* (DG, Employment, Social Affairs and Equal Opportunities 2008); Udo Reifner, Johanna Niemi, Nick Huls and Helga Springeneer, *Consumer Law and Consumer Debts: Credit and Insolvency Regulation in the European Union* (IFF 2003); J Johanna Niemi and Anna Henrickson, *Report on Legal Solutions to the Debt Problems in Credit Societies* (Council of Europe 2005).

this in his political theory of regulation, arguing that success for groups depends on the distribution of the costs and benefits of particular policies.[107] Where costs are concentrated but benefits are diffuse, as in the case of financial regulation, 'entrepreneurial politics' was necessary, where an individual or group could exploit a scandal or crisis to mobilize public opinion. The Great Recession provides the crisis, and the 'safety model' championed by Elizabeth Warren[108] has animated numerous reform proposals. Whether consumer groups, such as Consumers International, or coalitions of groups will be able to bring about long-term changes in financial product markets is difficult to answer. Greater consumer input into the financial regulation process is now recognized as necessary to the provision of legitimacy to regulation. Financial interests are a powerful group in the UK, France and the EU, but the French/English comparison indicates that the financial industry is not homogenous: French banks supported controls on *crédit gratuit* because they feared losing business to financial intermediaries (which they now own). On the other hand, consumer groups are not homogenous in their regulatory preferences across the two countries. The development of an EU-wide consumer position on consumer credit must involve negotiating these differences and recognizing the heterogeneity of consumer preferences.

Returning to Christine Lagarde's comment quoted at the outset of this chapter, establishing institutions that ensure the 'right' level of credit is not easy to achieve within the EU, given the various credit and social welfare economies of the EU member states. Europe is entering a difficult era in which welfare states and the 'social market' are under challenge. The role and regulation of credit may differ between countries. In some countries with only modest welfare states, credit is a relatively novel development after decades of communism. In the early 2000s the EU provided the model of responsible lending that may have provided international inspiration for other regions of the world. However, there remains substantial disagreement on many issues of consumer credit market regulation. This means, therefore, that a European model of credit regulation cannot be said to exist.

---

107 James Wilson, *The Politics of Regulation* (Basic Books 1980).
108 Elizabeth Warren, 'Unsafe at Any Rate' (2007) Democracy: A Journal of Ideas (Issue 5) 8.

Chapter 5

The Responsible Lending Response

Therese Wilson

1 Introduction

In the wake of concerns regarding over-indebtedness and, more recently, the global financial crisis, 'responsible lending' regulations or directives have been made or enacted in Australia, South Africa, the US and Europe. These regulatory regimes have varied in terms of the extent of their concern with 'responsible lending' or 'responsible borrowing' and their reliance on tests, such as 'suitability', 'creditworthiness' or 'recklessness'. Some appear to have been motivated by consumer protection – that is, the protection of consumers transacting in financial markets – while others seem to be more about protecting financial markets from the irresponsible actions of consumers. In every case, responsible lending regimes have at their base a requirement that lenders or potential borrowers assess the borrowers' capacities to repay the loans in question before lending or borrowing. Some regimes impose penalties for lenders' failures to make those assessments, while others do not, relying on borrowers to commence proceedings to complain about the lender's conduct.

All of these regimes have developed in neoliberal contexts which, it is argued, contribute to their reactive natures. In other words, they have been developed in response or reaction to concerns regarding a particular failure of the free market, whether that is consumer over-indebtedness and the broader social consequences that accompany it, or the sub-prime mortgage crisis and consequent global financial crisis. They are therefore limited in their scope, seeking only to address the narrow concern which motivates their enactment and not interfering with *laissez-faire* approaches beyond that. A clear example of this is the limitation of responsible lending obligations in the US to mortgage lending.

To the extent that regulation requires 'responsible borrowing', it clearly embraces the neoliberal 'responsibilization' of the consumer[1] which emphasizes the need for consumers to protect themselves against the potential harms of the market, arming them with opportunities for financial literacy and education, as well as information disclosure by lenders. The need for consumers to behave responsibly has been emphasized by the Organization for Economic Cooperation

---

1 Iain Ramsay, 'Consumer Law, Regulatory Capitalism and the "New Learning" in Regulation', (2006) 28 Sydney Law Review 9, 13.

and Development (OECD)[2] and the Financial Stability Board (FSB)[3] in the wake of the global financial crisis, in order to 'prevent financial instability'.[4] It is a strange approach to in effect blame consumers for entering into loan agreements that they could not afford, given the abusive and predatory lending practices which led to the US sub-prime mortgage crisis.[5] This approach also ignores the structural causes of over-indebtedness which will be referred to below, and which include a marketplace in which disadvantaged consumers have limited choice in the credit market.[6]

This chapter argues that responsible lending regimes should ideally be focused on consumer protection, not market protection, and should be developed proactively, not reactively, seeking to avoid not only social and economic harms that have already arisen as a result of free-market failure, but also harms that might arise in the future. It will begin by noting the continuation of neoliberal policies in Western liberal democracies, notwithstanding the global financial crisis, and will consider the impact of those policies on the regulation of consumer credit, including responsible lending requirements. The chapter will then describe the responsible lending regimes in Australia, the US, Europe and South Africa, before considering the motivations for those regimes and characterizing those as largely exemplifying neoliberal reactivity. It will conclude by describing a proactive responsible lending regime motivated by effective consumer protection.

2 The impact of a neoliberal context on a responsible lending regime

Whereas the term 'liberalism' has come to embrace both social and economic liberalism, 'neoliberalism' focuses on economic liberalism and advocates free markets and limited regulation, promoting competitive markets as the most efficient means of managing human society. Where neoliberalism has had to operate in democratic contexts, there has had to be some compromise, as evidenced by a tolerance for government regulation and spending to ensure a social welfare 'safety net'.[7] Nevertheless, regulation, including financial regulation, has tended to be

---

2   OECD, *G20 High-Level Principles on Financial Consumer Protection* (OECD 2011), 4.

3   Financial Stability Board, *Consumer Finance Protection with Particular Focus on Credit* (FSB 2011) 1.

4   Ibid 3.

5   See the discussion in Kathleen Engel and Patricia McCoy, *The Subprime Virus: Reckless Credit, Regulatory Failure, and Next Steps* (OUP 2011) 17.

6   See the discussion in Jean Braucher, 'Theories of Overindebtedness: Interaction of Structure and Culture' (2006) 06-04 Arizona Legal Studies Discussion Paper, 5–6 <http://ssrn.com/abstract=826006> accessed 1 June 2012.

7   Colin Crouch, *The Strange Non-Death of Neoliberalism* (Polity Press 2011) 21; Heikki Patomaki, 'Neoliberalism and the Global Financial Crisis' (2009) 31/4 New Political Science 431, 435.

reactive, responding to free market failures as they have arisen on an ad hoc basis, rather than attempting to proactively avoid harms. With respect to the impacts of financial globalization, for example, Picciotto has noted that '[f]inancial regulation has focused on trying to manage the diseases caused by financial globalisation, rather than tackling their root causes'.[8]

An example of this is the focus on irresponsible lending and borrowing following the global financial crisis, whereby the harms of irresponsible lending in terms of widespread damage to the global economy have been recognized. The FSB, for example, has noted that irresponsible lending practices with respect to mortgages have had significant economic impacts:

> The effects of irresponsible lending practices can be transmitted globally through the sale of securitised risk, particularly mortgages which are by far the largest single credit for many consumers.[9]

In the same report the FSB clearly links consumer protection to financial stability, suggesting that financial stability is the 'end goal' rather than consumer protection for its own sake.[10] The OECD has also asserted that financial consumer protection is important because it contributes to strengthening financial stability.[11] Similarly, even defenders of consumer protection laws acknowledge that while these laws may be 'a nuisance or impediment to the pursuit of short term profits' they should be tolerated because 'they are essential to sustaining economic growth and stability over the long term'.[12] One danger of this reactive approach is that consumer protection will be overlooked where threats to financial stability are not perceived to arise, and in fact will be regarded as less important than prudential regulation for financial institutions, given the clear links drawn between financial stability and prudential supervision and regulation. The FSB has noted the potential conflict between prudential regulation, which is concerned with the viability of a financial institution, and market conduct regulation, which is concerned with consumer protection. This potential conflict is evident in a UK proposal which will enable the prudential regulator of financial institutions to veto decisions made by the consumer protection regulator.[13]

---

8   Sol Picciotto, 'Disembedding and Regulation: The Paradox of International Finance' (The Social Embeddedness of Transnational Markets Conference, Bremen, February 2009) 1.

9   Financial Stability Board, *Consumer Finance Protection* (n 3) 1.

10   Ibid 3.

11   OECD, *G20 High-Level Principles on Financial Consumer Protection* (n 2).

12   James Nehf, 'Consumer Credit Regulation and International Financial Markets: Lessons from the Mortgage Meltdown' (2011) <http://ssrn.com/abstract=1923883> accessed 2 June 2012.

13   See the discussion in Financial Stability Board, *Consumer Finance Protection* (n 3) 10.

Why has there persisted a neoliberal focus on maintaining the efficacy and stability of financial markets and regulating only to the extent perceived necessary to achieve that stability, notwithstanding that it was the behaviour of free-market participants that caused the global financial crisis? As Crouch has noted:

> Already we have seen how a crisis caused by appalling behaviour among banks has been redefined as a crisis of public spending. Bankers' bonuses are returning to their pre-crisis level, while thousands of public employees are losing their jobs.[14]

It in fact seems as if the power and influence of the banking sector has strengthened in the wake of the crisis. One commentator argues that:

> The banks' leverage to extract booty from their customers has been enhanced. The dimensions of their operations that embody recklessness, incompetence and unconscionability will go unchecked.[15]

Crouch's hypothesis is that the financial sector has been successful in demonstrating to Western governments that Western economies are dependent on its operations, and that it therefore deserves protection, not punishment and more intrusive regulation.[16] Suggestions for example, that financial intermediaries need to be regulated to separate their roles as managers of consumer savings and investments from their more speculative activities seem to have fallen on deaf ears.[17] Crouch notes that '[a]lthough it was the behaviour of the banks that caused the 2008–9 crisis, they emerged from it more powerful than before'.[18]

In wielding significant economic power, financial institutions have also come to wield significant political power. Neoliberal policies that have lead to a weakening of unions and cuts in corporate tax rates, as well as regulatory support for takeovers and consolidation of market power,[19] have strengthened not only the economic strength of financial corporations, but arguably also their political power. This has impacted on the ability or desire of state regulators to act against them.[20] This chapter argues that limited, reactive regulatory responses have been

---

14   Crouch, *The Strange Non-Death of Neoliberalism* (n 7) 175.

15   Evan Jones, 'The Crisis and the Australian Financial Sector' (2009) 64 Journal of Australian Political Economy 91, 113.

16   Crouch, *The Strange Non-Death of Neoliberalism* (n 7) 2.

17   Picciotto, 'Disembedding and Regulation' (n 8) 11–12.

18   Crouch, *The Strange Non-Death of Neoliberalism* (n 7) 1.

19   For discussion in relation to such policies in Australia, see Jones, 'The Crisis and the Australian Financial Sector' (n 15) 104–105.

20   See the discussion in Laureen Snider, 'The Conundrum of Financial Regulation: Origins, Controversies, and Prospects' (2011) 7 Annual Review of Law and Social Science 121, 130–131.

the result. Not only does this limit the extent to which financial consumers enjoy regulatory protection, but it potentially leaves the door open for significant social and economic harms, including risks to financial stability not yet experienced or anticipated.

3 Describing the responsible lending response

In this section the responsible lending regimes of Australia, the US, Europe and South Africa will be described, and some preliminary observations made in relation to those regimes. These will be further developed in the next section which addresses motivations and reactivity.

Australia

In Australia, as part of the transfer of credit regulation from state governments to the federal government, the National Consumer Credit Protection Act 2009 (Cth) (NCCPA) was enacted, and provisions contained within it, imposing responsible lending obligations on credit providers, commenced in 2011. The NCCPA applies to credit for personal, domestic or household purposes, or credit relating to the purchase or improvement of a residential investment property provided to a natural person or strata corporation.[21]

Under the NCCPA, a credit provider must not enter into a credit contract with a consumer without first making a preliminary assessment as to suitability of the loan.[22] The preliminary assessment must be made within 90 days before the provision of credit, or within 120 days before the provision of credit for the purchase of residential property to be secured by a mortgage on that property.[23] Prior to making the preliminary assessment, the credit provider must make reasonable enquiries about not only the consumer's requirements and objectives in relation to the credit contract, but also the consumer's financial situation, and must take reasonable steps to verify the consumer's financial situation.[24]

The credit contract must be assessed by the credit provider as 'unsuitable' if the consumer will be unable to comply with the consumer's financial obligations under the contract or could only comply with those obligations with substantial hardship; or if the contract will not meet the consumer's requirements or objectives. It is presumed that if the consumer could only comply with his or her financial obligations under the contract by selling his or her principal place of residence, the consumer could only comply with those obligations with 'substantial hardship',

---

21 National Credit Code (Schedule 1, National Consumer Credit Protection Act 2009 (Cth)), s 5.

22 National Consumer Credit Protection Act 2009 (Cth), ss 128, 129.

23 Ibid s 128; National Consumer Credit Protection Regulations 2010 (Cth), s 26.

24 National Consumer Credit Protection Act 2009 (Cth), s 130.

unless the contrary is proved.[25] Failing to make the preliminary assessment, failing to make reasonable enquiries before undertaking the assessment or failing to assess the credit contract as unsuitable where required to do so incurs a penalty of up to AUD 220,000 for individuals, or AUD 1.1 million for corporate bodies.[26] The regulator, the Australian Securities and Investments Commission (ASIC), can apply for these pecuniary penalties within six years of a relevant contravention.[27] The ASIC can also apply to the court for an injunction restraining conduct in contravention of the NCCPA or mandating compliance with the NCCPA.[28] The ASIC, or a person who has suffered loss as a result of a contravention of the NCCPA, may apply to the court for an order for compensation within six years of the contravention.[29] Where a credit provider will not have sufficient financial resources to pay both compensation and a pecuniary penalty, the NCCPA requires the court to give preference to the order for compensation.[30]

This responsible lending regime is likely to be more effective than the previous regime under the state-based Uniform Consumer Credit Code which has more or less been preserved in schedule 1 to the NCCPA, entitled the National Credit Code (NCC). It therefore now provides an additional or alternative mechanism to enforce responsible lending. Under section 76 of the NCC a court may reopen an 'unjust' transaction on the application of the borrower. In determining whether a transaction is unjust, the court may have regard to a number of factors, including whether at the time the contract was entered into, the credit provider knew, or could have ascertained by reasonable enquiry at the time, that the borrower could not pay in accordance with its terms or not without substantial hardship. Under section 76 NCC, a number of orders may be made by the court on the reopening of the transaction, including setting aside or revising or altering the agreement or relieving the debtor of the obligation to make any payment under the agreement. The main shortcoming of this regime is the reliance on the borrower to initiate legal proceedings. Vulnerable low-income consumers who might be most at risk of entering into loan obligations that they do not have capacity to meet are unlikely to be in a position to pursue litigation.[31] The ability of the ASIC to pursue credit providers in relation to contraventions of the responsible lending requirements under the NCCPA, and in fact to pursue compensation on behalf of consumers, increases the likelihood of action being taken with respect to irresponsible

---

25   Ibid s 131.
26   Ibid ss 128, 130, 131.
27   Ibid s 167.
28   Ibid s 177.
29   Ibid s 178.
30   Ibid s 181.
31   See the discussion in Hazel Genn, *Paths to Justice: What People Do and Think About Going to Law* (Hart Publishing 1999) 101; Christine Coumarelos, Zhigang Wei and Alber Zhou, *Justice Made to Measure: NSW Legal Needs Survey in Disadvantaged Areas, 3 Access to Justice and Legal Needs* (Law and Justice Foundation of NSW 2006) 99.

lending. Further, the NCCPA introduces credit licensing for credit providers,[32] and a credit licence can be suspended or cancelled by the ASIC for failure to comply with the NCCPA, which will include a failure to comply with responsible lending obligations.[33]

A potential limitation of the Australian regime is the inability of the regulator, the ASIC, to monitor and enforce the statutory obligations imposed on lenders, largely due to a lack of resources. The ASIC has been criticized by one commentator for its failure to take action with respect to unconscionable conduct by banks,[34] and it is notable that notwithstanding a recent ASIC report listing breaches of responsible lending obligations by micro lenders, no action against them appears to be contemplated.[35] In particular, lenders' files were identified where: no purpose for the loan was recorded; there was limited documentation verifying the consumer's situation; lenders had not recorded verification of the consumer's expenses; or there was no record of how lenders had calculated a consumer's ability to meet repayment of the loan without substantial hardship.[36] The report does not suggest that any action will be taken with respect to these breaches. Rather, the ASIC indicates that it will 'work with' the lenders to assist them in meeting the requirements of the legislation.[37] This somewhat relaxed approach to the enforcement of market conduct requirements, as compared, for example, to the steps that one might expect the prudential regulator, the Australian Prudential Regulatory Authority, to take with respect to prudential breaches,[38] may be indicative of a greater concern with market stability and protection than with consumer protection.

Notable features of the Australian responsible lending regime, which can be compared to other regimes, are: the use of 'suitability' as a requirement which incorporates ability to repay without hardship but extends beyond that to meeting a consumer's needs; the fact that the obligation is on the credit provider to take reasonable steps to verify the consumer's financial situation but that there are no obligations of disclosure imposed on the consumer;[39] and the fact that the regime

---

32 National Consumer Credit Protection Act 2009 (Cth), ch 2.

33 Ibid ss 55, 47.

34 Jones, 'The Crisis and the Australian Financial Sector' (n 15) 109–110.

35 ASIC, *Review of Microlenders' Responsible Lending Conduct and Disclosure Obligations* (ASIC November 2011).

36 Ibid 7–8.

37 Ibid 8.

38 See, for example, enforcement actions referred to at <http://www.apra.gov.au/MediaReleases/Pages/06_13.aspx>.

39 Further, under National Consumer Credit Protection Act 2009 (Cth), s 131, the credit provider may only take into account information which he or she had reason to believe was true, very much placing the onus on the credit provider. A credit provider can be relieved from liability for a contravention of the NCCPA where he or she has acted honestly and, having regard to all of the circumstances, ought fairly to be excused: National Consumer Credit Protection Act 2009 (Cth), s 183.

applies to all consumer credit and is not limited to residential mortgage credit. These factors suggest that the regime focuses on consumer protection as its goal, rather than 'responsibilization' of the consumer.[40] A consumer responsibility focus would require the consumer to be a responsible borrower, thus protecting financial markets from his or her lack of responsibility, particularly where default under the particular form of credit can have significant impacts on the economy, as is seen to be the case with residential mortgages. The US responsible lending provisions found in the Dodd–Frank Wall Street Reform and Consumer Protection Act [41] (Dodd–Frank Act) arguably have more of a focus on 'market protection' and are more reactive than the Australian regime, if only because of their focus on residential mortgage loans rather than consumer credit more generally. They do not go so far, however, as to mandate responsible borrowing.

The US

The Dodd–Frank Act of 2010 imposes an obligation on lenders to assess a consumer's ability to repay a residential mortgage loan, before making such a loan. It does not focus more generally on consumer credit. Section 1411 of the Dodd–Frank Act requires a creditor to make 'a reasonable and good faith determination based on verified and documented information that, at the time the loan is consummated, the consumer has a reasonable ability to repay the loan'. It has been noted that the requirement to verify information will mean the end of low-doc and no-doc mortgage loans in the US, which have been a feature of sub-prime mortgage lending.[42]

In making the reasonable and good-faith determination, the residential mortgage lender must consider a range of factors including the consumer's credit history, current income, expected income, current obligations and residual income after paying mortgage-related and non-mortgage-related obligations, employment status and other financial resources. Further, the ability to repay must be determined on the basis of the payment schedule over the full loan term.[43]

Unlike the Australian NCCPA, the Dodd–Frank responsible lending provisions do not require a loan to be 'suitable' – in the sense of meeting the consumer's needs – beyond the consumer having an ability to repay the loan. The US legislators rejected a 'suitability' approach on the basis that it was too vague and subjective a standard to be applied.[44]

---

40   See the discussion in Iain Ramsay, *Consumer Law and Policy: Text and Materials on Regulating Consumer Markets* (2nd edn, Hart Publishing 2007) 551.

41   Pub L.No 111–203, 124 Stat 1376 (2010).

42   Engel and McCoy, *The Subprime Virus* (n 5) 229.

43   Dodd–Frank Wall Street Reform and Consumer Protection Act, Pub.L.No 111–203, 124 Stat 1376 (2010), s 1411.

44   John Pottow, 'Ability to Repay', University of Michigan Law School Public Law and Legal Theory Working Paper No 237 (May 2011) <http://ssrn.com/abstract=1844570> accessed 3 October 2011.

Further, the Dodd–Frank Act does not explicitly require ability to repay *without substantial hardship*, although it may implicitly do so by referring to a consumer's residual income after meeting all obligations.

The Dodd–Frank Act does allow lenders to rely on a rebuttable presumption of ability to repay, where mortgages can be classified as 'qualified mortgages'. This is known as a 'safe harbour' provision, where lenders can feel some level of protection if their residential mortgage loans satisfy designated criteria, which involve certain debt–to–income ratios, certain income levels and a borrower's ability to pay regular expenses after payment of periodic mortgage debt.[45] Reliance on the safe harbour provision may lead to inflexible credit assessment by lenders, which could exacerbate financial exclusion as discussed below.

In terms of enforcement, a borrower can defend mortgage foreclosure proceedings on the basis of a violation of the responsible lending requirement.[46] More significant is the establishment of a Consumer Financial Protection Bureau (CFPB) with enforcement powers under the Dodd–Frank Act.[47] The bureau may pursue civil actions for violation of the responsible lending and other consumer protection laws, and will track consumer complaints against financial institutions. It will be interesting to see how highly the consumer protection role of the CFPB will be valued in the US in the event of conflict with the prudential regulators of banks, given the potential conflict between the two roles noted by the FSB and discussed above.[48]

Europe

While Ramsay's chapter in this book highlights the difficulties inherent in identifying a consistent 'European approach' to credit regulation, the European parliament's directives on responsible lending are of interest in the context of this chapter. In Europe there has been a similar focus on residential mortgage lending when seeking to enact responsible lending requirements. Two directives of the European parliament are relevant here: the 2008 directive on credit agreements for consumers (2008 directive);[49] and the 2011 directive on credit agreements relating to residential property (2011 directive).[50] A comparison between the two directives demonstrates a greater concern with ensuring both 'responsible lending'

---

45 Dodd–Frank Wall Street Reform and Consumer Protection Act (2010), s 1412.

46 Ibid s 1413.

47 Engel and McCoy, *The Subprime Virus* (n 5) 227.

48 See the discussion in Financial Stability Board, *Consumer Finance Protection* (n 3) 10.

49 Council Directive 2008/48/EC of 23 April 2008 on credit agreements for consumers.

50 *Proposal for a Directive of the European Parliament and of the Council on Credit Agreements Relating to Residential Property* (EC 2011) <http://eur-lex.europa.eu/LexUriServ/LexUriServ.do?uri=com:2011:0142:FIN:EN:PDF>.

and 'responsible borrowing' for residential mortgage lending than for consumer credit loans more broadly.

While the 2008 directive does include a requirement that a creditor assess a consumer's 'creditworthiness' before the conclusion of a credit agreement, there is no prohibition against lending if the assessment is unfavourable.[51] The 2011 directive related to residential mortgage lending includes the same obligation,[52] but additionally requires that the creditor refuse credit where the assessment 'results in a negative prospect for [the consumer's] ability to repay the credit over the lifetime of the credit agreement'.[53] The 2011 directive also imposes an obligation of disclosure on the part of the consumer, being an obligation to provide creditors 'with complete and correct information on their financial situation and personal circumstances in the context of the credit application process'.[54]

Aspects of the European regime worth noting here are: the importance attached to responsible lending in residential mortgage lending; the use of the term 'creditworthy' to refer to consumers, which arguably incorporates some degree of judgement as to a consumer's status, as opposed to a lender's conduct; and, consistent with that, the obligation of disclosure on the part of the consumer, thus ensuring that a residential mortgage borrower is a responsible borrower.

South Africa

In an earlier piece of legislation, the South African National Credit Act 2005 prohibits reckless, rather than irresponsible, lending. Reckless lending undoubtedly refers to conduct more egregious than providing credit in circumstances where it might be unsuitable for a consumer's needs. Recklessness is an established English common-law concept, understood to refer to something in the order of gross negligence or a reckless disregard of a serious harm.[55] The South African legislation links reckless lending to over-indebtedness, over-indebtedness being defined as an inability to satisfy in a timely manner all the obligations under all credit agreements to which the consumer is a party.[56] A credit agreement is reckless where entering into that credit agreement would make the consumer over-indebted.[57] While this could be interpreted to equate to irresponsible lending in the sense of being concerned with lending where a borrower will not have capacity to

---

51   Article 8, Council Directive 2008/48/EC of 23 April 2008 on credit agreements for consumers.

52   *Proposal for a Directive of the European Parliament and of the Council on Credit Agreements* (n 50) Article 14.1.

53   Ibid Article 14.2(a).

54   Ibid Article 15.

55   See the discussion in Geoffrey Rapp, 'The Wreckage of Recklessness' (2008) 86 Washington University Law Review 111.

56   National Credit Act 2005, Republic of South Africa, s 79.

57   Ibid s 80.

repay, it is at least possible that the use of the word 'reckless' will lead to a more restrictive interpretation of the types of lending that will offend the Act.

The consumer is called upon to 'prevent' reckless credit by 'fully and truthfully' answering any requests for information made by the credit provider as part of its assessment that the credit agreement would not be reckless.[58] It will be a complete defence to an allegation of reckless credit if a credit provider establishes that the consumer failed to fully and truthfully answer those requests for information.[59] The consumer is therefore responsible for 'reckless' borrowing.

Like the previous Uniform Consumer Credit Code regime in Australia, enforcement of the reckless lending obligations seems to rely on the consumer to bring proceedings before the court, which is argued above to be a shortcoming of the predecessor Australian system. Where in such proceedings a court declares the credit agreement to be reckless, then the court may make an order setting aside all or part of a consumer's obligations under that credit agreement.[60]

The South African regime applies broadly to all credit agreements for loans below a threshold amount prescribed from time to time.[61] It seems concerned with preventing over-indebtedness rather than more explicitly protecting financial markets, but sets the bar high in terms of the standard of lending prohibited under it. There is an aspect of 'responsible borrowing' in the legislation, discernible from the obligation on the part of consumers to provide full and truthful answers to requests for information. Interestingly, within the same legislation there is a recognition of a consumer 'right' to apply for credit, and to only have credit refused on reasonable commercial grounds, as opposed to unfairly discriminatory grounds.[62] The legislation therefore seems to accept that the concepts of financial inclusion and avoiding over-indebtedness are not necessarily inconsistent, and commentators have noted that 'over-indebtedness' should not be interpreted under the legislation so as reduce the availability of credit in the low-income market.[63]

4 Reactivity: motivations for responsible lending regimes

The differences in approaches outlined under the legislation or directives considered above can, to some extent, be explained by the motivations behind them and the perceived links between irresponsible lending and over-indebtedness or the global financial crisis. In a sense, the regimes are all reactive in that they respond to

---

58   Ibid s 81(1).
59   Ibid s 81(4).
60   Ibid s 83.
61   Ibid s 4.
62   Ibid ss 60–62.
63   Ruth Goodwin-Groen and Michelle Kelly-Louw, *The National Credit Act and its Regulations in the Context of Access to Finance in South Africa* (Finmark Trust 2006) 53.

particular market failures and, in accordance with a neoliberal approach, do not seek to go beyond what is perceived as necessary in that response.

The question of who is to 'blame' for over-indebtedness and the financial crisis also influences the regulatory response in terms of both the extent to which 'responsible lending' or 'responsible borrowing' is required and whether the focus is on consumer protection generally or market protection from potentially harmful mortgage lending.

The resulting language used as part of the different regulatory responses may be significant in terms of the interpretation and implementation of those responses.[64]

Over-indebtedness

Over-indebtedness can have significant financial consequences for both individual consumers and the economy at large. The contribution of lenders to over-indebtedness through irresponsible lending might best be exemplified in the fringe credit market, where low-income consumers access high-cost, short-term loans.[65] It has in fact been argued that irresponsible lending, in the sense of not expecting a borrower to be able to repay at the conclusion of the short-loan term, is an essential aspect of the payday lending business model. In this model borrowers need to 'roll over' the loan at the end of the loan term on payment of an additional fee and may end up paying, over time, an amount well in excess of the original loan amount without reducing the principal owed. The 'roll-over' feature has been described as:

> ... one of the most controversial features of payday loans because it carries great financial risk for consumers and is perhaps the key to the lucrative nature of the business for lenders.[66]

A recent Australian Parliamentary Joint Committee report noted that repayments required under such loans 'can constitute a significant proportion of the borrower's income'.[67] This can reduce household disposable income and household consumption and have a negative impact on household welfare.[68]

---

64 See the discussion on textual interpretation in James Nehf, 'Textualism in the Lower Courts: Lessons from Judges Interpreting Consumer Legislation' (1994) 26 Rutgers Law Journal 2 <http://ssrn.com/abstract=1924446> accessed 12 December 2011.

65 See, for example, Therese Wilson, 'The Inadequacy of the Current Regulatory Response to Payday Lending' (2004) 32(3) Australian Business Law Review 159.

66 Sue Lott and Michael Grant, *Fringe Lending and 'Alternative' Banking: The Consumer Experience* (Public Interest Advocacy Centre 2002), 22.

67 Australian Parliamentary Joint Committee on Corporations and Financial Services, *Inquiry into Consumer Credit and Corporations Legislative Amendment (Enhancements) Bill* (2011) 116.

68 Goodwin-Groen and Kelly-Louw, *The National Credit Act and its Regulations* (n 63) 51.

Such lending has been criticized as 'a form of cultural exploitation, resulting in redistribution from the poor and from minorities to creditors' investors'.[69]

These effects flow through to the broader economy in that over-indebted consumers cannot meet rates and tax obligations, and may become a drain on legal, health and social welfare systems.[70]

Concerns regarding over-indebtedness and its impacts are most explicitly the motivation behind the South African National Credit Act 2005, which defines reckless lending in terms of its relationship to over-indebtedness, and also the Australian National Consumer Credit Protection Act 2009, which concerns itself with a borrower being unable to repay without substantial hardship. Given the recognized limitations of information disclosure and financial literacy and education as consumer protection mechanisms, responsible lending is an appropriate response to concerns about over-indebtedness.[71] It should, however, not lead to restrictive lending practices that exacerbate financial exclusion and, in that way, further exacerbate over-indebtedness as discussed below.

Financial crisis

The global financial crisis, which saw the collapse of financial institutions and financial systems in 2008, has been largely attributed to irresponsible, predatory lending practices facilitated by a *laissez-faire*, neoliberal approach. In the US there had been a view that borrowers should be responsible for their own protection when entering into credit agreements, and that they could be adequately empowered through disclosure and financial literacy and education programmes.[72] The idea that lenders should only recommend loans that were suitable, given a borrower's individual circumstances, was apparently met with derision in some circles.[73] As it transpires, the global financial crisis provides clear evidence of the link between allowing individual over-indebtedness and broader economic consequences, and, as a result, over-indebtedness now seems to be taken more seriously by Western regulators.

Through mortgage securitization, whereby loan repayments could be 'bundled' into bonds and sold to investors, lenders removed default risks from their own

---

69   Braucher, 'Theories of Overindebtedness' (n 6).

70   See the discussion in Goodwin-Groen and Kelly-Louw *The National Credit Act and its Regulations* (n 63) 51.

71   See Iain Ramsay, 'From Truth in Lending to Responsible Lending' in Geraint Howells, André Janssen and Reiner Schulze (eds), *Information Rights and Obligations: A Challenge for Party Autonomy and Transactional Fairness* (Ashgate 2005) 57; and Geraint Howells, 'The Potential and Limits of Consumer Empowerment by Information' (2005) 32 Journal of Law and Society 349, 355–357.

72   See the discussion in Engel and McCoy, *The Subprime Virus* (n 5) 7.

73   Ibid 6.

balance sheets.[74] The incentive on the part of lenders to ensure that borrowers had capacity to repay mortgage loans was severely diminished, and rating agencies were apparently happy to rate bonds highly as long as there was adequate property security supporting the loan. Engel and McCoy have noted that:

> If lenders had kept their subprime loans on their books, they probably would have made fewer loans and taken greater care with the ones they made. With securitisation, however, they could write risky loans and shed them quickly for cash. The buyers, mostly Wall Street banks, converted the loans into securities and passed the risk onto investors.[75]

This led to asset-based lending, where lenders would:

> ... ignore a borrower's income and cash flow as indicators of the borrower's ability to repay a debt and instead make 'asset-based' loans primarily based on the borrower's home equity.[76]

US regulators were not responsive to concerns regarding abusive, predatory lending practices. According to Engel and McCoy:

> The dominant ideology was that if there were problems with mortgage lending, the market would solve them. In addition, if consumers were taking on credit they couldn't afford, that was their choice and their problem. The market's job was to offer consumers choices, and consumers' job was to take personal responsibility for the choices they made. On the corporate side, responsibility meant maximising the bottom line for the benefit of shareholders, without regard for the consequences of abusive lending to consumers or society.[77]

Engel and McCoy tell an alarming tale of increasingly lax lending assessment standards and the use of low-doc or no-doc loans where loan applicants could simply state their income without providing proof or, in the case of no-docs, not state their income at all. This undoubtedly encouraged borrowers to 'stretch the truth', with 60 to 70 per cent of loan applications reportedly containing false information.[78] Ultimately, the price was paid not only by borrowers who lost their homes, but also by those who invested in the highly risky mortgage-backed securities, including large financial institutions. In true 'domino style', this in turn affected the financial system at large, most prominently in the US and Europe.

---

74   Ibid 17.

75   Ibid 43.

76   Cassandra Jones Harvard, 'To Lend or not to Lend: What the CRA Ought to Say about Sub-prime and Predatory Lending' (2005–2006) 33 Florida Coastal Law Review 1.

77   Engel and McCoy, *The Subprime Virus* (n 5) 17.

78   Ibid 35–36.

It is unsurprising that moves to require 'responsible lending' in the US and Europe at least have been largely motivated by a desire to protect against such events being allowed to reoccur and have focused on responsible residential mortgage lending and borrowing.

Attaching blame

In recent years in Western liberal democracies there has been a regulatory emphasis on consumers being able to protect themselves, including in relation to consumer credit agreements. Ramsay has referred to this as the 'responsibilization' of the consumer:

> ... where governments are investing heavily in projects to ensure that individuals become responsible consumers through the use of information, the development of financial capability, and financial literacy programs.[79]

The question of whether to 'blame' the creditor or the consumer where 'irresponsible loans' are made has also arisen in the context of bankruptcy laws, and the extent to which those laws should, on the one hand, operate to provide relief from debt to consumers through discharge of their liabilities or, on the other hand, operate to protect creditors through facilitating repayment of debt to them.[80] In the same way, the regulation of 'irresponsible' credit agreements may seek to emphasize relief from liability for the consumer or enforceability by the creditor, depending on who is to 'blame' for the loan having been made.

Where problems of over-indebtedness and financial crisis are attributed to a failure on the part of consumers to behave responsibly in relation to the credit contracts into which they choose to enter – for example, by failing to make full and true disclosure of their financial positions to lenders – a logical regulatory response might seem to be to punish such behaviour. This arguably ignores a structural cause of over-indebtedness, namely a credit market where individuals are excluded from access to mainstream providers and have no real choice in relation to the agreements into which they enter.[81] Ensuring the availability of safe, affordable, responsibly provided credit would surely be a more effective response, so that borrowers do not have the incentive to acquire harmful credit products.[82] At the

---

79 Iain Ramsay, 'Consumer Law, Regulatory Capitalism and the "New Learning"' (n1) 9, 13.

80 See the discussion in Iain Ramsay, *Between Neo-Liberalism and the Social Market: Approaches to Debt Adjustment and Consumer Insolvency in the EU, Consumer bankruptcy in Europe. Different Paths for Debtors and Creditors* (European University Institute Department of Law 2011).

81 See the discussion in Braucher, 'Theories of Overindebtedness' (n 6) 5–6.

82 See the discussion in Therese Wilson, 'Supporting Social Enterprises to Support Vulnerable Consumers: The Example of Community Development Finance Institutions and

least, there should be a regulatory focus on minimizing the availability of harmful, irresponsible credit by imposing responsible lending, rather than responsible borrowing, obligations. This would, however, involve proactive regulatory steps and would go beyond a neoliberal, minimalistic regulatory approach.

Responsible borrowing obligations, and possible sanctions for those obligations not being met, can be found in the 2011 EU directive and the South African legislation. The 2011 directive requires member states to 'ensure' that consumers provide creditors with 'complete and correct information', and the manner in which members states do that will vary. Sanctions may well follow the South African model of providing a complete defence to creditors to an allegation of reckless lending where the borrower has not fully and truthfully answered any requests for information. This might be regarded as a reasonable 'sanction' in the sense that a creditor should not be penalized for acting on information which turns out to have been false, although it would be preferable for the emphasis to remain on the creditor's obligation to take all reasonable steps to ascertain the consumer's true financial position. The Australian model, for example, requires the credit provider to 'take reasonable steps to verify the consumer's financial situation'.[83] It is not appropriate for a credit provider to receive a 'get out of jail free' card because the borrower has provided false information, in circumstances where the lender could, by reasonable enquiry, have ascertained the true state of affairs. This ignores the structural factors which deprive consumers of real choice in having their credit needs met in a responsible way, which might incentivize the provision of false information to access credit.

Language

It is worth considering the language used in the pieces of responsible lending legislation or directives which are the focus of this chapter. A recent study involving consumer protection legislation showed that statutes were predominantly interpreted textually, relying on the statutory language itself as a source of meaning, but also using that language to interpret more broadly the public policy sought to be advanced by the statute.[84] This is on the basis of an understanding that '[t]he most persuasive evidence of intent or purpose is the language the legislature chose to convey its meaning'.[85]

The term 'creditworthy' used in the 2008 and 2011 EU directives is a value-laden term which may lead to an interpretation which blames the consumer for not being 'worthy' of the loan and therefore 'blameworthy' at the same time as being 'uncreditworthy'. This is unfortunate in that it overlooks the possibility that, in an environment where loan products which are structured responsibly so as

---

Financial Exclusion' (2011) 35 Journal of Consumer Policy 197.

   83   National Consumer Credit Protection Act 2009 (Cth), s 130.

   84   James Nehf, 'Textualism in the Lower Courts' (n 64) 18.

   85   Ibid 4.

to be safe and affordable and 'suitable' for a low-income consumer, a consumer who at first glance appears to be 'uncreditworthy' may in fact be able to manage a loan well. Standard bank credit scoring models may be inflexible and discriminate against consumers on the basis of their income level alone, thus denying access to credit and generating what the World Bank has referred to as 'persistent income inequality'.[86]

Community sector organizations and community development finance institutions that provide credit to otherwise financially excluded individuals use more flexible risk assessment methods that involve carefully assessing capacity to repay on an individualized basis and then providing ongoing financial capability support and advice.[87] This is responsible lending at its best, and it overcomes the problem of the otherwise 'uncreditworthy', financially excluded consumer.

The term 'reckless lending' used in the South African legislation is likely to be understood to refer to more egregious conduct than irresponsible lending, given the common-law understanding of recklessness referred to above.[88] This may lead to a narrow reading of the circumstances in which a credit provider will be found to have breached the South African Act. This is particularly so given the relief from liability accorded to credit providers wherever a consumer has failed to fully and truthfully answer requests for information.[89] This may result in fairly limited circumstances in which a credit provider will risk losing its rights under a credit agreement, notwithstanding a failure to take reasonable steps to ascertain the borrower's financial position.

Other significant language is the use of 'suitability' in the Australian legislation,[90] compared with 'affordability' and 'ability to repay'.[91] The word 'suitability' is a wider term than 'affordability' and could encompass a range of factors and circumstances that would make a particular loan product appropriate or inappropriate to meet a consumer's needs. A concern may be that no credit provider could ascertain on reasonable enquiry all of those factors and circumstances. The credit provider should not be at a disadvantage in this regard, as the Australian legislation only requires it to make reasonable enquiries about the consumer's requirements and objectives, and factors and circumstances that could not have been discovered by reasonable enquiry will not be required to have been taken into account. Nevertheless, the use of the broad term 'suitability' may lead to an interpretation of the 'reasonable enquiry' obligation which results in a finding

---

86   World Bank, *Finance for All? Policies and Pitfalls in Expanding Access* (World Bank 2008) ix.

87   See, for example, Community Development Finance Association, *Inside Out 2010: The State of Community Development Finance* (CDFA 2010) <http://www.cdfa.org.uk/wp-content/uploads/2010/12/Inside-Out-20101.pdf> accessed 28 September 2011.

88   National Credit Act 2005, Republic of South Africa, ss 80 and 81.

89   Ibid s 81.

90   National Consumer Credit Protection Act 2009 (Cth), ss 129–131.

91   Dodd–Frank Wall Street Reform and Consumer Protection Act (2010), s 1411.

of irresponsible lending exceeding that which is necessary to protect consumers from harmful products that might lead to over-indebtedness. Of the legislation and directives considered in this chapter, the Australian legislation seems most heavily slanted towards consumer – rather than lender – protection.

5 Describing a proactive responsible lending regime

The goal of any responsible lending regime should be first and foremost to protect consumers from the harms of irresponsible lending, in that way avoiding over-indebtedness for individuals, as well as the broader economic consequences of that over-indebtedness, including financial crisis. Consumer protection and the welfare of consumers should, however, be enough of an 'end goal' in itself, without the need to justify regulatory intervention by reference to broader economic consequences.

Further, to focus on responsible borrowing, as opposed to lending, ignores the structural causes of over-indebtedness where consumers lack choice and must accept inappropriate, high-cost credit products in order to meet their credit needs.[92] It also ignores theories of behavioural bias, which hold that consumers will display overoptimism and overconfidence when entering into credit agreements.[93]

Additionally, to focus on residential mortgage lending misses an opportunity to address the causes of over-indebtedness more comprehensively, given that high-cost, small-sum personal loans can have significant impacts on consumers' financial positions.[94]

Another potential shortcoming of a responsible lending regime is that it will be interpreted in such a way that it leads to restrictive lending practices which exacerbate financial exclusion. Financial exclusion has been defined by the European Commission as referring to people's difficulties in accessing:

> [f]inancial services and products in the mainstream market that are appropriate
> to their needs and enable them to lead a normal social life in the society in which
> they belong.[95]

While financial exclusion can lead to over-indebtedness through consumers accessing high-cost, exploitative credit products, and broader social and economic consequences flowing from that, financial inclusion through access to appropriate,

---

92   Braucher, 'Theories of Overindebtedness' (n 6) 5–6.

93   See the discussion in Ramsay, *Consumer Law and Policy* (n 40) 162; and Lauren Willis, 'Against Financial Literacy Education' (2008) 94 Iowa Law Review 197.

94   Australian Parliamentary Joint Committee, *Inquiry into Consumer Credit Bill* (n 67) 1, 116.

95   European Commission, DG Employment, Social Affairs and Equal Opportunity, *Financial Services Provision and the Prevention of Financial Exclusion* (PROGRESS Program Overview Paper, EC 2007) 9.

responsibly structured credit products has been shown to have social and economic benefits beyond the meeting of an immediate need.[96]

In a modern consumerist society, most consumers will occasionally need credit to meet what are considered to be basic needs in the context in which they live. In this regard, the term 'financialization' has been coined, to refer to:

[t]he growing necessity, even sometimes the constraint, to use financial products to meet everyday needs e.g. from the most basic needs such as accommodation to other social needs which are necessary to participate in society ... financialisation means that financial products are less and less avoidable to lead a 'normal' life.[97]

Where a product or service is necessary to enable a person to lead a 'normal life', Wilhelmsson argues that it might be conceived as a 'social right':

Many financial services and information society services are now central to the infrastructure of society, and the consumer cannot reasonably be expected to live without them. These aspects of those services can be treated as social rights in that same way that services provided by 'traditional' public utilities are.[98]

Whether in recognition of access to credit as a 'right', or in the interests of avoiding over-indebtedness caused by financial exclusion, responsible lending regimes should not encourage restrictive lending practices any more than they should allow for lax lending practices. The main cause of over-restrictive lending practices seems to be inflexible credit assessment methods. For example, standard credit scoring models used in Australia automatically exclude most low-income consumers from being eligible for loans.[99] This is despite the evidence that low-income individuals can indeed repay loans provided that they are given the chance to do so through an appropriate, individualistic credit assessment process, and provided that the loan term and repayments are structured so that borrowers can repay them without substantial hardship.[100]

---

96   See the discussions in Michael Barr, 'Microfinance and Financial Development' (2005) 26 Journal of International Law 271, 280; and Valerie Ayres-Wearne and Janet Palafox, *NILS. Small Loans – Big Changes* (Good Shepherd Youth and Family Service 2005) 36.

97   Georges Gloukiezoff, *The Link between Financial Exclusion and Overindebtedness* (PROGRESS Program Working Paper, EC 2007) 3.

98   Thomas Wilhelmsson, 'Services of General Interest and European Private Law' in Charles Rickett and Thomas Telfer (eds), *International Perspectives on Consumers' Access to Justice* (CUP 2003) 149, 154–155.

99   See the discussion in Rosanna Scutella and Genevieve Sheehan, *To Their Credit: Learning about Personal Loans for People on Low Incomes* (Brotherhood of St Laurence 2006) 10; and Ayres-Wearne and Palafox, *NILS. Small Loans – Big Changes* (n 96).

100   See the discussion in Scutella and Sheehan *To Their Credit* (n 99); Ayres-Wearne and Palafox, *NILS. Small Loans – Big Changes* (n 99); and Vawser and Associates, *Progress*

Ramsay has noted a conflict between standardized models of credit scoring and truly responsible lending:

> There is a tension between the thrust of the responsible lending standard and the development of credit scoring ... The responsible lending standard envisages a more individualised lending process, perhaps based on a meeting with the borrower. Credit scoring, however, permits a lender to grant credit without ever meeting the borrower.[101]

If a responsible lending regime is not structured to encourage individualized credit assessment, then it is likely to lead to over-restrictive lending practices and to exacerbate over-indebtedness.[102]

A responsible lending regime also risks being ineffective where there is no regulatory agency charged with enforcement – for example, through pursuing penalties or compensation orders against irresponsible lenders.

There are four criteria which this chapter uses to assess the likely effectiveness of the responsible lending regimes described above, in terms of consumer protection and a fair and accessible consumer credit market. These involve a proactive, as opposed to a reactive, regulatory approach, and are: (1) a focus on responsible lending in order to avoid over-indebtedness, rather than responsible borrowing; (2) a focus on consumer credit in general, not limited to residential mortgage loans; (3) an encouragement of flexible, individualized credit assessment practices, or at least not an encouragement of rigid and inflexible credit assessment practices; and (4) the existence of a regulatory agency charged with enforcement, which is adequately resourced to properly monitor and enforce compliance with market conduct regulation, including responsible lending obligations.

Responsible lending, not responsible borrowing

The European and South African regimes include an unfortunate focus on responsible borrowing. Under the South African Act consumers must provide full and truthful answers to requests for information, and a failure to do so will provide a complete defence to a lender to an allegation of reckless lending.[103] In Europe it will be up to the European nations as to how the 2011 directive is implemented, but the directive imposes an obligation on consumers to provide creditors with 'complete and correct' information,[104] and it is possible that, as is the case in

---

Loans: Towards Affordable Credit for Low-Income Australians (ANZ and Brotherhood of St Laurence 2009).

    101   Ramsay, 'From Truth in Lending to Responsible Lending' (n 71) 59.

    102   See the discussion in Ramsay, *Consumer Law and Policy* (n 40) 555.

    103   National Credit Act 2005, Republic of South Africa, s 81.

    104   *Proposal for a Directive of the European Parliament and of the Council on Credit Agreements* (n 50) Article 15.

South Africa, a failure to do so may provide a defence against an allegation of irresponsible lending.

This shifting of responsibility will minimize the impact of the responsible lending regimes in terms of their ability to protect consumers against over-indebtedness.

Consumer credit not just residential mortgages

The European and US responsible lending regimes focus on residential mortgage lending. This is undoubtedly a response to concerns for the health of financial markets following the subprime mortgage crisis in the US For example, the explanatory memorandum to the European directive refers specifically to the financial crisis and the mortgage lending practices that led to it.[105]

It seems short-sighted and reactive, rather than proactive, to focus on the aspect of irresponsible consumer lending which has caused the most economic harm to date. There are many difficulties faced by consumers arising out of small amount, personal loans, which might have broader economic consequences.[106]A requirement that lenders lend responsibly regardless of the nature of the consumer credit loan is necessary to protect all consumers of credit products.

The need for individualistic, flexible credit assessment practices

In an ideal world, responsible lending regimes would mandate individualistic, flexible credit assessment models that would facilitate responsible credit access to a broader range of consumers than is possible under rigid and inflexible credit assessment models. This would alleviate, rather than exacerbate, both financial exclusion and over-indebtedness.

None of the regimes contains such a positive mandate, although the suitability requirement in the Australian NCCPA does involve individualistic enquiry and assessment at least insofar as the consumer's particular needs and requirements are concerned.

The US regime incorporates the 'safe harbour provision' pursuant to which the law will presume that loans are affordable where specific lending requirements are met.[107] This 'obviates the need for creditors to conduct manual assessments of borrowers' ability to repay'.[108] This is likely to reduce the availability of mortgage credit, which is actually regarded as one of the clear intentions of the Act:

---

105 *Proposal for a Directive of the European Parliament and of the Council on Credit agreements Relating to Residential* Property (EC 2011) 2 <http://eur-lex.europa.eu/LexUriServ/LexUriServ.do?uri=com:2011:0142:FIN:EN:PDF.>.

106 Market Intelligence Strategy Centre, *Consumer Credit Report* (MISC 2006); Lott and Grant, *Fringe Lending and 'Alternative' Banking* (n 66); Michael Stegman, 'Payday Lending' (2007) 21(1) Journal of Economic Perspectives 169.

107 Dodd–Frank Wall Street Reform and Consumer Protection Act (2010), s 1412.

108 Engel and McCoy *The Subprime Virus* (n 5) 229.

> One of the intended consequences of Dodd–Frank is for fewer people to acquire mortgages – those who lack the ability to repay them in the cold calculus of rigorous underwriting.[109]

This effectively amounts to 'punishing' potentially 'creditworthy' borrowers for the sins of predatory lenders in the lead-up to the sub-prime mortgage crisis.

Enforcement

As was the case under the predecessor to the Australian NCCPA, under the South African legislation any breaches of the reckless lending provisions must be pursued by the affected borrowers themselves. By contrast, in the US and Australia, the Consumer Financial Protection Bureau and the Australian Securities and Investments Commission respectively may pursue lenders in relation to breaches of the responsible lending provisions. Consumers themselves may not be aware of their rights under the legislation and, in any event, may not have the finances or inclination to pursue litigation in the courts.[110] Reliance on consumers to 'protect themselves' in this way can turn otherwise well-constructed regulation into a 'toothless tiger'.

As discussed above, however, the CFPB and ASIC must be adequately resourced to monitor and enforce compliance with the responsible lending regimes in the US and Australia respectively. Further, as regulators of market conduct and consumer protection, they should not be regarded as having secondary roles to prudential regulators because of neoliberal concerns with the integrity and stability of financial markets over and above the protection of consumers.

6 Conclusion

Regulating to require lenders to lend responsibly is potentially an effective way to protect consumers from the harms of over-indebtedness and, in turn, to protect national and global economies from the follow-on effects of having over-indebted citizens. Neoliberal approaches, which regard state regulation as having only a limited role 'in guaranteeing the effectiveness of market forces',[111] continue to dominate regulatory approaches in Western liberal democracies, even in the wake of the global financial crisis. This has led to limited, reactive approaches – including approaches to the design of responsible lending regimes – in which regimes may only seek to address clearly perceived market failures rather than avoid harms yet to be experienced or perceived. It is argued that consumer protection in and of itself

---

109 Pottow, 'Ability to Repay' (n 44) 36.

110 Genn *Paths to Justice* (n 31) 101; Coumarelos, Wei and Zhou *Justice Made to Measure* (n 31) 99.

111 Crouch, *The Strange Non-Death of Neoliberalism* (n 7) 7.

should be the 'end goal' of consumer protection regimes, rather than being accepted as necessary only because of its relevance to the quest for financial stability.

In particular, this chapter has argued that an effective, 'consumer protection-focused' responsible lending regime should not seek to shift responsibility to consumers for harmful loans that consumers are unable to repay without substantial hardship – for example, by referring to consumer's 'creditworthiness' or relieving lenders from liability where consumers have not provided 'full and truthful' information to them. To shift responsibility in this way ignores both the structural causes of over-indebtedness, such as a consumer credit market in which many consumers have no choice of product and will be driven to enter into any credit agreement that they can, and the tendency towards behavioural optimism and overconfidence that consumers have been found to demonstrate when entering into credit contracts. Lenders should not be excused from an obligation to make reasonable enquiries regarding consumers' financial situations in order to assess their capacity to repay. In this regard, the test should ideally be one that sanctions irresponsible lending, not only the more egregious standard of reckless lending. A negligent failure to make reasonable enquiries, as opposed to a wilful or grossly negligent failure, should be enough to offend responsible lending regulation.

An effective responsible lending regime should extend beyond protection against irresponsible mortgage lending to all forms of consumer credit provision. Consumers might face significant harms from personal loans or loans secured by chattels, where those loans are made irresponsibly. To focus only on the form of lending that is perceived to have caused the greatest harm to the global economy is both short-sighted and reactive, and moreover demonstrates a lack of genuine engagement with the issue of consumer protection.

An effective responsible lending regime should encourage individualistic, flexible credit assessment practices, or at least should not encourage rigid, inflexible credit assessment practices. While the latter may lead to financial exclusion and cause borrowers to access high-cost and exploitative forms of credit, the former may lead to more inclusive, well-informed, responsible lending and therefore financial inclusion.

Finally, an effective responsible lending regime will be enforceable at the instance of a well-resourced consumer protection agency, not relying on potentially under-resourced and ill-informed consumers to commence their own enforcement proceedings. That consumer protection agency should not be undermined in its activities by being subject to the veto of a prudential regulator which has a neoliberal focus on market protection over and above consumer protection.

This analysis of the responsible lending regimes of Australia, South Africa, the US and Europe suggests that those regimes might all be found wanting in terms of their ability to protect consumers against the harms of irresponsible lending, and against the broader economic consequences of those harms. This chapter has attributed the shortcomings of those regimes to a reactive, limited, neoliberal approach to financial regulation, which has continued to influence regulatory policy notwithstanding the impacts of the global financial crisis.

PART IV
Possible Future Initiatives

Chapter 6

Extending Responsible Lending to Small Business: A 'Consumer' Categorization?

Eileen Webb

Modern courts recognise that the signer may be theoretically and technically a merchant but functionally a consumer in terms of education, business acumen and experience.[1]

1 Introduction

Deliberations about the global financial crisis have, for the most part, focused on the conduct of financial institutions and the ultimate consequences of that conduct on consumer borrowers. There has also been considerable debate about the various regulatory responses and the most appropriate means of protecting consumers from the excesses of irresponsible lending practices in the future. This chapter moves the focus from the consumer to small business.

Acquiescing to traditional norms, small businesses are presumed to possess the business acumen and resources of larger counterparts and, as a consequence, are often excluded from the ambit of consumer laws.[2] Yet, in many cases, small businesses have far more in common with the conventional notion of a consumer due to their 'absence of choice, ignorance, naivety in the particular market, standard form contracts and absence of negotiating strength'.[3] Imbalances of the nature that exist between consumers and financiers may occur as readily in small-business transactions as in consumer transactions.[4]

---

1 *Germantown Mfg Co v Rawlinson* 341 Pa Super 42 491 A.2d 138, 146 n 5 (1985); John Edward Murray Jr, 'The Standardized Agreement Phenomena in the Restatement (Second) of Contracts' (1982) 67 Cornell Law Review 735, 778–779; Jane Mallor, 'Unconscionability in Contracts between Merchants' (1986) 40 Southwestern Law Journal 1065, fn 116.

2 Indeed, Professor Bigwood has referred to this approach by the courts as a caricature: Richard Bigwood, 'Curbing Unconscionability: *Berbatis* in the High Court of Australia' (2004) 28 Melbourne University Law Review 203, 204. At 215 Bigwood states: '... their Honours proceeded upon an overly caricatured conception of free competitive bargaining enterprise.'

3 Susan Bright, 'Protecting the Small Business Tenant' (2006) March/April Conv 137, 146.

4 Sarah Brown, 'Protection of the Small Business as a Credit Consumer: Paying Lip Service to Protection of the Vulnerable or Providing a Real Service to the Struggling

To date most legislative, governmental and public attention concerning contentious credit practices has been focused on lending to consumers. Although it is, of course, important to preserve ethical practices in relation to consumer lending, business conduct issues associated with small-business finance should not be ignored. Like the ubiquitous 'consumer', small-business owners vary markedly in terms of business and personal experience, financial liquidity, education and literacy. Again, like consumers, small-business lending is routinely in the form of security over residential property, lines of credit and/or on credit cards. Yet, a small businessperson may be in an even more precarious position in the event of irresponsible or unfair conduct associated with borrowings securing the business. Since the global financial crisis, financial institutions are insisting on higher levels of secured lending for business – particularly small-business – loans. A common financial arrangement involving a small business is a loan from the bank secured by a mortgage over real property; usually the family home. Guarantees, by the small businessperson themselves or close family or associates, are sought as a matter of course. If a business fails, the consequences are dire from a personal, financial and employment perspective. Indeed, the impact on an individual small businessperson may be greater than that occasioned by a default by a 'mere' consumer because of the complexity of the arrangements and the likelihood that larger sums have been borrowed. Moreover, in the event of changing economic conditions, a lender is more likely to intervene in, or modify, the agreement to protect its security. It is important, therefore, that small businesses have safeguards that are at least comparable, if not identical, to consumers with regard to credit.

In the wake of the global financial crisis and, in an Australian context, the mooted extension of the responsible lending provisions of the National Consumer Credit Protection Package to small businesses,[5] it is timely to acknowledge the impact of irresponsible lending practices on small businesses and consider a 'consumer categorization' to ensure appropriate standards of protection for small-business borrowers.

Section 2 of this chapter discusses the nature of small business and outlines the similarities and differences between consumer and small business lending. Broadly, small businesses are privately owned sole traders, partnerships or corporations. Although there is no uniform definition of 'small business', this

---

Entrepreneur?' (2012) 41 Common Law World Review 59, 70–71; Martijn Hesselink, 'Towards a Sharp Distinction between B2B and B2C? On Consumer, Commercial and General Contract Law after the Human Rights Directive' (2010) 18(1) European Review of Private Law 57, 102. See also Geraint Howells and Stephen Weatherill, *Consumer Protection Law* (2nd edn, Ashgate 2005), 31.

5 Australian Government, The Treasury, *National Credit Reform: Enhancing Confidence and Fairness in Australia's Credit Law* (Green Paper, Australian Government July 2010) <http://archive.treasury.gov.au/documents/1852/PDF/National_Credit_Reform _Green_Paper.pdf> accessed 23 July 2012.

may be a positive as general definitions tend to result in a 'one size fits all' approach. Such an approach does not concur with the realities of small business and would not take heed of the diversity within the small-business sector. Section 3 examines the impact of the global financial crisis on small-business lending, particularly the measures utilized by governments to maintain access to credit and the measures introduced by financial institutions to protect their securities. This raises a troubling divide between the attention paid by governments and agencies to small-business *access* to finance and, in some cases, a neglect of small-business *protection* once finance is obtained. In section 4 the availability of consumer credit protection to small businesses in selected jurisdictions is surveyed in some detail. Section 5 focuses on the Australian consumer credit framework and examines some common complaints by small businesses in relation to their credit arrangements. Australian consumer and credit laws are applied to the complaints to determine whether that law can be of assistance to a small businessperson. The section also considers consumer credit laws that are currently unavailable to small businesses to ascertain whether an extension of their application to small businesses would be beneficial. The chapter concludes in section 6 with an assertion that a 'consumer characterization' of small business is desirable and justifiable, and that its impact, though considerable, is worthwhile.

2 The nature of small business

It would be logical to commence an examination of the nature of small business with a definition but, perhaps surprisingly, there is no uniform definition of 'small business' even in similar contexts and/or in the same jurisdiction.[6] In circumstances where small business is defined, the definitions rarely extend beyond simple criteria such as number of employees, turnover and/or some form of monetary threshold. While simplicity has its virtues, such quantitative definitions do not lend themselves to a consideration of the varied types of enterprise the term 'small business' encapsulates. A more qualitative approach would consider the diversity of the persons, natural and corporate, involved in small businesses.[7]

---

6 In Australia, the Parliamentary Joint Committee on Corporations and Financial Services has recommended that the Commonwealth government assess the value of developing uniform definitions of micro-, small and medium business to be applied for data-gathering, policy development and analysis by Commonwealth and state agencies: PJCCFS, *Access for Small and Medium Business to Finance* (Australian Government 2011) [1.21].

7 Indeed, the OECD has warned that focusing on a quantitative definition, rather than on a qualitative definition, causes important characteristics to be forgotten: OECD Statistics Directorate, *Towards Better Structural Business and SME Statistics* (OECD 2005) <http://

Quantitative definitions

In an Australian context, the Australian Bureau of Statistics (ABS) defines small businesses as private-sector businesses employing less than 20 people.[8] It also defines small businesses in other related, and at times overlapping, categories, including non-employing businesses, micro-businesses, small medium enterprises (SMEs) and medium businesses.[9] The number of employees is also used in relation to some workplace legislation, although the number in these circumstances is 15.[10]

---

www.oecd.org/dataoecd/32/14/35501496.pdf page 4>; The OECD Centre for Private Sector Development, *Effective Policies for Small Business: A Guide for the Policy Review Process and Strategic Plans for Micro, Small and Medium Enterprise Development* (OECD 2004) <http://www.oecd.org/dataoecd/2/56/33926971.pdf>. See also Leah Hertz, *In Search of a Small Business Definition: An Exploration of the Small-business Definitions of the U.S., the U.K., Israel, and the People's Republic of China* (University Press of America 1982); Tim Mazzarol, 'Seeking a Common Definition for Small Business – Why is it Important?' (The Conversation 2012) <http://theconversation.edu.au/seeking-a-common-definition-for-small-business-why-is-it-important-6763>.

8   Small businesses are businesses in the private sector which employ less than 20 people. Nearly half do not employ other people. They are in all industries, but agricultural businesses are not normally included in small-business statistics. Small businesses are generally considered to have the following characteristics:

They are independently owned and operated.
They are closely controlled by owners/managers.
Decision-making is principally done by the owners/managers.
The owners/managers contribute most, if not all, of the operating capital.

Australian Bureau of Statistics, *Small Business in Australia 2001* Catalogue no 1321.0 (ABS 2001) < http://www.abs.gov.au/AUSSTATS/abs@.nsf/mf/1321.0>.
In June 2006, 92 per cent of all small-business operators conducted one business, 6 per cent operated two businesses and 2 per cent operated three or more businesses: Australian Bureau of Statistics, *Characteristics of Australian Business 2006* <http://www.abs.gov.au/AUSSTATS/abs@.nsf/0/E49E3B4DC3595C92CA2568A900139377?OpenDocument#SELECTED> accessed 9 March 2011.

9   The Australian Bureau of Statistics, *Small Business in Australia 2001* (n 8) uses the following classifications:

Small businesses: employing fewer than 20 people. They include non-employing businesses, in which one person or two or more partners work, but there are no employees. People who work in these businesses are referred to as 'own account workers'.
Micro-businesses: employing fewer than five people, including non-employing businesses.
Medium businesses: employing between 20 and 199 people.
Small and medium enterprises (SMEs): employing fewer than 200 employees.

10   For the purposes of the Fair Work Act 2009 (Cth), a small business is described as an employer with fewer than 15 employees at a particular time: ss 12, 23.

In comparison, both the Australian Taxation Office and the Privacy Commissioner use turnover to establish that an enterprise is a small business, although the amount of turnover differs quite considerably; less than $2 million dollars (excluding GST) for taxation purposes[11] and less than $3 million for the purposes of the Privacy Act.[12]

In the EU, enterprises are classified as micro,[13] small and medium-sized[14] enterprises[15] and are defined by reference to the number of employees and turnover or annual balance-sheet total.[16] In the UK, again there is no commonly accepted definition (see generally Table 6.1, below).[17] The Companies Act defines small and medium-sized *companies* for accounting purposes as those with a turnover of not more than £6.5 million, a balance-sheet total of not more than £3.26 million and not more than 50 employees.[18] The Small Business Administration in the US utilizes the average number of employees for the preceding 12 months or on sales

---

11   Income Tax Assessment Act 1997 (Cth), s 328.110.

12   Privacy Act 1988 (Cth), s 6D.

13   A micro-enterprise is defined as an enterprise which employs fewer than ten people and whose annual turnover and/or annual balance-sheet total does not exceed €2 million: Commission Recommendation 2003/361/EC of 6 May 2003 concerning the definition of micro-, small and medium-sized enterprises [Official Journal L 124 of 20.05.2003] Article 1.

14   A medium-sized enterprise employs fewer than 250 people and has a an annual turnover not exceeding €50 million or an annual balance-sheet total not exceeding €43 million: Commission Recommendation 2003/361/EC of 6 May 2003 concerning the definition of micro-, small and medium-sized enterprises [Official Journal L 124 of 20.05.2003] Article 1.

15   Enterprise: an enterprise is considered to be any entity engaged in an economic activity, irrespective of its legal form. This includes, in particular, self-employed people and family businesses engaged in craft or other activities, and partnerships or associations regularly engaged in an economic activity: Commission Recommendation 2003/361/EC of 6 May 2003 concerning the definition of micro-, small and medium-sized enterprises [Official Journal L 124 of 20.05.2003] Article 1.

16   In this case, a small enterprise employs fewer than 50 persons and has an annual turnover and/or annual balance-sheet total that does not exceed €10 million. Commission Recommendation 2003/361/EC of 6 May 2003 concerning the definition of micro-, small and medium-sized enterprises [Official Journal L 124 of 20.05.2003] Article 2. See also 'Definition of Micro, Small and Medium-sized Enterprises' (Europa Summaries of European Legislation 2007) <http://europa.eu/legislation_summaries/enterprise/business_environment/n26026_en.htm>.

17   Brown, 'Protection of the Small Business as a Credit Consumer' (n 4) 90.

18   A medium-sized company has a turnover of not more than £25.9 million, a balance-sheet total of not more than £12.9 million and not more than 250 employees. For definitions of small and medium-sized enterprises, see <http://www.lib.strath.ac.uk/busweb/guides/smedefine.htm>.

volume averaged over a three-year period[19] although the calculation differs from industry to industry.[20]

'One size fits all': legal approaches to classifications of business

For understandable reasons of consistency and simplicity, the law often regards businesses as one and the same. The commercial character of business – even the smallest of businesses – relegates them to the 'arms-length' category of commercial transactions regardless of the business's size or the education and experience of the proprietors.[21] Such a business categorization suggests that such entities are better resourced and informed than consumers and can bargain on an equal footing with other businesses. Laws, such as those available to protect consumers, are not necessary because businesspeople can protect their own interests. Therefore, all businesspeople are regarded as 'equals' in a manner reminiscent of the commercial bargains in the classical period.

---

19   Caron Beesley, *What is a Small Business? What You Need to Know and Why* (US Small Business Administration 2009) <http://www.sba.gov/community/blogs/community-blogs/small-business-matters/what-small-business-what-you-need-know-and-wh>. In some industries a combination of employee numbers and turnover is utilized: <http://www.sba.gov/content/what-sbas-definition-small-business-concern>.

20   Examples of Small Business Administration general size standards include the following:

> Manufacturing: maximum number of employees may range from 500 to 1500, depending on the type of product manufactured;
> Wholesaling: maximum number of employees may range from 100 to 500, depending on the particular product being provided;
> Services: annual receipts may not exceed $2.5 to $21.5 million, depending on the particular service being provided;
> Retailing: annual receipts may not exceed $5 to $21 million, depending on the particular product being provided;
> General and heavy construction: general construction annual receipts may not exceed $13.5 to $17 million, depending on the type of construction;
> Special trade construction: annual receipts may not exceed $7 million;
> Agriculture: annual receipts may not exceed $0.5 to $9 million, depending on the agricultural product.

21   Miller notes that: '… in the absence of a meaningful definition of sophistication, courts are not actually addressing the context of the deal. Rather, they are simply reciting well-worn clichés about "sophisticated parties dealing at arms' length"': Meredith Miller, 'Contract Law, Party Sophistication and the New Formalism' (2010) 75 Missouri Law Review 1 available at SSRN < http://ssrn.com/abstract=1468647>; Blake Morant, 'The Quest for Bargains in an Age of Contractual Formalism: Strategic Initiatives for Small Businesses' (2003) 7 Journal of Small & Emerging Business Law 233.

Table 6.1   Use of business finance across different-sized firms in the United Kingdom

Smallest micro-businesses	Micro-businesses	SMEs	Mid-size companies
Below £50k Cash-based firms, often part-time business; few tangible assets; local operations Limited mainly to overdraft, loans and credit cards or personal finance products Some asset-backed lending (ABL) – mainly vendor finance Banks, credit card providers and point of sale (vendor finance)	£50k to £1m Increasingly full-time firms with staff, premises and assets; local activity normally limited to a single region; occasional exporting Overdraft, loans, and credit cards Increased use of structured ABL Occasional use of trade finance products Banks, credit card providers, specialized providers for ABL and trade products	£1m to £25m Full-time, larger multiregional and national firms; increasing export/ import activity Overdraft, loans Still some use of ABL, factoring and invoice discounting, export finance, some equity finance Banks, credit card providers, specialized providers, business angels, private equity	£25m up to £500m Larger national and international firms, often multinational operations Overdraft (or a revolving credit facility), some loans Export finance, invoice finance, asset finance and equity funding Banks, venture funds, equity funds and stock-market listing

Source: Based on Table 2.1, *Supporting UK Business: The Report of the Business Finance Taskforce* (Business Finance Taskforce 2010) <http://www.bba.org.uk/downloads/bba/Business_Finance_Taskforce_report.pdf> accessed 1 June 2012.

In 2004 Professor Garvin wrote about the tendency of the law to adopt 'simplifying divides'[22] such as legal,[23] subject[24] and 'status-driven' dichotomies.[25] 'Status-driven dichotomies cut across legal lines such as consumers and business and consumer and commercial transactions.[26] There is no doubt such classifications are useful, and attempts to merge categories can be difficult and artificial.[27] A problem arises, however, when those classifications become so generalized that they effectively become caricatures. In such a case, the classification attracts a

---

22   Larry Garvin, 'Small Business and the False Dichotomies of Contract Law' (2005) 40 Wake Forest Law Review 295.

23   For example, criminal or civil law: ibid 296.

24   For example, contract or tort: ibid.

25   Ibid.

26   Ibid 295–296.

27   Ibid 296.

particular perception and is deemed to have certain characteristics. This affects the legal perspective from which the legislature and the courts proceed.[28]

Looking deeper: the substance of small business

As a snapshot of the general population, small-business owners come from a variety of backgrounds, levels of business and personal experience, financial liquidity, education and literacy.[29] Even within the category of small business, the size of such businesses varies, from one-person operations often conducted from home to larger enterprises with numerous employees. Small business is also inclusive of groups which, in some circumstances, are marginalized from the wider workforce, such as women[30] and migrants.[31]

---

28   An example of this approach can be seen in the Australian decision, *Australian Competition and Consumer Commission v C G Berbatis (Holdings) Pty Ltd* (2003) 214 CLR 51 (*Berbatis*) where the majority of the High Court approached the relationship between the landlord and the tenants as being on an equal legal footing, as both were commercial parties. Gleeson CJ concluded that that the tenants had no legal entitlement to a new lease, and as such a disability routinely affects tenants at the end of a lease term; it could not be said to be a 'special' disadvantage in the sense known to equity. Gummow and Hayne JJ acknowledged that the tenants were in a vastly inferior bargaining position when compared with the landlord, but considered they were not under a disabling condition which affected their ability to make a judgement as to their own best interests. Callinan J responded in terms of commercial choice. In this respect the High Court's approach can be likened to Garvin's discussion of the 'rational actor' model. Professor Bigwood is critical of the High Court's approach: 'I criticise the majority judges' rather perfunctory handling of the facts of the case, which was made worse by their failure to link the elements of unconscionable dealing to a sophisticated conceptual account of interpersonal exploitation in market exchange contexts': Bigwood, 'Curbing Unconscionability' (n 2) 204, 215.

29   In the US literature, such businesses are often referred to as 'mom and pop' enterprises: *United States v Von's Grocery Co* (1966) 384 US 270, 288 per Stewart J dissenting; Joshua Wright, Comment, 'Von's Grocery and the Concentration–Price Relationship in Grocery Retail' (2001) 48 UCLA Law Review 743, 752, 773; Brian Blum, 'The Goals and Process of Reorganizing Small Businesses in Bankruptcy' (2000) 4 Journal of Small & Emerging Business Law 181, 188; Luz Nagle, 'E-Commerce in Latin America: Legal and Business Challenges for Developing Enterprise' (2001) 50 American University Law Review 859, 901.

30   In June 2006, 68 per cent of small-business operators were male and 32 per cent were female: Australian Bureau of Statistics, *Characteristics of Australian Business 2006* <http://www.abs.gov.au/AUSSTATS/abs@.nsf/0/E49E3B4DC3595C92CA2568A900139 377?Open Document#SELECTED> accessed 13 October 2012.

31   In June 2006, 71 per cent of all Australian small-business operators were born in Australia, with the remaining 29 per cent born overseas.

The diversity of individuals captured within the term 'small business' has been the subject of academic discussion, particularly in the US.[32] For example, Professor Abril coined the term 'acoustic segregation'[33] to describe the obstacles faced by many small-business owners when participating in the business marketplace. Abril distinguishes between what she refers to as Chamber 2 and Chamber 3 merchants:[34] Chamber 2 comprises 'experienced business owners, educated Anglophones with Internet access, and those with the financial wherewithal to obtain legal counsel' and Chamber 3 comprises people with 'limited access to education, business and contract-related information'.[35] Under the Uniform Commercial Code (UCC), a Chamber 3 merchant will be regarded as having the same qualities as a Chamber 2 merchant, when often this is clearly not the case. The law is said to contribute to this inequity because, in Abril's view, it does not 'explicitly recognize the existence of, particularly, the disadvantages of Chamber 3 merchants'.[36] While Abril's research is focused on the most disadvantaged small businesspeople, she is careful to note that a person can be classified as a Chamber 3 merchant if there is evidence of only one of the criteria.[37] Similarly, other research has been undertaken on the economic, societal and practical reality of many small businesses.[38] In an Australian context, the Trade Practices Act 1974 (Cth),[39] recognized that small businesses may require protection from the unconscionable conduct of, in particular, larger landlords and franchisors.[40]

---

32   Patricia Abril, '"Acoustic Segregation" and the Hispanic Small Business Owner' (2007) 10 Harvard Latino Law Review 1, 3–4; Miller, 'Contract Law, Party Sophistication and the New Formalism' (n 21); see also Meredith Miller 'Party Sophistication and Value Pluralism in Contract' (11 July 2012) <http://papers.ssrn.com/sol3/papers.cfm?abstract_id=2103351> accessed 23 July 2012.

33   Abril, '"Acoustic Segregation"' (n 32) 3.

34   I acknowledge that here I am not heeding Professor Garvin's warning regarding the dangers of such classifications.

35   Abril, '"Acoustic Segregation"' (n 32) 3–4. These may include 'non-English speakers, recent immigrants, the unschooled, the illiterate, and those that cannot pay for legal or business services'. Members of Chamber 3 receive little information about normative information and conduct rules. For a discussion of Abril's thesis in an Australian context see Eileen Webb, 'Unconscionable Conduct in *Australian Competition and Consumer Commission v Dukemaster Pty Ltd*' (2010) 18 Australian Property Law Journal 48.

36   Abril '"Acoustic Segregation"' (n 32) 8.

37   Ibid 8.

38   For example, Jane Mallor, 'Unconscionability in Contracts Between Merchants' (1986) 40 SW LJ 1065, 1066; Tansel Yilmazer and Holly Schrank, 'Financial Intermingling in Small Family Business' (2006) 21 Journal of Business Venturing 726; George Haynes and R J Avery, 'Family Businesses: Can the Family and the Business Finances be Separated?' (1997) 5 Journal of Entrepreneurial and Small Business Finance 61.

39   Now the Australian Consumer Law, Schedule 2 Competition and Consumer Act 2010 (Cth).

40   Eileen Webb, 'The Productivity Commission Inquiry Report: The Market for Retail Tenancy Leases in Australia' (2009) 16 Australian Property Law Journal 219; Neil

A recent decision has highlighted the disadvantages some businesspeople have in relation to other better-resourced and informed entities. *Australian Competition and Consumer Commission v Dukemaster Pty Ltd*[41] underscores some of these disadvantages in relation to language, information and/or financial limitations.

Appreciating the existence of this diversity is especially important when considering whether small businesses should be excluded from consumer protection laws because of their business character. Given this diverse nature of the small-business 'populace' and the fact that small businesspeople share many characteristics with consumers, it is artificial for two individuals to suffer the same wrong but for only one to be entitled to recourse. Such denial disregards the iniquity of the conduct and focuses instead on a rather perfunctory classification.

3 Common impediments impacting on small businesses' ability to obtain and retain credit

Why protect small-business lending?

Access to finance provides small businesses with stability and the ability to consolidate and expand, thus leading to consequent benefits in the economy as a whole.[42] As a general rule, constraints on private funding to small businesses are an impediment to economic recovery and growth.[43] Recently, the Organization for Economic Cooperation and Development (OECD) analysed data from 18 countries regarding business loans to SMEs before and since the global financial crisis.[44]

Crosby, Sandi Murdoch and Eileen Webb, 'Landlords and Tenants Behaving Badly? The Application of Unconscionable and Unfair Conduct to Commercial Leases in Australia and the United Kingdom' (2007) 33 University of Western Australia Law Journal 207; Eileen Webb, 'Almost a Decade On – A (Reid) Report Card on Retail Leasing' (2006) 13 Australian Property Law Journal 240.

41   (2009) FCA 682. See generally Eileen Webb, '*ACCC v Dukemaster*: A Recognition of Acoustic Segregation in Australian Retail Leasing?' (2010) 18 Australian Property Law Journal 48.

42   At the Pittsburgh Summit in 2009, G20 Leaders recognized that small–medium enterprises are crucial engines of economic growth, jobs and social cohesion, according to the OECD. In many countries they represent around 99 per cent of all firms. Access to finance remains one of the biggest challenges in the creation, survival and growth of small firms: Global Partnership for Financial Inclusion, 'SME Finance: Stepping up to the Challenge' (OECD 2012) <http://www.oecd.org/dataoecd/5/18/50105000.pdf> accessed 19 April 2012.

43   Ibid.

44   OECD, *Financing SMEs and Entrepreneurs 2012: An OECD Scoreboard* (OECD 2012) <http://www.oecd-ilibrary.org/industry-and-services/financing-smes-and-entrepreneurship_9789264166769-en>.

The OECD survey concluded that securing bank and other forms of debt had become more difficult for SMEs. Reasonable lines of credit have become increasingly difficult to obtain and, despite record falls in interest rates, the gap between interest paid by large and small firms has widened.[45]

In some cases, governments assisted SMEs to ensure lending was maintained. Mazarol notes that the OECD identified ten different methods by which governments assisted SMEs during the financial crisis.[46] Of all the options, government loan guarantees were the most favoured option.[47] For example, in the US, the Small Business Administration (SBA) introduced loan programmes to help small businesses secure loans. The SBA guaranteed a portion of the loan to the issuing bank, thus relieving financial institutions of some of the risk of extending the loan to a small business. For their part, business owners had to pledge personal assets and sign a personal guarantee. Such guarantees were often combined with special guarantees and loans for start-ups, usually comprising some business advisory support services.[48]

In Australia, the financial crisis impacted on SME business finance, though not to the extent seen elsewhere. Growth in business lending slowed as a result of tighter lending criteria and standards by financial institutions and reduced demand for credit from small businesses due to the prevailing economic conditions.[49] Also,

---

45   Ibid.

46   Interestingly, more than 170 countries had introduced government loan guarantees prior to the GFC. Obviously, many schemes were enhanced in the wake of the crisis. The impact of the global crisis on SME and entrepreneurship financing and policy responses meant that many countries increased the level of support financing for exporters, and in Sweden there was some government co-financing of businesses. Direct lending to SMEs by government was observed in Chile, Hungary, Korea and Slovenia, while Portugal and Thailand offered subsidized interest rates. Other schemes included credit mediation, tax exemptions and tax deferments, venture capital equity funding and business advice services.

47   For example, some nations increased the level of support financing for exporters, government co-financing of businesses, direct lending to SMEs by government, subsidized interest rates, credit mediation, tax exemptions, tax deferments, venture capital equity funding and business advice services: Tim Mazarol, 'The Small Business Sector: What Has Been the Impact of the GFC?' (The Conversation 2012) <http://theconversation.edu.au/financing-the-small-business-sector-what-has-been-the-impact-of-the-gfc-6894> accessed 12 June 2012.

48   NSW Business Chamber, *Submission to the Manufacturing Industry Action Plan Taskforce* (NSW Business Chamber 2011) <http://www.business.nsw.gov.au/__data/assets/pdf_file/0010/21340/NSW-Business-Chamber.pdf> accessed 12 June 2012; Mazarol, 'The Small Business Sector' (n 47).

49   Australian Treasury, *National Credit Reform* (n 5) 5; Reserve Bank of Australia, *Submission to the Inquiry into Access of Small Business to Finance* (RBA 2010): 'This tightening reflects a combination of increased cyclical risk of business loans and the global repricing of risk more generally. Further, a number of financial intermediaries scaled back their lending to small business during the global financial crisis, due to a combination of factors including rising funding costs resulting from the dislocation in financial markets and

during the crisis many 'second-tier' financial institutions, which had provided an alternative source of consumer and business lending, merged with various members of the 'Big Four' Australian banks,[50] thus undermining competition for business lending.[51] A combination of these factors has affected SME lending in Australia, particularly in relation to:

- greater insistence by lenders for secured lending; and
- lenders requiring enhanced information requirements from businesses.[52]

Sources of capital for small businesses

Small businesses typically obtain their funding for start-up and early-stage growth from a combination of self-financing through savings, an equity loan on the business owner's home, and/or other assets and credit cards.[53] Banks will usually insist on a personal guarantee by the business owner. In an Australian context, the Australia and New Zealand Banking Corporation (ANZ), one of the larger small-business lenders, has described its small-business lending profile thus:

- 61 per cent of small-business lending customers has a business credit card;
- 39 per cent have a property mortgage; and
- 3.5 per cent have a personal loan.[54]

---

weaker conditions in foreign lenders' home economies. This placed additional pressure on credit conditions.'

50   The Commonwealth Bank, Australia and New Zealand Banking Corporation, The National Australia Bank and Westpac Banking Corporation.

51   During and after the global financial crisis many small banks merged with the larger Big Four banks, thus undermining competition within the Australian banking market.

52   CPA Australia, *SME Access to Finance: Recent Experiences of SME's in Accessing Finance* (CPA Australia 2012) 15; Reserve Bank of Australia, *Recent Developments in Interest Rates on Bank Lending* (RBA 1999) <http://www.rba.gov.au/publications/bulletin/2002/feb/pdf/bu-0202-2.pdf> accessed 31 May 2012. Other examples include cash-flow lending, debtor finance, full-drawn advance credit, mortgage equity loans, interest-only loans and chattel mortgages.

53   For example, the Business Finance Taskforce in the UK has identified the use of different financial products depending on the size of the business (see Table 6.1 above).

54   ANZ Banking Corporation, *Submission to Treasury – National Credit Reform Green Paper* (ANZ 2010) 7: <http://archive.treasury.gov.au/consumercredit/content/consultation/submissions/downloads/reform_green_paper/ANZ.pdf> accessed 5 June 2012. It should be noted, however, that in 2008 CPA Australia concluded that the main forms of small-business credit were via credit cards, leasing, overdrafts and hire purchase: CPA Australia, *Small Business Survey August – Financial Management of Small Business* (CPA Australia 2008). Small businesses do not appear to be as familiar with alternative forms

Elsewhere it has been noted that since the crisis additional security is often required in relation to existing loans, and lenders are no longer prepared to provide finance on soft unsecured security, such as cash flow or goodwill.[55] Reporting requirements for both new and existing borrowers have also been significantly enhanced.[56]

Access versus protection

Certainly, stricter requirements were placed upon small-business financing in the wake of the global financial crisis. It was soon recognized, however, that lending to SMEs was critical to the rebuilding process, and governments adopted a variety of strategies to ensure that SME finance was maintained to some extent. But, although the flow of funds is regarded as essential, consumer-like protections are, for the most part, not regarded as necessary to business borrowers. Indeed, the restriction of funds has been used as an argument against enhanced protections for small-business borrowers, the assertion being that more regulation will result in less lending. It is suggested that the discussions in sections 4–6 of this chapter will dispel this myth.

4 The applicability of consumer credit protection to small businesses in selected jurisdictions

At this point in the chapter it is instructive to consider what measures, if any, have been adopted in selected jurisdictions to extend consumer or consumer credit legislation to small-business borrowers.

Protections in consumer credit laws that do not extend to small businesses as businesses of any size are excluded from the definition of 'consumer'

Europe: a 'rigorous' divide
The European Community pursues an objective of achieving an internal market – this concept is pivotal to discussions of EU consumer law generally.[57] The internal

---

of finance, such as international trade finance, inventory financing and vendor and debtor financing: Australian Treasury, *National Credit Reform* (n 5) 2.

55   CPA Australia, *SME Access to Finance* (n 52), 15–16.

56   Ibid.

57   Referring to Reich, Wilhelmsson notes that 'EC consumer law and policy has been characterised as Janus-faced, on the one hand aiming at creating a common internal market, on the other hand striving at some protective goals as well': Thomas Wilhemsson 'The Abuse of the "Confident Consumer" as a Justification for EC Consumer Law' (2004) 27 Journal of Consumer Policy 317; Norbert Reich, *Europäisches Verbraucherrecht* (Nomos 1996) 56.

market seeks to guarantee free movement of goods, persons, services and capital throughout member states. However, member states retain powers to provide protection for their citizens.[58] The Treaty of Lisbon[59] lists the internal market and consumer protection as areas of 'shared competence' between the EU and member states.[60]

The directive most relevant to this chapter is the Consumer Credit Directive.[61] Despite acknowledging the importance of small-business access to finance[62] and, at some levels, recognizing that small businesses may be as vulnerable in credit transactions as consumers,[63] the definition of 'consumer' in the Consumer Credit Directive is very narrow. This is a feature common to all consumer-oriented directives and has caused one commentator to note that European law evinces 'a rigid distinction between commercial and consumer law'.[64]

---

58   Norbert Reich, Hans Micklitz and Peter Rott, *Understanding EU Consumer Law* (Intersentia 2009) 7.

59   After a turbulent process, the Lisbon Treaty took effect on 1 December 2009. The treaty does not affect the basic regulatory structure of the internal market. It was signed by EU member states on 13 December 2007 but was put on hold due to its rejection by a majority of voters in a referendum held in the Republic of Ireland. The treaty will have considerable impact on the internal operation of the EU and amends several pivotal treaties such as the Treaty on European Union (TEU, Maastricht 1992) and the Treaty establishing the European Community (TEC, Rome 1957). See generally <http://europa.eu/lisbon_treaty/index_en.htm> accessed 1 December 2011.

60   Reich et al, *Understanding EU Consumer Law* (n 58). In order to foster consumer confidence in the internal market, there has been a recent shift in policy by the European Commission towards maximum harmonization of European consumer laws rather than the minimum harmonization utilized in earlier consumer law directives. In summary, if a directive decrees minimum harmonization, legislation in member states is required to meet a certain threshold but, if desired, the member state may enact laws which exceed the terms of the directive. In circumstances of maximum harmonization, member states must abide by the terms of the directive and cannot impose additional provisions in domestic legislation.

61   Directive 2008/48/EC of 23 April 2008 of the European Parliament and of the European Council. The Consumer Credit Directive covers unsecured lending products (so excludes mortgages, second mortgages and secured loans) such as credit cards, loans and current accounts where an overdraft facility is offered. 'Consumer' is not defined in the EC Treaty although there is an obligation to maintain a high degree of consumer protection. The directive states in Article 3(a) that a consumer for the purpose of the directive 'means a natural person who, in transactions covered by this directive, is acting for purposes which are outside his trade, business or profession': Hesselink, 'Towards a Sharp Distinction between B2B and B2C?' (n 4) 71.

62   'Opinion of the European Economic and Social Committee on Credit and Social Inclusion in an Affluent Society' (2008) Official Journal of the European Union C44/19, para 4.1 <http://eur-lex.europa.eu/LexUriServ/LexUriServ.do?uri=OJ:C:2008:044:0074:0074:EN:PDF> accessed 5 June 2012.

63   Brown, 'Protection of the Small Business as a Credit Consumer' (n 4) 64.

64   Hesselink, 'Towards a Sharp Distinction between B2B and B2C?' (n 4) 102.

'Consumer' is defined in Article 3(a) as '*a natural person*' who, in transactions covered by the directive, '*is acting for purposes which are outside his trade, business or profession*'[65] (emphasis added). In summary, in Europe 'consumer' is limited to a natural person entering into a transaction for private purposes.[66] Clearly, no incorporated entities may avail themselves of the provisions, and the necessity for the transaction to be external to a consumer's trade, business or profession prevents any business, even small-business, application.[67]

This issue also impacts on the applicability of other directives that could have potentially assisted small businesses. For example, the Unfair Commercial Practices Directive (UCPD)[68] prohibits unfair commercial practices such as misleading conduct and harassment in business-to-consumer (B2C) transactions.[69] Despite lobbying from member states where relevant laws are equally applicable to business-to-business (B2B) transactions, the directive remained focused on B2C transactions.[70]

Protection through extension of relevant definitions to include some small businesses, in particular partnerships and unincorporated businesses

Domestic law of some EC member states
Within the domestic law of member states, however, there is some flexibility regarding the definition of 'consumer', thus permitting an extension to some small

---

65 Note that the definition varies slightly in some directives. For example, in Germany 'consumer' refers only to trade or profession.

66 Martin Ebers, 'Comparative Analysis Part 3A, the Notion of Consumer' in Martin Ebers, Hans Schulte-Nolke and Christian Twigg-Flesner (eds), *EC Consumer Law Compendium* (Sellier European Law Publishers 2008); Brown, 'Protection of the Small Business as a Credit Consumer' (n 4) 64.

67 For example, ECJ c-361/89 *Patrice Di Pinto* [1991] ECR 1-1189.

68 Directive 2005/29/EC of the European Parliament and of the Council of 11 May 2005 concerning unfair business to consumer commercial practices in the internal market and amending Council Directive 84/450/EEC, Directives 97/7/EC and 2002/65/EC of the European Parliament and of the Council.

69 Article 3(1): 'This Directive shall apply to unfair business-to-consumer commercial practices, as laid down in Article 5, before, during and after a commercial transaction in relation to a product. Commercial practices will be unfair if they are misleading as set out in Articles 6 (misleading actions) and 7 (misleading omissions) or are aggressive as set out in Articles 8 (aggressive commercial practices) and 9 (use of harassment coercion and undue influence).' Most terms are clearly defined. The directive contains a 'black list' of practices which will always be regarded as unfair.

70 Howells and Weatherill, *Consumer Protection Law* (n 4). Howells provides several examples, including reference to the Danish Marketing Practices Act, Swedish Marketing Act and the Austrian, German and Greek Acts against Unfair Competition. Indeed, Howells notes that several member states had traditionally enacted legislation that extended beyond B2C transactions but contained, for example, different approaches to how the law applied to consumers and competitors.

businesspeople. Therefore, in some cases, protection will extend to businesses operating outside their usual business operations.[71] This can result from a wider interpretation of national laws or through the inclusion of a different definition of 'consumer' adopted for national purposes.[72] For example, relevant French and Italian laws have been held to provide protection so long as an individual is not acting directly for the purposes of the business.[73] In Germany, paragraph 13 BGB states that a consumer is 'every natural person who enters into a legal transaction for a purpose that is outside his trade, business or *autonomous* profession' (emphasis added).[74] It has been suggested, therefore, that transactions caught by the provision extend to employed field representatives who use the loan to finance the purchase of a car for professional purposes.[75] Bulgarian,[76] and it seems Estonian, law provides protection where businesses contract outside their usual field of business.[77] The Netherlands is a particularly interesting case for the purposes of this discussion as Dutch domestic law does not distinguish between B2B and B2C transactions – a stark contrast to the European situation. Hesselick contrasts the domestic approach of treating 'like treated alike' with directives introduced as *lex specialis* or general private law.[78] Indeed, it seems there is pressure in some circles for greater adherence to the directives in the domestic law with 'more business like contract with less heed of good faith'.[79] In relation to the Consumer Credit Directive, some member states have extended the scope of its application to other agreements not covered by the directive as well as the personal scope of application.[80]

---

71   Brown, 'Protection of the Small Business as a Credit Consumer' (n 4) 65.

72   The scope of the directive has been extended in many member states; see generally European Parliament Directorate General for Internal Policies, Policy Department A, *Economic and Scientific Policy Implementation of the Consumer Credit Directive* <http://www.europarl.europa.eu/studies>.

73   Ebers, 'Comparative Analysis Part 3A, the Notion of Consumer' (n 66).

74   Margus Kingisepp and Age Värv, 'The Notion of Consumer in EU Consumer Acquis and the Consumer Rights Directive – A Significant Change of Paradigm?' 44 Juridica International <http://www.juridicainternational.eu/index.php?id=14841> accessed 15 May 2012; Christoph Kramer, 'National Report Germany' <http://www.zoll.jura.uni-osnabrueck.de/files/National_Report_Germany.pdf>.

75   Furthermore, the German legislation extends the scope of certain provisions to founders of a new business (para 502 BGB). This group is not covered by the European notion of 'consumer'.

76   Ebers, 'Comparative Analysis Part 3A, the Notion of Consumer' (n 66); Brown, 'Protection of the Small Business as a Credit Consumer' (n 4) 66.

77   Karin Sein, 'Transposition of the New Consumer Credit Directive in Estonia' (2012) 20(2) European Review of Private Law 435.

78   Hesselink, 'Towards a Sharp Distinction between B2B and B2C?' (n 4) 104.

79   Ibid.

80   European Parliament Directorate General for Internal Policies: Policy Department A, *Economic and Scientific Policy Implementation of the Consumer Credit Directive* (n 72) 12.

The United Kingdom
The Consumer Credit Act (1974)   The UK has a long history of protecting
small business in credit transactions. As early as 1971 the Crowther Committee[81]
recognized that small businesses can be vulnerable in relation to their borrowing
as consumers. The Consumer Credit Act (1974), as amended in 2006 extends
protections to certain sole traders, certain partnerships[82] and unincorporated
bodies. The legislation does not extend to incorporated small businesses. The 2008
Consumer Credit Directive is in the process of being implemented.

Unlike in Europe, there is no specific definition of 'consumer'. A consumer
credit agreement is an agreement between an individual debtor and the creditor
by which the creditor provides the debtor with credit of any amount.[83] There are
some exemptions, particularly if the transaction involves a first mortgage on a
dwelling.[84] Also, a borrower receives protection if the borrowings do not exceed
£25,000 for business purposes or, in the case of individuals, where the net worth
exceeds £150,000.[85]

Although this extension to some business credit arrangements is, no doubt,
of some assistance to small businesses, the relatively small sum means that any
significant business borrowings will be excluded. Questions can also be raised
about the rationale behind the monetary threshold. The threshold was set at
£25,000 as borrowers of sums above this amount were likely to be able to protect
their own interests and, indeed, seek legal or accounting advice. Leaving aside the
fact that, in 2012, £25,000 is not a considerable loan, the threshold for a perceived
vulnerability justifying legislative protection is reached at the relatively low sum
of £25,000 in comparison to an individual's vulnerability at net worth of £150,000.
Sarah Brown highlights the fact that those borrowing larger sums may indeed
exhibit greater vulnerabilities:

> ... borrowing larger amounts may in fact simply indicate greater need or an
> inability to calculate risks/consequences. Inequality in bargaining power and
> vulnerability may be an issue here, relevant in relation to small businesses
> struggling with cash flow, often under pressure from suppliers to pay but unable

---

81   Committee on Consumer Credit, *Consumer Credit Report of the Committee* (Cmnd
4596, HMSO 1971). See the discussion by Brown, 'Protection of the Small Business as a
Credit Consumer' (n 4) 63–65.

82   Consumer Credit Act (CCA), s 189(1). The purpose of the loan is irrelevant and
'individual' includes a partnership of stwo or three persons not all of whom are bodies
corporate. This does not include incorporated bodies. See Elizabeth Halle, 'When is a
Company a Consumer?' (2004) 13(2) Nottingham Law Journal 52.

83   CCA, ss 2, 8. Note amendments via the Consumer Credit Act 2006. See also Sarah
Brown, 'The Consumer Credit Act 2006: Real Additional Mortgagor Protection?' (2007)
71 Conveyancer 321.

84   Financial Services Act, s 140C.

85   Exemptions are listed in ss 16, 16A and 16B.

to get their own invoices paid, or new businesses needing finance to purchase stock or assets such as machinery. (footnotes omitted)[86]

Unfair credit relationship test   The Consumer Credit Act 1974 enables borrowers to challenge unfair credit agreements in court and obtain redress, if the overall relationship is unfair to the borrower. The courts have a wide range of powers where a credit relationship is unfair.[87] Interestingly, the provisions apply to parties otherwise exempted, namely high net worth borrowers and businesses borrowing more than £25,000.[88]

Recent developments   There are some other interesting developments afoot. The Business Lending Taskforce, in response to the UK government's Green Paper, *Financing a Private Sector Recovery*[89] has proposed that service levels to micro-enterprises be improved.[90] A new Lending Code will stipulate the levels of service that banks will provide and outline additional sources of help and advice.[91] A recent consultation[92] proposes a more streamlined framework for

---

86   Brown, 'Protection of the Small Business as a Credit Consumer' (n 4) 87.

87   S 140A provides that a court may determine that the relationship between a lender and a borrower arising out of a credit agreement (or the agreement taken with any related agreement) is unfair to the borrower because of any of the terms of the credit agreement or a related agreement; the way in which the lender has exercised or enforced its rights under the credit agreement or a related agreement; or any other thing done (or not done) by or on behalf of the lender either before or after the making of the credit agreement or a related agreement. For an excellent overview of the legislation, see Sarah Brown, 'The Unfair Relationship Test, Consumer Credit Transactions and the Long Arm of the Law' (2009) LMCLQ 90. For a discussion of the desirability of such a provision in the Australian law, see Andrew Serpell 'Treating Consumers Fairly in the Australian Financial Services Sector' (2010) 25 Australian Journal of Corporate Law 26.

88   Agreements that are exempt under ss 16, 16A or s 16C (buy-to-let agreements) of the Act, para 1.4. See Office of Fair Trading, *Unfair Relationships: Enforcement Action under Part 8 of the Enterprise Act 2002* (OFT May 2008, updated August 2011) <http://www.oft. gov.uk/shared_oft/business_leaflets/enterprise_act/oft854Rev.pdf> accessed 12 June 2012. For a recent judicial consideration of the provisions see *Patel v Patel* [2010] 1 All ER (Comm) 864 but compare *Harrison v Black Horse Ltd* EWCA CIV 1128.

89   HM Treasury, *Financing a Private Sector Recovery* (HM Treasury 2010) <http:// www.bis.gov.uk/assets/biscore/corporate/docs/f/10-1081-financing-private-sector-recovery> accessed 1 June 2012.

90   Business Finance Taskforce, *Supporting UK Business: The Report of the Business Finance Taskforce* (Business Finance Taskforce 2010) <http://www.bba.org.uk/downloads/ bba/Business_Finance_Taskforce_report.pdf> accessed 1 June 2012. In the report, micro-businesses are described as businesses with fewer than ten employees and turnover or a balance sheet under €2 million.

91   Ibid.

92   HM Treasury, *Financing a Private Sector Recovery* (n 89) 1.17.

consumer credit protection and pays heed to the 'different rights and divergence in protection for consumer and small-business borrowers'.[93]

Protection through specifically directed provisions that specifically catch commercial parties, including small businesses

South Africa
Of all the jurisdictions discussed in this chapter, South Africa's consumer and consumer credit legislation provides the most comprehensive protection to small businesses.[94] Unfortunately, the protections in the National Credit Act (NCA) do not extend to businesses affected by reckless lending practices.

National Credit Act (NCA) 2005   The National Credit Act 2005 contains a wide definition of 'consumer', including within its scope mortgagors,[95] borrowers under a secured loan[96] and guarantors.[97] Subject to some qualifications, the NCA also extends to 'juristic persons'.[98] This is important in the context of the application of the NCA to business because a juristic person includes a partnership, association or other body of persons, corporate or unincorporated.[99] However, not all businesses obtain the protection of the Act.[100] A monetary threshold limits the application of the NCA to juristic persons with an asset value or annual turnover of less than R1 million,[101] so long as such a juristic person enters into a large

---

93   Ibid.

94   Three types of credit agreements are distinguished in the Act: (1) a credit facility – for example, a credit card, line of credit, overdraft protection; (2) a credit transaction which subdivides into several 'subspecies' of agreement – for example, a mortgage (of immovable property), lease of personal property, secured loan (secured by pledge of personal property), instalment account, discount account, pawn transaction, incidental credit agreement, i.e. a prepaid transaction or outstanding account, or any other similar transaction like an unsecured loan; and (3) a credit guarantee.

95   National Credit Act 2005, s 1(d).

96   Ibid s 1(e).

97   Ibid s 1(g).

98   Ibid s 1:

'juristic person' includes a partnership, association or other body of persons, corporate or unincorporated, or a trust if–
(a) there are three or more individual trustees; or
(b) the trustee is itself a juristic person,
but does not include a stokvel.

99   In some circumstances the term also catches certain trusts.

100   See National Credit Act 2005 ss 5 and 6.

101   S 4(1) of the NCA states:

Subject to sections 5 and 6, this Act applies to every credit agreement between parties dealing at arm's length and made within, or having an effect within, the Republic, except–

agreement (more than R250,000).[102] Also, some provisions of Chapters 4 and 5 NCA do not apply to juristic persons.[103] These exclusions include, *inter alia*, the credit marketing and reckless credit provisions of Chapter 4 Part C.

The NCA provides for certain types of credit agreements relevant to small and emerging businesses: for example, a Developmental Credit Agreement is a distinct category of financing that includes loans for the development of small businesses.[104] Such credit agreements attract comprehensive protection and special provisions within the legislation.

Consumer Protection Act   It is also relevant to mention the Consumer Protection Act which affects a wide range of consumers and transactions. Again, 'consumer' is defined broadly, being a natural or juristic person to whom goods or services are promoted or supplied. The legislation is applicable to businesses; however, a similar approach to the monetary threshold test in the NCA is applied. 'Consumer' includes a juristic person if the asset value or annual turnover is less than R2 million a year. Therefore, in such cases, small businesses and sole proprietors who fall within this turnover will enjoy the same protection from suppliers as an individual consumer. In a credit context it is important to note that 'services' include banking services.[105]

---

a credit agreement in terms of which the consumer is–
(i) a juristic person whose asset value or annual turnover, together with the combined asset value or annual turnover of all related juristic persons, at the time the agreement is made, equals or exceeds the threshold value determined by the Minister in terms of section 7(1).

102   In some circumstances it is necessary to consider the amount of money involved in a particular transaction as the NCA differentiates between small, intermediate and large agreements. Monetary thresholds are contained in the National Credit Regulations: a small agreement (credit limit of R15,000 or less); intermediate agreement (credit facility with a credit limit over R15,000 or a credit transaction with a credit limit over R15,000 but less than R250,000); and a large agreement (a mortgage agreement or a credit transaction where the principal debt exceeds R250,000).

103   The following provisions of this Act do not apply to a credit agreement or proposed credit agreement in terms of which the consumer is a juristic person:

Chapter 4 – Parts C and D;
Chapter 5 – Part A - section 89 (2)(b);
Chapter 5 – Part A - section 90(2)(0); and
Chapter 5 – Part C.

104   NCA s 1; s 10(1)(b)(iii)(a).

105   Section 1 (definition of services)(c): 'any banking services, or related or similar financial services, or the undertaking, underwriting or assumption of any risk by one person on behalf of another, except to the extent that any such service constitutes advice or intermediary services that is subject to regulation in terms of the Financial Advisory and Intermediary Services Act, 2002 (Act No 37 of 2002); or is regulated in terms of the Long-

Overview

The jurisdictions reviewed are generally consistent in that they tend to offer some, but not universal, protection for small-business borrowers. The differing approaches can be best understood by contrasting the rationale for EC directives with the internal laws of member states. The focus of the EU is on improving conditions for the efficient functioning of the internal market[106] and, it seems, law-makers are of the view that this purpose is best served by focusing on the rights of a narrowly defined 'consumer'. The result is the exclusion of B2B transactions. On the other hand, domestic laws in some European member states have not historically made such distinctions, and the domestic focus is on addressing problems arising between parties.[107] The UK features some useful extensions to small business, but the approach is inconsistent and is presently subject to review. The South African legislation exhibits the broadest protections in this context, but it is unfortunate that small-business borrowers do not seem to have received the benefit of the relevant responsible lending provisions.

5 Focus on Australia

When considering a 'consumer categorization' for small business credit customers, it is instructive to examine the Australian approach in some detail. Although not 'covering the field', some Australian consumer laws do encompass business, and an extension of consumer credit protections to small business is mooted.[108]

Concerns regarding small-business lending

In Australia, conduct issues surrounding small-business lending have been the subject of consideration for some time. In 1997 the Reid Committee examined the business conduct of banks and financial institutions, *inter alia*, when providing finance to small business.[109] In particular, concerns were raised about

---

term Insurance Act 1998 (Act No 52 of 1998), or the Short-term Insurance Act 1998 (Act No 53 of 1998).'

106   EC Treaty Article 95 enables the Community to harmonize national regulation in order to establish or facilitate free movement within the internal market.

107   Hesselink, 'Towards a Sharp Distinction between B2B and B2C?' (n 4) 66.

108   Stage 2 National Consumer Credit Protection Package as discussed in Australian Treasury, *National Credit Reform* (n 5).

109   Joint Select Committee, *Finding a Balance: Towards Fair Trading in Australia: Report on Retailing* (Parliament of the Commonwealth of Australia 1997) Chapter 5, Para 5.1. Hereafter the Reid Report. The serious business conduct issues relating to small business finance raised in evidence to the Reid Committee concerned: lack of disclosure of the terms of a loan; limited client access to information about bank accounts; failure of banks and finance companies to live up to their side of loan agreements; harsh conduct in

the considerable amount of security required from small businesspeople[110] and the conduct of repossession and mortgage sales.[111] Also, in 1997 the *Financial Systems Inquiry Final Report*[112] examined the availability and cost of small-business finance, noting that small businesses faced higher borrowing costs and more onerous loan conditions than larger businesses.[113] Both inquiries identified a lack of access to dispute resolution as a major impediment for small businesses.[114]

Until recently, the Uniform Consumer Credit Code (UCCC)[115] provided a means by which borrowers could make application for hardship variations or to set aside an unjust credit contract. The UCCC was, however, limited to persons borrowing for personal, domestic or household purposes, and parties could 'contract out' of the UCCC through the use of a 'business purpose declaration'.[116] In addition, some states had introduced related legislation such as the Contracts Review Act 1980 (NSW) and the Finance Brokers Control Act (1975) (WA).[117] The Trade Practices Act 1974 (Cth), and, later, the Australian Securities and Investments Commission Act 2001 (Cth) (ASIC Act)[118] provided some recourse

---

relation to repossession and mortgagee sales; breach of client confidentiality; and banks obstructing dispute resolution by recourse to costly court action.

110   Ibid paras 5.1, 5.5.57–5.67, recommendation 5.4.

111   Ibid paras 5.1, 5.35–5.48, recommendation 5.2. The Reid Report (n 109) made five recommendations regarding small-business finance. It also recommended that, should an unfair conduct provision be introduced, it should extend to such transactions.

112   Australian Treasury, *Financial Systems Inquiry Final Report (The Wallis Report)* (AGPS 1997) <http://fsi.treasury.gov.au/content/FinalReport.asp> accessed 12 June 2012.

113   Small business was particularly reliant on debt rather than equity finance: Reid Report Para 5.8.

114   Reid Report (n 109) paras 5.12–5.16, recommendation 5.1.

115   The Uniform Consumer Credit Code (UCCC) commenced operation on 1 November 1996. Operating as a uniform national legislative scheme, it was enacted as template legislation in Queensland and adopted in the other states and territories. With the transfer of responsibility for consumer credit to the Commonwealth, the UCCC has been largely incorporated in the National Credit Code: Schedule 1 National Consumer Credit Protection Act 2009.

116   Persons borrowing for business or investment purposes were required to execute a business purpose declaration that excluded them from the provisions of the UCCC. This has continued in the NCC.

117   For example, the Contracts Review Act 1980 (NSW) prohibited, *inter alia*, unjust contracts and provided that where the Court found a contract or a provision of a contract to be unjust, it could refuse to enforce all or any provisions of the contract or making variations to the contract. In Western Australia the Finance Brokers Control Act (1975) (WA) introduced a comprehensive system to regulate the education and conduct of brokers.

118   In 2001 the Australian Securities and Investments Commission (ASIC) commenced its regulatory and enforcement role in relation to financial products and services. Some prohibitions equivalent to the consumer protection provisions in the TPA

to small business through the prohibition of misleading or deceptive and unconscionable conduct.[119] Voluntary codes of conduct were also developed or their operation expanded.[120]

The 2012 legal landscape: credit protection for small business

In 2012 Australia has a limited, but patchwork, extension of consumer and credit laws to business. Nevertheless, the lending practices and conduct of financial institutions in relation small-business loans continue to attract criticism.[121] Figure 6.1 summarizes the existing regulatory arrangements.

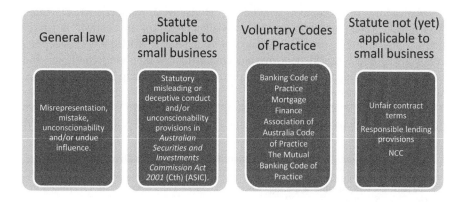

Figure 6.1   Existing regulation of small-business borrowing in Australia

The general law
For aggrieved small-business borrowers, possible causes of action under the general law include, *inter alia*, misrepresentation, mistake, unconscionability and/or undue influence. Nevertheless, it is a difficult task to establish these causes of action in a business context. Also, the decision in *ANZ Banking Group v Karam*[122]

– in particular, unconscionable conduct and misleading or deceptive conduct – were incorporated in the ASIC legislation.

119   S 12CC will be discussed below. Although the Reid Committee had recommended that the mooted unfairness provision also apply to dealings between small businesses and financial institutions, a provision mirroring s 51AC was adopted. Therefore, regulation of such conduct, whether directed at consumers or business, became the responsibility of the ASIC.

120   For example, the Code of Banking Practice and the Credit Union Code of Practice (in July 2009 the Code was renamed the Mutual Banking Code of Practice).

121   See, for example, Lee Aitkin, 'A Duty to Lend Reasonably – New Terror for Lenders in a Consumer's World? (2007) 18 JBFLP 18.

122   (2005) 64 NSWLR 149.

illustrates the difficulty of establishing economic duress in a small business dispute.[123]

The Australian Securities and Investments Commission Act 2001 (Cth)

The ASIC Act regulates conduct issues in relation to financial products and services. Division 2 contains prohibitions regarding unconscionable conduct and consumer protection. It is important to note, however, that not all provisions are applicable to businesses. For example, while the prohibitions of unconscionable conduct[124] and misleading or deceptive conduct[125] provide recourse for businesses, the unfair contract terms provisions[126] and those involving conditions and warranties[127] do not.[128]

Misleading or deceptive conduct   Division 2, Subdivision D, titled 'Consumer protection' lists several provisions relevant to conduct in credit transactions, including misleading or deceptive conduct.[129] Misleading or deceptive conduct has been identified in myriad circumstances involving consumer and business lending, including the giving of advice,[130] the granting of loans[131] and the taking of guarantees[132] and mortgages.[133]

Unconscionable conduct   Division 2, Subdivision C contains various prohibitions of unconscionable conduct. Of most consequence is[134] section 12CB

---

123   Peter Gilles, 'Banks, Unconscionability and Economic Duress – A Small Step towards Deregulation?' (2006) 17 Journal of Banking and Finance Law and Practice 177; JessicaTuffin, 'Responsible Lending Laws: Essential Development or Overreaction?' (2010) 9 QUTLJJ 280.

124   Part 2 Division 2, Subdivision C: S 12CA-CB. S 12CC informs s 12CB.

125   S 12DA. Note the related provisions in Part 2 Division 2, Subdivision D.

126   Part 2 Division 2, Subdivision BA, in particular s 12BF.

127   Part 2 Division 2, Subdivision E.

128   For a discussion on these inconsistencies and some possible solutions see Lynden Griggs, Aviva Freilich and Eileen Webb, 'Challenging the Notion of a Consumer: Time for Change' (2011) Competition and Consumer Law Journal 19.

129   For example, false or misleading representations, false or misleading representations in relation to financial products that involve interests in land, and certain misleading conduct in relation to financial services.

130   *Ines v Commonwealth Bank of Australia* [2008] FCA 1608; cf. *Mahlo v Westpac Banking Corp*oration [1999] NSWCA 358.

131   *Plum v Commonwealth Bank of Australia* [2005] FCA 790; *Australian Securities & Investments Commission, in the matter of Money for Living (Aust) Pty Ltd (Administrators Appointed) v Money for Living (Aust) Pty Ltd (Administrators Appointed) (No 2)* [2006] FCA 1285.

132   *First for Finance Pty Ltd v Westpac Banking Corp* (unreported SC Vic 7 May 1998).

133   *Arbest Pty Ltd v State Bank of NSW Ltd* (1996) ATPR 41-470.

134   In summary, s 12CA prohibits a person in trade or commerce from 'engaging in conduct in relation to financial services if the conduct is unconscionable within the meaning of the unwritten law, from time to time, of the States and Territories'. In other words, the

which prohibits a person, in trade or commerce, in connection with the supply or acquisition or possible supply or acquisition of financial services to a person (other than a listed public company) from engaging in conduct that is, in all the circumstances, unconscionable. Pursuant to section 12CC, the court may refer to a non-exhaustive list of factors in determining whether conduct is unconscionable. The list of factors is the 'starting-point' in making a determination as to unconscionability.[135]

It is fair to say that judicial interpretation of the prohibition of unconscionable conduct to business transactions in the ASIC legislation and equivalent provisions elsewhere[136] has been cautious. Although it seems that a dictionary interpretation of 'unconscionable' is appropriate, a high standard of wrongdoing is required to evince unconscionable conduct in a commercial transaction.[137]

Therefore, in a majority of cases, a lender may have behaved, in common parlance, 'unfairly' or 'harshly' and the borrower may have suffered a resultant detriment, yet the conduct will not be held to be unconscionable. The reason for this is that the entitlement to safeguard one's own business is regarded as paramount and, so long as in doing so the conduct is not regarded as excessive, the courts are seeking to ensure that this high threshold remains and the unconscionability standard is not blurred by notions of unfairness or unjustness.[138] There have been several decisions

---

provision represents the equitable doctrine of unconscionable dealing as it develops over time but makes statutory remedies available to aggrieved parties. The provision is applicable to commercial transactions. The provision is virtually identical to ACL s 20 / AATPA s 51 which has had little success due to the narrow interpretation of unconscionable, particularly in a business context.

135   This section is capable of applying to conduct in respect of loans: *Tonto Home Loans Australia Pty Ltd v Tavares* [2011] NSWCA 389.

136   For example, AC TPA s 51, now ACL s 21.

137   For example, see the rather extreme fact situation in *Coggin v Telstar Finance Company (Q) Pty Ltd* [2006] FCA 191 where the conduct was held to be unconscionable. Also, the concept of unconscionability in this section involved 'serious misconduct or something clearly unfair or unreasonable' and contemplates actions which show 'no regard for conscience, or that are irreconcilable with what is right or reasonable' or involve 'a high degree of moral obloquy': *Hurley v McDonald's Australia Pty Ltd* (2000) ATPR 41-741; *Australian Competition and Consumer Commission v 4WD Systems Pty Ltd* (2003) 200 ALR 491 at [184]; *Hall v Kennards Storage Management Pty Ltd* [2009] VCAT 153; *Transaero Pty Ltd v Goulthorpe* [2009] VCAT 2146, [92]; *Attorney General of New South Wales v World Best Holdings Ltd* (2005) 63 NSWLR 557; *In the matter of Free Wesleyan Church of Tonga in Australia Inc (administrators appointed) Phoenix Lacquers & Paints Pty Limited v Free Wesleyan Church of Tonga in Australia Inc (administrators appointed) & Ors* [2012] NSWSC 214.

138   It seems that recently some courts and tribunals have embraced the 'gloss' of moral obloquy: *Attorney General of New South Wales v World Best Holdings Ltd* (2005) 63 NSWLR 557, 583 per Spiegelman J, applied in, *inter alia, Canon Australia Pty Ltd v Patton* (2007) 244 ALR 759, 768. See, too, the comments in *In the matter of Free Wesleyan Church of Tonga in Australia Inc (administrators appointed) Phoenix Lacquers & Paints Pty Limited v Free*

involving financial services which seem to restrain any significant extension of the unconscionability standard, particularly in relation to small-business refinancing.[139] While not all these decisions involve section 12CC, in combination the cases exhibit a restrained view of the standard of conduct which would be regarded as 'unconscionable' in terms of the equitable doctrine and pursuant to statute. It seems that not only will such decisions inform considerations of whether conduct, in all the circumstances of the financial services transaction, exceeded good conscience, but also that only examples of extreme, egregious conduct will satisfy the threshold.[140]

Unfair contract terms in credit contracts   Section 12BF(1) ASIC Act renders a term in a relevant consumer contract void if that term is unfair. A term will be unfair if: it would cause a significant imbalance in the parties' rights and obligations arising under the contract; it is not reasonably necessary in order to protect the legitimate interests of the party who would be advantaged by the term; and it would cause detriment (whether financial or otherwise) to a party if it were to be applied or relied on.[141] A list of factors assists the court in determining whether a contract is unfair.[142] To date, the unfair contract terms legislation does not apply to small-business finance.

National Consumer Credit Protection Act 2009

Stage 1 NCCPP   In relation to the applicability of the consumer credit protections, such as responsible lending and assistance in circumstances of unjust credit contracts, Australia is in a state of transition. In 2009 the Commonwealth government introduced the National Consumer Credit Protection Package (NCCPP). Stage 1, introduced by the National Consumer Credit Protection Act 2009 (NCCP Act), mandates responsible lending and requires finance brokers and lenders to be licensed. All providers and brokers of financial services are required to be members of an external dispute resolution (EDR) scheme.[143] The UCCC has been renamed the

---

Wesleyan Church of Tonga in Australia Inc (administrators appointed) & Ors [2012] NSWSC 214 at [24] in relation to *Tonto Home Loans Australia Pty Ltd v Tavares* [2011] NSWCA 389: conduct could contravene the section where it demonstrated a high degree of moral obloquy on the part of the person said to have acted unconscionably; where it was irreconcilable with what is right or reasonable; where factors similar to those arising under the Contracts Review Act were relevant; and where conduct involves 'taking advantage of vulnerability or lack of understanding, trickery or misleading conduct'. The President observed that the conduct requires at least 'some degree of moral tainting in the transaction of a kind that permits the opprobrium of unconscionability to characterise the conduct of the party'.

139   In particular, the decision in *Australia and New Zealand Banking Group Ltd v Karam* (2005) 64 NSWLR 149; also refer again to the cases listed in n 138.

140   Indeed, although the statutory provisions generally involved are s 12CC, the comments of the courts in many of the cases seem to reflect the views of the majority of the High Court in *Berbatis*.

141   S 12BG.

142   S 12BH.

143   Stephen Cavanagh, Katrina Banh and Alena Cher, 'National Consumer Credit Protection Act 2009 – What is Responsible Lending?' (2010) 25(10) BLB 172; Bruce

National Credit Code (NCC) and is incorporated into the NCCP as schedule one. The NCC is, subject to some enhancements, identical to the provisions of the UCCC.

Stage 2 NCCPP   The second stage of the NCCPP, addresses, *inter alia*, unsolicited credit card limit extension offers; interest rate caps and reverse mortgages. A pivotal and controversial issue has been the proposal to extend some, if not all, of the Stage 1 reforms to small businesses. Three options have been proposed by the Commonwealth government and are summarized in Figure 6.2.

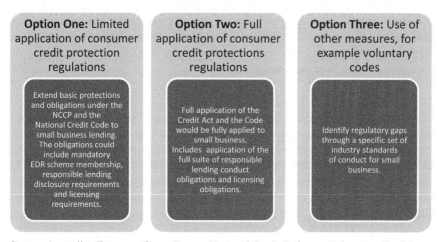

Source: Australian Treasury, *Green Paper: National Credit Reform – Enhancing Confidence and Fairness in Australia's Credit Law* (Australian Government 2010) 12–14.

Figure 6.2   Proposed options for the extension of consumer credit protections to small businesses

While Option 2 proposes full application, Option 1 proposes that the extension should be limited to 'basic protections'. It is unfortunate that there is no guidance as to the nature of the 'basic protections' referred to. Option 3 proposes a specific set of industry standards of conduct for small business lending.

Other possible avenues for aggrieved small-business borrowers
Financial arrangements entered into by small business do not attract the protections of the NCCP Act, including the responsible lending provisions, or the NCC.[144] Various industry codes of practice,[145] – in particular, the Code of Banking Practice

---

Taylor 'New National Responsible Lending Obligations' (2012) 40 ABLR 43.

144   Although the Code of Banking Practice does address this anomaly to an extent through provisions such as cl 24.4 which states that statements will be issued to small business customers in line with the requirements of the UCCC.

145   The Code of Banking Practice, the Mortgage and Finance Association of Australia Code of Practice and the Mutual Banking Code of Practice.

(CBP) – have jurisdiction involving small-business lending and provide a benchmark for service and conduct. However, while the CBP places obligations on the banks regarding the provision of information to small-business clients[146], assistance during financial difficulties and compliance with procedures involving guarantees,[147] the Code is voluntary and, to date, not all banks have adopted it.[148] Also, the provisions are not applicable to the wider financial services industry. EDR services are available to small businesses pursuant to the Financial Services Ombudsman and Credit Services Ombudsman, although there is controversy over the relevant terms of reference and the level of the monetary and compensation thresholds.[149] Depending on their terms of reference, some EDR schemes have jurisdiction to consider small-business complaints.[150] Otherwise, recourse, including for unconscionable or misleading or deceptive conduct, is to the courts.

Common issues for small-business borrowers

The Consumer Ombudsman Service Ltd (COSL) has identified several issues of concern for small businesses regarding their dealings with financiers.[151] It is instructive, therefore, to examine these problems and assess whether the Australian law, at present, can address these issues or whether an extension of other laws to encompass small business would be beneficial. Interestingly, and consistent with the overall thesis in this chapter, all are concerns common to both consumers and small-business lenders.

Failure or delay in following client instructions   At present, such concerns are addressed in the Banking Code of Practice and other relevant codes, but remedies are limited. In most cases, it is unlikely that such conduct would be misleading or deceptive, or so egregious as to establish unconscionable conduct. If the NCCPA was applicable, however, section 47(1)(a) requires a licensee[152] to do all things necessary to ensure that the credit activities authorized by the licence are engaged in efficiently, honestly and fairly. The licensee is required to conduct itself in a way that is consistent with, and reflects an appreciation of, the need to

---

146   For example, CBP cl 24.4, cl 25.

147   CBP cl 28.

148   A list of banks which have adopted the Banking Code of Practice are listed at http://www.bankers.asn.au.

149   The BFSO cannot consider disputes involving financial institutions' general practices and policies or an exercise of commercial judgement.

150   Clauses 3.1 and 3.2 and Schedule 1 of FOS Terms of Reference, *FOS Circular, Dealing with Customers in Financial Difficulty: Small Business*, Issue 2 April 2010. Clauses 9.1 and 9.2, definitions 44.1 in COSL Rules (March 2010). The monetary compensation limit increased to $280,000 on and from 1 January 2012 and will be adjusted thereafter every three years using the higher of the increase in the MTAWE or CPI (COSL Member Alert, 8 September 2009).

151   Australian Treasury, *National Credit Reform* (n 5) 6.

152   A person who holds an Australian credit licence. A person cannot engage in credit activities without holding an Australian credit licence.

meet community standards of efficiency, honesty and fairness.[153] It seems that, in the event of a conflict between efficiency of banking procedures and fairness to the client, fairness will prevail.[154]

Fees   The fee structure imposed by banks is a common bugbear for consumers and small businesses alike. Fees are contained in the relevant contract, and the nature of the complaint about the fees will determine whether there is some recourse available to a small businessperson. Disclosure and information obligations regarding changes in fees are regulated by the CBP.[155] Also, high rates of interest and onerous terms regarding default interest and compounding interest in a contract may, in certain circumstances, be held to be unfair as well as unjust or unconscionable. As yet, however, these avenues are unavailable to small businesses.

Unfair contract terms   The most obvious contention is that such a term is unfair. Indeed, unfair bank fees are currently the subject of pending litigation in Australia,[156] and there has been much criticism by both consumers and small business about the unilateral variation of contracts.[157] Although in long-term and ongoing standard-form contracts there is a legitimate need to amend terms unilaterally,[158] there seems no reason why an extension to small-business contracts should be resisted. So long as such terms are used in a manner 'which is reasonably necessary in order to protect the legitimate business interests of the party advantaged by the term',[159] a term is likely to be upheld.[160] Also, the provisions are not intended to allow customers to challenge the lender's right to unilaterally vary the interest rate under a credit agreement[161] or undermine securitization arrangements[162] – two principal areas of concern for financiers.

Unconscionable charges   Section 78 NCC empowers a court to annul or reduce certain fees if the change is unconscionable.[163] The NCC also contains the

---

153   Explanatory memorandum, National Consumer Credit Protection Act 2009, cl 176

154   Ibid cl 177.

155   Code of Banking Practice, Part C.

156   Maurice Blackburn Lawyers, *Bank Fees Class Action* <http://www.mauriceblackburn.com.au/areas-of-practice/class-actions/current-class-actions/bank-fees-class-action.aspx> accessed 29 May 2012.

157   In the examples listed in s 12BH, subsections (a), (b), (d), (e), (f), (g) and (h) refer to various forms of unilateral conduct.

158   *The Australian Consumer Law: Consultation on Draft Unfair Contract Terms Provisions* (ACL 11 May 2009) 13 <http://www.consumerlaw.gov.au/content/Content.aspx?doc=ACL_consultations.htm> accessed 5 May 2012.

159   Ibid, referring to *Director of Consumer Affairs Victoria v AAPT Ltd* [2006] VCAT 1493.

160   In *Kowalczuk v Accom Finance Pty Limited* (2008) 252 ALR 55.

161   *The Australian Consumer Law* (n 158) 14.

162   Ibid 15.

163   Any change in the annual percentage rate, any establishment fee or charge or fee payable on early termination of a contract. A change is unconscionable if: the change occurs

right for consumers to be able to have a credit contract, consumer lease, mortgage or guarantee reopened on the grounds that it is unjust.[164]

Allegations of unconscionable interest rates have been considered in a small-business context in several cases.[165] Although a finding of unconscionability is not unusual in relation to consumer issues, it is more difficult to establish in commercial matters. In two notable cases the courts seemed to regard it as relevant that two commercial parties were involved[166] and should have therefore appreciated the risks involved, and the fact that the businesses had very little option, as all lenders would have offer the same rates, was disregarded. Nevertheless, there certainly appears to be scope for a successful allegation of unconscionable conduct, especially when combined with a lack of business acumen on the part of the businessperson and questionable conduct on the part of the lender.[167] High interest rates may be balanced by the risk involved in the transaction, the borrower's credit history and/or the duration of the loan term. However, additional expenses imposed in the event of a default in payment – for example, 'risk fees', in combination with the high interest rates, may suggest unconscionable conduct.[168]

Contracting out of the NCC

A contentious issue under the UCCC, and now the NCC, is the ability of parties to 'contract out' of the NCC and their associated obligations by nominating loan purposes that take the transaction outside the scope of the legislation. Small-business advocates assert that, in many cases, the purposes listed are not genuine, are secured by the borrower's principal place of residence or are guaranteed

---

in an unreasonable manner, having regard to the advertised rate and the period of time since the contract was entered into; or the change discriminates against the debtor compared to other similar debtors. A court has to decide if a charge is unconscionable, taking into account the credit provider's reasonable costs.

164   Interestingly, there is presently no general remedy provided for unjust conduct by brokers or other intermediaries (as the Code only provides a remedy where there has been unjust conduct by lenders).

165   These actions have been commenced under the Contracts Review Act 1980 (NSW) and the ASIC Act.

166   *Joelco Pty Ltd v Balanced Securities Limited* [2009] QSC 236 (unreported, de Jersey CJ, 26 August 2009); *Commonwealth Bank of Australia v Ridout Nominees Pty Ltd* [2000] WASC 37 (unreported, Wheeler J, 28 February 2000).

167   For example, in *No Fuss Finance Pty Ltd v Miller* [2006] NSWSC 630 (unreported, Barrett J, 27 June 2006); Ms Miller entered into a loan for three months at 72 per cent per annum which was secured over her home. Ms Miller was investing with an acquaintance and the proceeds of the loan were paid wholly to this person. In all the circumstances, which included Ms Miller's lack of business acumen, unconscionability was also alleged but, after making the finding on the CRA, the matter was not pursued. *Galadriel Lothlorien Pty Ltd v Station 1 Pty Ltd* [2008] NSWSC 91 (unreported, Hamilton J, 15 February 2008).

168   *Kowalczuk v Accom Finance Pty Limited.* (2008) 252 ALR 55.

by a third party, usually a family member.[169] Loans involving a principal place of residence are of particular concern due to the dual nature of the transaction. Although used to secure a business loan, it seems incongruous that it should lose its character, and thus protection, from unfair lending practices. Yet, a business-purpose declaration is all that is required to remove the borrower from these protections.

Financial hardship
Hardship may arise through irresponsible lending practices or events subsequent to lending may befall a borrower, thus leading to hardship. The issue then becomes the lender's ability and readiness to assist. Unfortunately, neither the responsible lending provisions nor the hardship variation procedure under the NCC is available to small-business borrowers.

Irresponsible lending   Part 3 NCCP Act addresses responsible lending and places responsibilities on licensees who are credit providers[170] in relation to disclosure, *inter alia*. The pivotal requirement is that a licensee must not enter a credit contract with a consumer unless, within the previous 90 days, the licensee has made a relevant assessment and has carried out the required inquiries and verification. The licensee must make an assessment as to whether the credit contract will be *unsuitable* for the consumer. The suitability assessment requires the credit provider to: make reasonable inquiries about the consumer's requirements and objectives in obtaining the credit and the consumer's financial situation; take reasonable steps to verify the financial situation; and carry out any inquiries or verification prescribed by the regulations.[171] A contract will be deemed unsuitable where: the consumer will be unable to comply with the consumer's financial obligations under the contract; the consumer will only be able to comply with substantial hardship; and the contract will not meet the consumer's requirements or objectives or in any circumstances prescribed in the regulations.[172] This includes reference to circumstances where the consumer could only comply with his or her financial obligations under the contract by selling his or her principal place of residence. It will be uncertain for some time, in practice, how far the reforms will go and how the yardstick of 'suitability' will be assessed.[173]

An example of the inconsistency in not extending the responsible lending provisions to small business is the problem of asset lending – that is, lending

---

169   For example, note the submissions in response to the 2010 Green Paper by Care Australia.

170   There are also provisions regulating credit representatives – for example, brokers.

171   Gail Pearson, 'Reading Suitability against Fitness for Purpose: The Evolution of a Rule' (2010) 32(2) Sydney Law Review 311.

172   *Silberman v Citigroup Pty Ltd* [2011] VSC 514.

173   ASIC, *Regulatory Guide No 209: Credit Licencing – Responsible Lending* (ASIC March 2011) <http://www.asic.gov.au/asic/pdflib.nsf/LookupByFileName/rg209-310311.pdf/$file/rg209-310311.pdf> accessed 5 June 2012.

money 'without regard to the ability of the borrower to repay by instalments under the contract, in the knowledge that adequate security is available in the event of default'.[174] In such a case, the loan is based entirely on the value of the security offered[175] and, if the borrower's income is such that the debt cannot be repaid, it is likely that the financier will sell the property to recover the monies owing.[176] In the absence of any duty of care[177] or substantive rule of law prohibiting this conduct,[178] financiers cannot be prevented from recovering the security when the borrower defaults.[179] Decided cases have considered asset lending as being 'unjust' under the CRA and also as unconscionable conduct, although it seems that the responsible lending provisions would be of assistance by nipping the problem in the bud.

---

174   *Perpetual Trustee Company v Khoshaba* [2006] NSWCA 41 (unreported, Spigelman CJ, Handley and Basten JJA), [128]. See *also National Australia Bank v Satchithanantham* [2009] NSWSC 21 (unreported, McCallum J, 6 February 2009) and, on appeal, *Satchithanantham v National Australia Bank Ltd* [2009] NSWCA 268; *Perpetual Trustees Victoria v Longobardi* [2009] NSWSC 654; *Big Kahuna Holdings Pty Ltd v Joanna Kitas* [2012] NSWSC 615.

175   Although this does in fact occur, as a general principle, banks should not lend solely against security.

176   Brereton J referred to asset lending in *Riz v Perpetual Trustee Australia Ltd* [2007] NSWSC 1153 (unreported, Brereton J, 18 October 2007, [70]. His Honour said that where borrowers could not service a loan from their own resources, 'then it is not in substance a loan but an asset sale, in which the lender risks nothing but the borrower risks the asset'.

177   Joan Wadsley, 'Bank lending and the Family Home: Prudence and Protection' (2003) 2 Lloyds Maritime and Commercial Law Quarterly 341, 343; Aitken, 'A Duty to Lend Reasonably' (n 121) 18.

178   Aitkin, 'A Duty to Lend Reasonably' (n 121) 18.

179   The perceived injustice in 'asset lending' is sourced in what is described in Khoshaba by Basten JA (at [128]) as the futility of the exercise:

... if the loan is not serviceable, then it is not in substance a loan but an asset sale, in which the lender risks nothing but the borrower risks the asset. Such a transaction involves no risk to the lender, but considerable risk to the borrower, given the likely inability of the borrower to perform and the probability if not certainty of resort to the security, with the lender being in a better position to protect itself against loss. The substantive unfairness lies in the imbalance of risk. Where that is voluntarily accepted, such a transaction may not be unjust. But where in the circumstances in which the transaction is made – particularly where the family home is involved – the borrower has a less than full appreciation of the risks or consequences, or is under some misapprehension or pressure, so as to provide an element of procedural unfairness, such a loan may be unjust. And even apparent comprehension of the transaction and its legal and practical effect and voluntariness is not entirely prophylactic: the purposes of the Contracts Review Act include protection of those who are not able to protect themselves, and while the Act is not a panacea for the greedy, it may come to the aid of the gullible. Permanent Trustee Company Limited v O'Donnell [2009] NSWSC 902 (unreported, Price J, 4 September 2009).

A contract which involves 'pure' asset lending is likely to be regarded as unconscionable conduct.[180] But instances where 'pure' asset lending has been established have been comparatively rare and, in such instances, the crucial issue has been the financier's complicity. If the financier has exercised the appropriate diligence – that is, internal procedures were complied with and the financier did not knowingly or recklessly advance the funds – the conduct is likely to be regarded as unjust, much less unconscionable.[181]

The responsible lending provisions impact on asset lending because the 'general position is that consumers should be able to meet the contract's obligations from income rather than equity in an asset'.[182] Therefore, it would appear that pure asset-based lending would be regarded as 'unsuitable' under the new legislation. Adhering to the responsible lending provisions in small-business transactions would not affect financiers that embrace appropriate procedures and is far preferable to a small businessperson having to establish unconscionable conduct before a court.

Other avenues where there has been irresponsible lending   Assistance for small businesspeople in financial difficulty may proceed, if applicable, via the CBP and access to IDR and EDR services.[183] Unfortunately, the statutory right to request variations in circumstances of hardship under the NCC is not available to small businesses. Consumer borrowers may request certain variations to their contract where they are reasonably unable, due to illness, unemployment or other

---

180   *Perpetual Trustees Australia Limited v Schmidt* [2010] VSC 67 at [207]: 'Acceptance of the concept of situational disadvantage extends the reach of the doctrine to cases involving asset lending where there is intentional moral obloquy , contrary to good conscience on the part of the financier or the procurer of the loan in relation to its dealings (including the processing of the loan application) with the borrower. It is not limited to knowledge of linguistic, educational or intellectual difficulties, but, I think, extends to a situation where the loan documentation alerts the financier or its representative to real issues (such as the patent discrepancies exposed in this case) concerning the borrower's ability to repay the loan, particularly where the security, in the form of the borrower's family home, is his or her only asset.' See also *Perpetual Trustee Company Ltd v Khoshaba* [2006] NSWCA 41; *Permanent Mortgages Pty Limited v Sibylle Ulrike MacFadyen* [2012] NSWSC 130.

181   *Kowalczuk v Accom Finance* (2008) 252 ALR 55; *Elkofairi v Perpetual Trustee Co Ltd* (2003) 11 BPR 20,841 at [57]–[59], [79] (Beazley JA (with whom Santow JA and MW Campbell AJA agreed)); *Khoshaba* [92] (Spigelman CJ (with whom Handley JA agreed on this point)), [128] (Basten JA); *Perpetual Trustee Company Ltd v Khoshaba* [2006] NSWCA 41 (unreported, Spigelman CJ, Handley and Basten JJA, 20 March 2006) but compare *Perpetual Trustee Company Ltd v Riz* (2008) NSW Conv R 56-198, [51].

182   Explanatory Memorandum, cl 105 See also ASIC *Regulatory Guide 209: Credit Licencing* (n 173).

183   Some credit providers have elected to become signatories to a voluntary industry code. These types of codes include requirements that signatories will assist consumers in financial hardship beyond meeting the statutory obligations required by the Code. While there is no statutory recourse to a court for review, the jurisdiction of EDR schemes can include monitoring compliance with industry codes.

reasonable cause, to meet their obligations where the value of their contract is under the monetary threshold. A court may also reopen a transaction if it considers that the contract, mortgage or guarantee was unjust at the time it was made.[184] In making this determination, the court has to consider a range of factors, including whether the lender knew or should have known that the borrower could not afford repayments or not without substantial hardship.

Guarantees

Casework experience documented in submissions to the 2010 Green Paper cite instances where vulnerable persons have been induced into providing their residential home as security for a friend's or relative's business loan.[185] Commonly, guarantees are entered into by relatives; a common instance might be an elderly parent guaranteeing the obligations of an adult child. Aside from the obvious risks associated with a transaction of this nature, other criticisms of guarantees include issues involving disclosure, unfair terms and continuing liability.

The NCC extends protection to guarantors as defined but does not extend this to small-business scenarios.[186] Part 3 Division 2 imposes obligations on the lender in relation to disclosure, rights of withdrawal and variation, and provides for limitations on the guarantor's liability. The NCC also provides that a guarantor may apply to have a contract reopened because it is unjust. In line with the responsible lending provisions, credit providers are obliged to make reasonable inquiries, including of third parties.

Guarantees of small-business debts by the small-business owners or their relatives or friends similarly do not receive protection under the NCCPA, NCC or the unfair contract terms provisions of the ASIC legislation.[187] The only recourse available to a guarantor in this situation is under the general law[188] or through an action for unconscionable conduct or misleading or deceptive conduct under the ASIC legislation – an expensive route fraught with risk. Part 28 of the Banking

---

184   *Perpetual Trustees Victoria Limited v Peter Van den Heuvel* [2009] NSWSC 57 (unreported, Price J, 20 February 2009); *RHG Mortgage Corporation Limited v Cran* [2009] QSC 183 (unreported, McMurdo J, 10 July 2009).

185   Australian Treasury, *National Credit Reform* (n 5).

186   S 7(1)(a), 8(1), nb 8(2), (3).

187   Janine Pascoe, 'Statutory Unconscionability and Guarantees' (2006) 18(2) Bond Law Review, Article 4. Available at <http://epublications.bond.edu.au/blr/vol18/iss2/4>.

188   Perhaps through an application of *National Australia Bank Ltd v Garcia* (1998) 194 CLR 395 where the High Court held that courts will intervene where a wife guarantees her husband's debt without fully understanding the guarantee agreement. It is mooted that this decision may extend to other relationships of trust and confidence – for example, *de facto* relationships and loans involving an adult child and elderly parent: Pascoe, 'Statutory Unconscionability and Guarantees' (n 188).

Code of Practice is applicable to guarantors, however, as noted; the consequences of a breach are minimal.

Residential investment properties
Interestingly, Australia has recently extended the responsible lending provisions to people purchasing investment properties.[189] Such purchasers could be individuals looking to invest for retirement purposes, or, could, in some cases, be a person's livelihood or 'business'. This development evinces recognition that some protection is required for people who may be vulnerable in business situations. This contrasts with the situation in the UK and Europe,[190] although it does seem consistent with the Australian track record of recognizing that certain people, operating in a business, may be at a disadvantage in a business context. However, in the context of consistency, a person may enter into a mortgage to purchase an investment property and use the rental to pay for the mortgage whereas another person may mortgage a residential property to finance a business. Rental markets fluctuate as do business conditions. It is inconsistent that one person has this protection whereas another does not. As for the complexity of the products packages, the purchasers of the investment property are likely to have a credit card, a personal loan and maybe more mortgages.

So where to now for Australia?

In sum, in 2012, Australian small-business borrowers are limited in their legal options in instances of inappropriate lending conduct by financiers.

Although the ASIC Act prohibitions are available, such claims can only be made in a court, and unconscionable conduct, in particular, is notoriously difficult to establish in a business context. Recourse through various IDR and EDR services is available in some circumstances, depending on the relevant thresholds. However, the main consumer protections – particularly an obligation to lend responsibly, variations for hardship and an opportunity to set aside an unjust contract, and the more streamlined procedures associated with these actions – are not available to small businesses. Similarly, there is little protection for people who guarantee small-business loans. Given these circumstances, it is suggested that that lenders providing credit to small business should be brought under the umbrella of certain aspects of the NCCP regime.

In relation to the three options being considered, it would seem that, given the inevitable backlash from the financial sector, the most likely outcome will be the adoption of Options 2 or 3. If Option 2 – the extension of basic protections and obligations under the NCCP Act and NCC to small-business lending – is to be adopted, it is suggested that this should, at least, extend to: licensing of

---

189 NCCP Act s 5.
190 Note the discussion by Brown, 'Protection of the Small Business as a Credit Consumer' (n 4) 78–80.

entities lending to small businesses and their representatives; responsible lending obligations; and procedures – for example, the service of default notices for relief and recourse from the NCC. These protections, where relevant, must be applicable to guarantors. EDR should be also made available as a matter of course to small businesses. If Option 3 is adopted, it would seem unlikely that the status quo would be altered. The Banking Code of Practice and other relevant codes have done little to allay small-business complaints and, indeed, the body established to oversee the codes has lamented the inability to make progress in addressing concerns. Formulation of a new code may be contemplated, but, again, progress towards even a review of the CBP has been convoluted.[191]

6 A consumer categorization?

This chapter has noted that, despite their business character, small businesses often demonstrate the same or similar vulnerabilities as consumers with respect to credit transactions. Also, although in some cases the financial arrangements associated with a business may be more complex than a 'straightforward' consumer arrangement, a significant number of business loans involve identical products and processes (secured property, credit cards, personal loans and guarantees) as consumer lending.[192] The chapter has also identified the paradox that sees access to small-business finance applauded and encouraged, although the same enthusiasm is not extended to safeguards during the course of the financial accommodation. Although there are varying degrees of protection in some jurisdictions, and some interesting developments afoot in Australia and abroad, for the most part small business is excluded from meaningful legislative protection involving credit. Indeed, the discussion of the Australian consumer credit framework evinces that, despite some attempts to extend protection to business borrowers, significant shortcomings in legislative protection and access to justice persist. Therefore, the chapter's remaining task is to assess the arguments for, and give due consideration to the arguments against, a consumer categorization for small business in credit arrangements.

---

191   A review of the Code of Banking Practice was undertaken by independent reviewer Jan McClelland, and her final report was published in September 2009. The Australian Bankers' Association (ABA) will provide quarterly updates on the implementation process to update the Code. Progress reports have been published in January and June 2010, and the process continues.

192   For example, the CPA Australia 2009 survey indicates that small businesses may not have a good understanding of financial services and could be as unsophisticated as individual consumers in their dealings with credit providers. Nearly 24 per cent of the small businesses surveyed did not have a good understanding of the interest rate on their borrowings and a further 15 per cent had a limited understanding: CPA Australia, *Small Business Survey – Asia Pacific Small Business Survey* (CPA Australia, Hong Kong 2009).

Arguments highlighting 'differences' in consumer and small-business lending

Throughout this chapter the diverse nature of small businesses has been emphasized. It follows, therefore, that credit arrangements for such businesses will take a variety of forms depending on, *inter alia*, the size of the business, the nature of the industry, trade or profession and the stage of the business's business cycle.

Financial institutions and their intermediaries assert that consumer credit protections should not be extended to small business because there is a fundamental difference in terms of purpose, complexity and risk between consumer and small-business lending.[193] The various arguments can be summarized as follows:

- Most consumer lending involves residential mortgages where risk is inherently low.
- Credit assessment is more complex due to the variables associated with small business. Consumer lending, in comparison, requires proof of income and savings, employment history and other debts – a simpler process that provides for speedier and less complex assessment.
- More products are involved in a single small-business account. A small business may have, for example, a business credit card, a loan secured on the home and possibly a personal loan or other form of credit arrangement.
- The nature of business lending requires, both during the application process and throughout the financial accommodation, closer scrutiny and oversight than consumer lending.[194]
- Businesses are advised by lawyers and accountants.

It is suggested that these arguments should not prevent an extension of consumer credit protections to small business. Although the variety of small-business financial arrangements is potentially enormous, it is acknowledged, even by financial institutions, that the majority of financial accommodation since the GFC involves secured lending, usually over real property. The most common 'packages' for small business involve these secured loans, credit cards and personal loans. Obviously there will be more complex financial arrangements in some circumstances, but this is the case even in relation to consumer lending. Many customers have several mortgages, credit cards and loans. As discussed, such mortgages many involve (multiple) investments in residential property in addition to their own home – a 'business' transaction that *does* attract protection under the NCCP Act and the NCC. Regular employment is a comfort for banks but, as can be observed in the current economic climate, such solace can be illusory.

---

193 MFAA, *MFAA Argues Further Regulation of Small Business Credit is Unnecessary* <http://www.mfaa.com.au/default.asp?artid=2464>.

194 Referred to as 'judgemental decision making': ANZ Banking Corporation, *Submission to Treasury – National Credit Reform Green Paper* (n 54).

There are countless successful small businesses whose cash flow, even in difficult financial times, provides the ability to fulfil financial commitments. Indeed, in an Australian context small-business borrowers have an excellent track record which has persisted even during the global financial crisis. 'Low doc' loans performed well in Australia with default rates being only marginally higher than standard loans.[195] In addition there was a greater equity position taken, and lender losses were minimized.[196]

Studies have regularly demonstrated that small businesses do not avail themselves of the services of lawyers and accountants to any great extent.[197] Many small businesspeople often cannot afford, or prefer not to take, advice. Other arguments raise concerns about such regulation: that it results in a lack of certainty and predictability; that it undermines the need for bad businesses to fail in order to ensure efficient use of capital;[198] and that it ensnares those people who are not in need, and do not want, protection.[199] Finally, it is often alleged that enhanced protection will result in reluctance by banks and financial institutions to lend to small business. Given that the recovery from the global financial crisis is, in most cases, slow and precarious, will a bad situation be made worse by enhanced regulation?[200]

Although such arguments are emotive, it is acknowledged that, in some cases, enhanced regulation will affect both the capacity of some people to borrow and the willingness of some institutions to lend. However, if the checks and balances are in place, risky borrowing would not, or should not, occur anyway. There can be no doubt that, in many cases, credit assessment in the case of small-

---

195   Around 0.50 per cent with most lenders. Finance Guide, 'No More Low Doc Loans?' (May 2012) <http://www.financeguide.com.au/index.php/2-uncategorised/15-no-more-loc-doc-loans> accessed 23 July 2012; but compare Rachel François, *The Dangers of Low Documentation Loans – The Litigation Perspective* (ANU Centre for Commercial Law & CARE Inc Public Forum 12 October 2007) <http://law.anu.edu.au/ccl/Rachel_Francois.pdf> accessed 23 July 2012.

196   Although Australian lending institutions did not lend money on the same basis as, for example, some US banks did prior to the global financial crisis. Also, it seems that Australian small-business borrowers tended to reduce borrowing after the crisis. In 2009, small businesses were more likely to access finance by selling business assets or by borrowing from family and friends: CPA Australia, *SME Access to Finance* (n 52).

197   CPA Australia, *Access to Finance: Recent Experiences of SMEs in Accessing Finance* (CPA Australia 2012) <http://www.cpaaustralia.com.au/cps/rde/xbcr/cpa-site/sme-access-to-finance.pdf> accessed 1 June 2012.

198   Hesselink, 'Towards a Sharp Distinction between B2B and B2C?' (n 4) 99; Brown, 'Protection of the Small Business as a Credit Consumer' (n 4) 73.

199   Ewoud Hondius, 'The Notion of Consumer: European Union versus Member States' (2006) 28 Sydney Law Review 90.

200   UK Department of Trade and Industry, 'Fair Clear and Competitive: The Consumer Credit Market in the 21st Century' (DTI 2003); Australian Treasury, *National Credit Reform* (n 5) 12.

business loans is complex. Yet, the scrutiny mandated by the responsible lending provisions for consumer lending is not inconsiderable. The banks make much of the rigorous processes they impose in relation to small-business lending – for example, consideration of financial information, business history, business plans and ongoing scrutiny. Yet, if these processes are already in place, seemingly to a greater extent than the responsible lending procedures impose, it seems strange that the banks are resisting responsible lending obligations in relation to small businesses. If they are already imposing responsible lending standards, it should be of no concern to them, and the regulation would only serve to ensure that *all* players in the banking and finance industry were bound by the same 'rules'.

Extension to small business: is this even possible?

Assuming that a consumer categorization for small business that extends credit protection legislation to small business is desirable, is it achievable? The next step is to examine briefly the potential ramifications and modification that may be necessary to achieve such an extension. The Australian provisions will be utilized.

Responsible lending
Given the recognized limitations of information disclosure, financial literacy and education as consumer protection mechanisms, responsible lending is an appropriate response to concerns regarding over-indebtedness.[201] Licensing would be advantageous for small-businesses borrowers because it would ensure that all lenders comply with the responsible lending provisions, thus reducing the opportunity for predatory business lending practices. It would also prevent most lenders from avoiding credit obligations. The extension would also necessitate compulsory membership of EDR schemes which, although available to some extent through the various codes of practice, do not 'cover the field'. As discussed above, it is essential, too, that those individuals providing guarantees are protected.[202]

These proposals cannot proceed, however, unless small-business lending is capable of being regulated through the key responsible lending provisions and, it is suggested, such an extension is conceivable. Under the relevant provisions,[203]

---

201   See Iain Ramsay, 'From Truth in Lending to Responsible Lending' in Geraint Howells, Andre Janssen and Reiner Schulze (eds), *Information Rights and Obligations: A Challenge for Party Autonomy and Transactional Fairness* (Ashgate 2005) 47, 57; and Geraint Howells, 'The Potential and Limits of Consumer Empowerment by Information' (2005) 32 Journal of Law and Society 349, 355–357.

202   National Legal Aid, *Submission to Green Paper on National Credit Reform* <http://www.legalaid.nsw.gov.au/__data/assets/pdf_file/0005/7592/NLA-Response-to-Green-Paper-on-National-Credit-Reform-Aug10.pdf>.

203   See generally NCCP Act Part 3.

an assessment must be made as well as a determination as to whether the proposed loan or refinancing is 'unsuitable'.[204] Therefore, reasonable inquiries must be made into the prospective borrower's financial situation, financial information should be verified and the requirements and objectives of the prospective borrower considered.[205] All have to be considered in the context of the period in which the loan or refinancing was determined, and an assessment of 'reasonable' will depend on all the circumstances surrounding the assessment.[206] A reading of submissions to the 2010 Green Paper[207] from various banks and the MFAA indicate that these standards are being met, or exceeded, already. Therefore, rather than the responsible lending provisions being regarded as an imposition on lenders, they may, on the other hand, be viewed as an endorsement of existing practices and as 'insurance' that all lenders maintain these standards. And, if these processes are already in place, there will be little cost or impost if legislation were to enshrine a situation that is already claimed to exist.

Finally, given that many small-business loans are secured by real estate, it is incongruous that protection extends to one business purpose, investment in residential property, and not to another business purpose, that of a small business.

The NCC
Small-business advocates recommend the extension of processes – for example, default notices and hardship provisions – consistent with the requirements of the NCC, to small business.[208] Default notices require, *inter alia*, a period of 30 days to remedy a default.[209] Financiers claim that this would place them in a precarious position because, if a business is failing, they need to move quickly to protect their security and there are serious ramifications for the financier if the business were to become insolvent.[210] Again, this can be disputed because, in many cases,

---

204   See ss 115–119 for credit assistance providers and ss 128–131 for licensees.

205   Ss 116–117, ss 129–130.

206   And in some circumstances the credit must be deemed unsuitable: for example, s 131.

207   MFAA, 'MFAA Argues Further Regulation of Small Business Credit is Unnecessary' <http://www.mfaa.com.au/default.asp?artid=2464> accessed 15 June 2012; ANZ Banking Corporation, *Submission to Treasury* (n 54).

208   See, for example, Financial Ombudsman Service, 'Dealing with Customers in Financial Difficulty: Small Business' (April 2010) <http://www.fos.org.au/centric/home_page/publications/the_circular/issue_2_april_2010/dealing_with_customers_in_financial_difficulty_small_business.jsp> accessed 4 June 2012; Council of Small Business of Australia, National *Credit Reform Green Paper Response: Credit for Small Business* (August 2010) <http://www.consumercredit.treasury.gov.au/consumercredit/submissions> accessed 4 June 2012.

209   National Credit Act s 88.

210   MFAA, 'MFAA Argues Further Regulation of Small Business Credit is Unnecessary' (n 208).

the financiers act very quickly, only giving a small business a few days or a week to rectify the situation. This is, in most cases, unnecessary and, if anything, a sensible approach with a view to trading out of the situation is preferable to a 'knee-jerk' reaction such as asking the small business to repay the loan in full, or to commence default proceedings.[211] Generally, a 30-day period equivalent to that accorded to individual consumers would be sufficient, especially when most security is over property anyway and, as such, time is needed to sell or refinance. In some instances there will be no other option for the lender, and an exception permitting a reduction in the 30-day period in particular circumstances could be incorporated into the legislation.

A related argument in relation to the hardship provisions is the purported conflict between obligations to assist during hardship and the need to protect the financier's security in the event of insolvency.[212] Again, this could be dealt with by minor modifications to the existing legislation, which would relieve obligations regarding hardship in instances of imminent insolvency.

The rationale for a consumer categorization
Protecting the vulnerable   The foundation of consumer regulation is the protection of vulnerable consumers from the excesses of the marketplace. It is, however, unrealistic to assert that the only people who experience vulnerability in a business context are 'traditional' consumers seeking goods or services for domestic purposes. Business relationships can also be profoundly imbalanced.[213]

The notion of 'consumer', and consequently the perception of a 'vulnerable consumer', is evolving.[214] In a European context 'the consumer', a vital component in ensuring Europe's internal market,[215] has evolved from a relatively ill-informed

---

211   Australian Treasury, *National Credit Reform* (n 5) 9.

212   Ibid.

213   See Howells and Weatherill, *Consumer Protection Law* (n 4) 31. BIS, *Consultation on Proposals for Implementing the Consumer Credit Directive: Government Response* (BIS December 2009) 366–371 <http://www.bis.gov.uk/files/file54098.pdf>; BERR, 'Implementation of the Unfair Commercial Practices Directive: Consultation on the Draft Consumer Protection from Unfair Trading Regulations 2007' (URN 08/554, February 2008) Annex D, Partial Regulatory Impact Assessment 2.

214   Hondius, 'The Notion of Consumer' (n 200). This has been seen as a problem for sole traders/small business in all types of transactions: Hesselink, 'Towards a Sharp Distinction between B2B and B2C?' (n 4) 102.

215   'In order to determine whether a statement or description designed to promote sales ... is liable to mislead the purchaser ... the national court must take into account the presumed expectations which it evokes in an average consumer who is reasonably well-informed and reasonably observant and circumspect': *Gut Springenheide GmbH, Rudolf Tusky v Oberkreisdirektor des Kreises Steinfurt–Amt für Lebensmittelüberwachung*, judgment of the Court of Justice (Fifth Chamber) of 16 July 1998, case C-210/96 [1998] ECR I-4657, § 31, cited by Cristina Poncibò and Rossella Incardona, 'The Average Consumer,

and needy character[216] to an 'average consumer'[217] who, in more recent times, has been endowed with enhanced characteristics.[218] Vulnerable consumers have tended to be regarded as those individuals displaying constitutional disadvantages such as mental or physical infirmity, age or credulity.[219] And, as the idea of 'a consumer' has evolved, so too it seems has the notion of a vulnerable consumer. As recently as May 2012, the European Parliament's *Report on a Strategy for Strengthening the Rights of Vulnerable Consumers* emphasized that consumers display vulnerabilities in certain *situations* rather than through more traditional constitutional defects.[220] This development confirms views

---

the Unfair Commercial Practices Directive, and the Cognitive Revolution' (2007) 30 Journal of Consumer Policy 21.

216   Hans Micklitz, 'The Expulsion of the Concept of Protection from the Consumer Law and the Return of Social Elements in the Civil Law: A Bittersweet Polemic (EUI Working Paper 2012/3), 1.

217   Described by Poncibò and Incardona, 'The Average Consumer, the Unfair Commercial Practices Directive, and the Cognitive Revolution' (n 216): a reasonably well-informed, or at least averagely informed, consumer. In other words, the consumer has a rough idea, but not necessarily a detailed knowledge, about the product or service in question.

218   For the purposes of the Unfair Commercial Practices Directive: 'a reasonably well-informed and reasonably observant and circumspect consumer, taking into account social, cultural, and linguistic factors, as interpreted by the Court of Justice (Recital 18)'. Article 2 of the Unfair Commercial Practices Directive defines the consumer and not the average consumer. Express reference to the average consumer is, however, made in Articles 5(2)b, 6(1), 7(1) and 8 of the Unfair Commercial Practices Directive.

219   Concibò and Incardona, 'The Average Consumer, the Unfair Commercial Practices Directive, and the Cognitive Revolution' (n 216) 29.

220   Committee on the Internal Market and Consumer Protection, Report on a Strategy for Strengthening the Rights of Vulnerable Consumers (European Parliament 2012) http://www.europarl.europa.eu/sides/getDoc.do?type=REPORT&reference=A7-2012-0155&language=EN-D:

> Notes that the diversity of vulnerable situations, both when consumers are placed under statutory protection and when they are in a specific situation of sectoral or temporary vulnerability, hinders a uniform approach and the adoption of a comprehensive legislative instrument, which has thus led the existing legislation and policies in place to address the problem of vulnerability on a case-by-case basis; stresses, therefore, that European legislation must address the problem of vulnerability among consumers as a horizontal task, taking into account consumers' various needs, abilities and circumstances.

This resembles the situation in Australia where disadvantages for the purposes of unconscionable conduct evolved from constitutional to situational characteristics.

such as those of Hondius[221] and Stuyck,[222] which pay heed to the diversity of potential disadvantages which may lead to vulnerability in particular commercial situations. As this recognition grows, and the notion of consumer becomes more sophisticated, there seems no reason why it would not be recognized that other groups, including small businesses, are in a position to deserve protection. Indeed, in an English context, Brown observes that:

> ... as it becomes perceived that the 'man on the street' is being adequately served by regulation, then thoughts turn to other contenders, one such example being small businesses.[223]

---

221   Hondius, 'The Notion of Consumer' (n 200) 246: 'The protection of the weak party has developed slowly over the last century, to include first employees, then tenants and hire-purchasers, and finally consumers and patients. This development has not come to an end. It is bound to continue, as new weak parties – such as asylum seekers and small businesses – emerge into the limelight, whereas the need to protect existing categories of weak parties may lose some of its importance.' Recall, too, Abril, '"Acoustic Segregation"' (n 32).

222   Jules Stuyck, Evelyne Terryn and Tom Van Dyck, 'Confidence through Fairness? The New Directive on Unfair Business-to-Consumer Commercial Practices in the Internal Market' (2006) 43 Common Market Law Review 107: 'it would have been – and still is – recommended to conduct sound empirical research, at EC level, about the correlation between the characteristics of certain groups of consumers and the likelihood of being specifically vulnerable for certain commercial practices.'

223   Brown, 'Protection of the Small Business as a Credit Consumer' (n 4), 70; see also Geraint Howells, Iain Ramsay and Thomas Wilhelmsson, 'Consumer Law in its International Dimension' in Geraint Howells, Iain Ramsay and Thomas Wilhelmsson with David Kraft (eds), *Handbook of Research on International Consumer Law* (Edward Elgar Publishing 2010) 3:

> To the extent that consumers need special rules, this raises the complex and sensitive issue of how the 'consumer' should be defined. Individuals purchasing for private purposes are normally unproblematically treated as consumers; but what about someone who purchases for a dual private and business purpose, a company director buying a car or a law professor purchasing a computer... Should businesses be able to benefit from consumer rules and if so, should it only be small – or medium-sized enterprises ... The answer should probably depend upon why one is protecting the consumer – lack of knowledge, lack of bargaining power – but legislators often agonise over these distinctions, which are not infrequently the subject of litigation in the courts.

See also Stephen Weatherill, 'The Evolution of European Consumer Law and Policy: From Well Informed Consumer to Confident Consumer?' in Hans Micklitz (ed.), *Rechtseinheit oder Rechtsvielfalt in Europa? Rolle und Funktion des Verbraucherrechts in der EG und den MOE-Staaten* (Nomos 1996) 423; Stephen Weatherill, 'The Rôle of the Informed Consumer in EC Law and Policy' (1994) 2 Consumer Law Journal, 49; Poncibò and Incardona, 'The Average Consumer, the Unfair Commercial Practices Directive, and the Cognitive Revolution' (n 216).

Research by Leff and Mallor[224] has noted how traditional notions of unconscionable conduct have already been extended, and there is no reason why it should not cover groups or classes who are vulnerable, including small business.[225]

In Australia, the vulnerability of small businesspeople, particularly in relation to leases, franchises and financial arrangements, was recognized in the seminal Reid Report.[226] After a period of evolution, the eventual introduction of section 51AC TPA created a prohibition of unconscionable conduct in relation to small business.[227] Although the provisions have had limited success to date, recent decisions suggest that the courts are taking heed of the commercial realities of these relationships and are making findings accordingly.[228] It is recognized that although persons may be skilled in their own trade or profession, this expertise will not extend to financial or business acumen. This is particularly the case in a credit context where, because of the circumstances of the relationship, there may be a disadvantage between the small businessperson and the financier.[229] If vulnerability can be recognized in the context of some conduct, such as unconscionable credit transactions, it is a small step to also recognize that the same person who may be vulnerable on account of his or her position vis-à-vis the person engaging in that conduct should also be protected by consumer credit legislation.

---

224   Refer generally to Mallor, 'Unconscionability in Contracts between Merchants' (n 1); and Arthur Leff, 'Unconscionability and the Code – The Emperor's New Clause' (1967) 115 University of Pennsylvania Law Review 485, 531–533.

225   Mallor, 'Unconscionability in Contracts between Merchants' (n 1) 1086; Manfred Ellinghaus, 'In Defence of Unconscionability' (1969) 78 Yale Law Journal 575; Melvin Eisenberg, 'The Bargain Principle and its Limits' (1982) 95 Harvard Law Review 241.

226   See n 109.

227   Initially, a monetary threshold of $1 million was set and this was later raised to $10 million. The equivalent ACL provision is now s 21, but the monetary threshold has been removed.

228   *Australian Competition and Consumer Commission v Dukemaster Pty Ltd* (2009) FCA 682.

229   CPA Australia, *SME Access to Finance* (n 52); Consumer Affairs Victoria Discussion Paper, *What Do We Mean by 'Vulnerable' and 'Disadvantaged' Consumers?* (CAV 2004) <http://www.consumer.vic.gov.au/CA256902000FE154/Lookup/CAV_Publications _Reports_and_Guidelines/$file/vulnerabledisadvantaged.pdf>. A vulnerable consumer is a person who is capable of readily or quickly suffering detriment in the process of consumption; see ACCC, *Don't Take Advantage of Disadvantage: A Compliance Guide for Businesses Dealing with Disadvantaged or Vulnerable Consumers* (ACCC 2011) <http:// www.accc.gov.au/content/item.phtml?itemId=704340&nodeId=a372b4f5e79c8e75c25a6e 22999bfe&fn=BS%20Don't%20take%20advantage%20.pdf>. See also UK Department of Trade and Industry, 'Fair Clear and Competitive' (n 201) 8.

Small businesses often cannot be separated from the individuals making up the business

The close relationship between the individual and the business means that such businesses may be more severely affected by everyday problems such as illness, marital discord and financial pressures. Indeed, it is difficult to separate small businesses from their owners in terms of mortgages and guarantees, and it has been noted that, in many respects, small businesspeople resemble overextended consumers.[230] In an Australian context, consumer and consumer credit laws have extended significant consumer protections to business from their inception. Although this was brought about by a constitutional imperative,[231] the end result the extension of several significant consumer protections to business transactions without an ensuing deterioration in business certainty and confidence.

The close relationship between the small business and the individuals that comprise it is exemplified by the mortgages on the family home to secure funding for the business. desirable Such mortgages are best treated as a separate case. The consequences of the loss of the home in the event of business failure provide a social and psychological imperative to additional measures of protection.[232] Brown has discussed this issue in an English context, although first mortgages in the UK seem to have more protection than in an Australian context.[233] It is suggested that the execution of a Business Purpose Declaration should not sever all protections for borrowers, especially in circumstances where the family home is involved.[234] Similar comments are applicable to those individuals granting guarantees secured by mortgages on their homes for the business purposes of relatives and friends.[235]

Finally, the education levels and business experience of small businesspeople resemble those of the population at large rather than corporate managers.[236] Also,

---

230 Garvin, 'Small Business and the False Dichotomies of Contract Law' (n 22) fn 50.

231 The necessity to base the legislation on Commonwealth heads of power, including the corporations and trade or commerce power.

232 Rosemary Hisclock, Ade Kearns, Sally MacIntyre and Anne Ellaway, 'Ontological Security and Psycho-social Benefits from Home: Qualitiative Evidence on Issues of Tenure' (2001) 18 Housing Theory and Society 50, 56.

233 Brown, 'Protection of the Small Business as a Credit Consumer' (n 4), 86.

234 In particular, refer to the submission by National Legal Aid <http://www. legalaid.nsw.gov.au/__data/assets/pdf_file/0005/7592/NLA-Response-to-Green-Paper-on-National-Credit-Reform-Aug10.pdf> accessed 23 July 2012 and that of Care Inc Financial Counselling Service and the Consumer Law Centre of the ACT <http://www.asic.gov. au/asic/pdflib.nsf/LookupByFileName/Care%20Inc%20and%20Consumer%20Law%20 Centre%20of%20the%20ACT%20non%20confidential%2020100816.pdf/$file/Care%20 Inc%20and%20Consumer%20Law%20Centre%20of%20the%20ACT%20non%20 confidential%2020100816.pdf> accessed 23 July 2010.

235 Ibid.

236 Garvin, 'Small Business and the False Dichotomies of Contract Law' (n 22) fns 70, 71.

because someone is a good businessperson in respect of his or her own trade or profession, this does not necessarily translate to being well versed in the nuances of business and the law.

Consistency

Simplicity, uniformity and consistency are desirable goals in any legislative framework and lead to maximum coverage and efficiency. Similarly, the reach of legislation should extend to all those it can assist unless there is some good reason to exclude certain groups. As discussed, however, in most jurisdictions there is a divide between business consumers and traditional consumers with only some of the protections available to the latter being available to the former.

In an Australian context, it seems strange that some provisions, such as unfair contract terms, will only provide protection for consumers once it has been recognized that there is clearly a need for small-business protection from unfair business conduct. There is no valid reason why, for example, the protection of the unfair contracts provisions and the unconscionability provisions should not apply consistently. Many contracts – for example, those for mobile telephones – are used by both business and by consumers. It defies common sense for a statute which promotes, *inter alia*, fair trading, to have the same contract subject to unfair contract terms provisions when a well-educated, experienced consumer purchases the telephone, but not when a less experienced, small businessperson does. In a credit context, the same contractual provisions are applicable in a mortgage whether for business purposes or for purely domestic purposes. Similarly, how is a natural person, who is the guarantor, different from any other natural person (consumer) who may enter into a credit arrangement?

An approach inclusive of small businesses as consumers would remove some arbitrary distinctions, again providing for more simplicity and efficiency. This could also extend to abolishing any distinctions between incorporated and unincorporated businesses.[237] As Griggs et al. note:

> To currently confuse and conflate only some business transactions as consumer in origin only devalues the protection that we are seeking to give a particular group of people or a particular set of transactions.[238]

Focus on conduct, not classifications

Some commentators have commented on the imperfect fit between contract doctrine and small-business status.[239] Two of the greatest challenges for small

---

237   Brown, 'Protection of the Small Business as a Credit Consumer' (n 4) 87.

238   Griggs et al, 'Challenging the Notion of a Consumer: Time for Change' (n 128).

239   David Audretsch, 'The Dynamic Role of Small Firms: Evidence from the US' (2002) 18 Small Business Economics 13; D Keith Robbins, Louis Pantuosco, Darrell Parker and Barbara Fuller, 'An Empirical Assessment of the Contribution of Small Business Employment to US State Economic Performance' (2000) 15 Small Business Economics 293.

businesses are the competitive nature of a free-market system dominated by large corporate entities and navigating the requirements of contractual formalism.

Those critical of merging business and consumer protections often rely on arguments focused on the formation of the contract and not on the course of the transaction itself. However, this position is being undermined.[240] In Australia, the ACL extends to conduct and permits a consideration of broader issues, beyond formation. This is especially the case with unconscionable conduct and the specific statement regarding the substantive nature of the contract. Contracts scholars are recognizing that examining the transaction rather than just its formation is appropriate.[241] Perhaps rather than focusing on the negatively affected party and making distinctions based on a 'divide',[242] conduct should be emphasized. If the conduct is inappropriate, it should not matter to whom it is directed.

Table 6.2   EDR jurisdiction schemes to consider small-business complaints

Service	Jurisdiction	Financial limits
Financial Ombudsman Service (FOS)	Disputes lodged before 1 January 2010	$280,000
	Disputes lodged after 1 January 2010	$500,000 with maximum compensation of $280,000.
Consumer Ombudsman Service Ltd (COSL)		Losses less than $500,000 with maximum compensation of $250,000.

Access to justice
It is essential that timely and inexpensive legal procedures are available to small businesses. For the most part, small businesses have only limited access to EDR procedures and if, for example, a person wants to pursue an action in misleading or deceptive or unconscionable conduct, the only recourse is to the court – an unlikely destination if a small business is in financial difficulty already. Although some access to EDR is available, as discussed above, the situation is again inconsistent and dependent on thresholds and the amount of compensation sought (see Table 6.2).

---

240   Poncibò and Incardona, 'The Average Consumer, the Unfair Commercial Practices Directive, and the Cognitive Revolution' (n 216); Larry DiMatteo and Blake Morant, 'Contract in Context and Contract as Context' 2010 45 Wake Forest L Rev 549; Miller, 'Contract Law, Party Sophistication and the New Formalism' (n 21).

241   Recently, Roger Brownsword has been taking a similar 'transactional' view in relation to his discussions of good faith: 'Regulating Transactions', paper delivered to the Consumer Law Conference (University of Manchester 2009).

242   See Garvin, 'Small Business and the False Dichotomies of Contract Law' (n 22); Abril, 'Acoustic Segregation"' (n 32).

7 Conclusion

This chapter has asserted that small-business borrowers should be categorized as consumers and that consumer credit protections be extended to them. Although it seems to be recognized that small-business borrowers are a curious hybrid of consumer and commercial components, to date arguments regarding commercial certainty, predictability and expediency remain persuasive. Even in jurisdictions where there has been some extension of consumer credit legislation to incorporate aspects of small-business lending, substantial limitations remain. It is suggested, however, that such an extension is desirable and achievable.

Such extension is consistent with the basis of consumer law and the protection of those persons vulnerable in a consumer or credit transaction. The nature of small business often makes it difficult to separate the individuals involved from the business itself. Although regarded as businesspeople, such individuals may be just as vulnerable as those who conform to the notion of a traditional consumer. In many jurisdictions the definition of 'consumer' is evolving, and it seems a logical step to incorporate small businesses within that classification. It is unlikely that this measure would undermine confidence and business certainty; in Australia, small businesses have enjoyed the protections of much consumer and credit law for some time. Such an extension would guarantee greater consistency and efficiency, and also ensure access to justice for more aggrieved parties.

So far as implementation is concerned, the processes, at least within the major lenders, are already in place. Consequently there would be not only little cost to these lenders if the consumer credit protections were extended to small business, but also little risk as their conduct would seem to meet the responsible lending conduct required. Obviously, some small-business situations might require some additional investigation and scrutiny but this would, of course, be taken into account when assessing the suitability and thus the ultimate reasonableness of the loan. On the other hand, those organizations which, to date, do not apply standards similar to those of the larger lenders would perhaps benefit from the necessity to do so. As noted, licensing is a way of ensuring that all players within the industry are registered and have to adhere to the same standards of regulation, thus lessening the likelihood of predatory lending in a small-business environment. Similarly, with perhaps a few modifications for problematic matters – for example, an imminent insolvency – there seems no reason why the protections in the NCC regarding default notices, hardship variations and provisions regarding unjust credit contracts should not be available for small-business loans.

Nehf has noted that even defenders of consumer protection laws acknowledge that while these laws may be 'a nuisance or impediment to the pursuit of short term profits', they should be tolerated because 'they are essential to sustaining economic growth and stability over the long term'.[243] Although an extension to

---

243   James Nehf, 'Consumer Credit Regulation and International Financial Markets: Lessons from the Mortgage Meltdown' <http://ssrn.com/abstract=1923883>.

small business may have the same or even greater 'nuisance' value, the benefits of a 'consumer characterization' exceed those of maintaining the existing inconsistent and unjustifiable status quo.

Chapter 7

Innovating for 'Safe Consumer Credit': Drawing on Product Safety Regulation to Protect Consumers of Credit

Luke Nottage[1]

1 Introduction

The global financial crisis in 2008 and the ensuing economic recession in most parts of the world have called into question many conventional understandings about financial markets. Policy-makers are no longer easily swayed by the assumptions that 'reputable firms do not place risky products on the markets, that innovation is stifled by regulation and that regulators are not as well placed as the market to judge the value of products'.[2] Pre-crisis *laissez-faire* approaches and 'light-handed' or 'principles-based' regulation are being reassessed, although neoliberalist views are proving remarkably resilient.[3] Financial markets re-regulation so far has been most evident at the 'wholesale' end of the market, namely in how financial institutions raise funds – by on-selling consumer loans through securitization, for example. But attention has also turned to the interrelated 'retail' end – how firms lend to consumers in the first place.[4]

---

1 I am grateful to Professor Souichirou Kozuka and the *Sydney Law Review* for allowing me to publish this chapter, under my own name, based on the second half of Luke Nottage and Souichirou Kozuka, 'Lessons from Product Safety Regulation for Reforming Consumer Credit Markets in Japan and Beyond' (2012) 34 Sydney Law Review 129. I also thank Alexandra Boxall, CAPLUS student intern (2012), for editorial assistance.
2 Iain Ramsay and Toni Williams, 'The Crash that Launched a Thousand Fixes: Regulation of Consumer Credit after the Lending Revolution and the Credit Crunch' in Kern Alexander and Niamh Moloney (eds), *Law Reform and Financial Markets* (Elgar 2011) 221, 222. See also generally Kevin Davis, 'Regulatory Reform Post the Global Financial Crisis: An Overview', Report prepared for the Melbourne APEC Finance Centre (March 2011) <http://www.apec.org.au/docs/11_CON_GFC/Regulatory%20Reform%20Post%20GFC-%20Overview%20Paper.pdf> accessed 24 May 2012.

3 John Quiggin, *Zombie Economics: How Dead Ideas Still Walk Among Us* (Princeton University Press 2010); Colin Crouch, *The Strange Non-Death of Neoliberalism* (Polity Press 2011).

4 See, for example, Daniel Lamb, 'A Specter is Haunting the Financial Industry – The Specter of the Global Financial Crisis: A Comment on the Imminent Expansion of Consumer

In the US, the Obama administration established, in 2010, the Consumer Financial Protection Bureau (CFPB), belatedly bringing together and strengthening disparate regulatory powers over consumer lending.[5] In July 2010 the UK government announced the creation of a new Consumer Protection and Markets Authority (CPMA) which was expected to take a tougher, more proactive and more focused approach to regulating conduct in financial services and markets than has the Financial Services Agency (FSA), whose functions it will take over as the FSA is now seen as having been too lax in regulating the mortgage loan market.[6] The Treasury (the UK's economics and finance ministry) also proposed to bring within the CPMA the powers of the Office of Fair Trading over other consumer credit (unsecured loans, credit card lending, and the provision of goods or services on credit), which is currently outside the FSA's jurisdiction. This market segment had already been reformed in 2010 partly to implement a revised EU Consumer Credit Directive (2008/48/EC).[7] Legislation introduced in 2011 renamed the CPMA as the Financial Conduct Authority (FCA).[8]

Even Australia, more sheltered from the global crisis thanks largely to a mining boom and close economic links with more buoyant Asian markets, has enacted a more harmonized national consumer credit regime centred on the National Consumer Credit Protection Act 2009 (Cth) (NCCP Act). The regime is also underpinned by the Australian Consumer Law[9] which regulates unfair terms in consumer contracts generally. Yet, a recent report shows how financial institutions are investing heavily in technology to profile their customers, offering

---

Financial Protection in the United States, the United Kingdom, and the European Union' (2011) 31 Journal of the National Association of Administrative Law Judges 213; OECD, *G20 High Level Principles for Consumer Financial Protection* (OECD October 2011) available at <http://www.oecd.org/document/2/0,3746,en_2649_37463_48455682_1_1_1_37463,00. html> accessed 27 April 2012.

5   Arthur Wilmarth, 'The Financial Services Industry's Misguided Quest to Undermine the Consumer Financial Protection Bureau' (2012) 31 Review of Banking and Financial Law <http://ssrn.com/abstract=1982149> accessed 24 April 2012.

6   HM Treasury, *A New Approach to Financial Regulation: Consultation on Reforming the Consumer Credit Regime* (2010) 7.

7   Iain Ramsay, 'Regulation of Consumer Credit' in Geraint Howells, Iain Ramsay and Thomas Wilhelmsson (eds), *Handbook of International Consumer Law and Policy* (Edward Elgar 2010).

8   Eilis Ferran, 'The Reorganisation of Financial Services Supervision in the UK: An Interim Progress Report' (2011) 49 University of Cambridge Faculty of Law Research Paper <http://ssrn.com/abstract=1952705> accessed 27 April 2012.

9   Australian Competition and Consumer Act (Cth) Sch 2, amended 2010. For a detailed analysis of these recent reform initiatives in general consumer law as well as consumer credit and other financial markets impacting on consumers, see Justin Malbon and Luke Nottage (eds), *Consumer Law and Policy in Australia and New Zealand* (Federation Press 2013).

them financial products often when they are at their most vulnerable.[10] The research, conducted by Deakin University and the Consumer Action Law Centre, with funding from the Australian Securities and Investments Commission (ASIC), links these new tactics to rising consumer debt. despite a temporary reprieve around 2007–2009.[11]

So far, in the UK and especially in the US,[12] re-regulation of consumer credit markets has tended to focus on filling in gaps in coverage of existing legislation and on merging regulatory functions. Fewer attempts have been made to introduce novel regulatory tools or to engage in fundamental re-evaluations of the empirical and theoretical grounds for credit regulation. Japan offers one interesting comparative reference-point, since, even before the global financial crisis, it comprehensively re-regulated unsecured consumer credit markets through the Moneylenders Law (Law No 115 of 2006). This renamed statute (replacing Law No. 32 of 1983) added new disclosure and 'responsible lending' requirements. The amendments also brought down a statutory interest cap, to between 15 and 20 per cent per annum (depending on the size of the loan). It is no longer possible to charge higher 'grey zone' interest under certain conditions, as had been provided in the 1983 legislation.[13]

Interest rate caps also remain common in other jurisdictions influenced by the 'civil law' tradition. However, they had been undermined in the US since the 1980s,[14] and price regulation for small consumer loans was only extended nation-wide in Australia from 2012.[15] The UK abolished interest rate caps as long ago as 1854, and the government decided not to reintroduce them in 2005, but the issue is now again under review.[16] Generally, interest rate controls have proven

---

10   Deborah Gough, 'Banking on Finding Your Weak Spots' *The Sun-Herald* (Sydney, 29 April 2012) 28 <http://m.smh.com.au/technology/technology-news/banking-on-finding-your-weak-spots-20120428-1xrfc.html> accessed 30 April 2012.

11   Paul Harrison and Charles Ti Gray, *'Profiling for Profit': A Report on Target Marketing and Profiling Practices in the Credit Industry* (Consumer Law Action Centre 2012) 15 <http://www.consumeraction.org.au/downloads/ProfilingforProfit-final-formatted.pdf> accessed 30 April 2012.

12   Wilmarth, 'The Financial Services Industry's Misguided Quest to Undermine the Consumer Financial Protection Bureau' (n 5).

13   Souichirou Kozuka and Luke Nottage, 'Re-regulating Unsecured Consumer Credit in Japan: Over-indebted Borrowers, the Supreme Court, and New Legislation' in Deborah Parry et al (eds), *Yearbook of Consumer Law 2009* (Ashgate 2008).

14   James White, 'The Usury Trompe l'oeil' (2000) 51 South Carolina Law Review 445.

15   See Denise McGill, Stephen Corones and Nicola Howell, 'Regulating the Cost of Small Loans: Overdue or Overkill?' (2012) 30 Company and Securities Law Journal 149; and Nicola Howell, 'Interest Rate Caps and Price Regulation in Consumer Credit' in Justin Malbon and Luke Nottage (eds), *Consumer Law and Policy in Australia and New Zealand* (Federation Press 2013).

16   Ramsay, 'Regulation of Consumer Credit' (n 7) 397–403.

controversial because they put in stark relief a basic problem in consumer lending markets.[17] How should policy-makers reconcile private interests (including making credit available to tide over cash-flow difficulties experienced temporarily by consumers) with public interests (a competitive and fair market)?

Japan's experience is also useful for testing explanations – from various economic, cultural and political theory perspectives – for the growth and the re-regulation of consumer credit markets.[18] Developments in Japan are often comparable to those in other industrialized countries. For example, suppliers of cash loans (popular in Japan) have developed a 'sweat box' business model similar to that found in the US for credit card lending.[19] This model aims to ensure that customers never really pay off the loan principal.

My previous work has therefore compared Japan with other jurisdictions to develop empirically informed but more normative perspectives on *why* we might need to re-regulate consumer credit more comprehensively in the present era.[20] That research began by querying the empirical basis and normative implications of Chicago School economics, which have been undermined more generally by the global financial crisis.[21] It argued that 'information economics' – and especially 'behavioural economics' – provide a stronger basis for policy-making innovation, in Japan and elsewhere. Particularly impressive is a study by Bar-Gill and Warren,[22] using theory and evidence informed by behavioural economics to press for the establishment of a new regulatory agency in the US.

However, my previous study also highlighted the empirical and normative challenges emerging from the 'cultural cognition of risk' studies of Dan Kahan and his co-researchers. His large-scale survey and other evidence from the US show that individuals adopt stances that express values defining their identities or world-views – that is, they assess risky activities by evaluating their social meanings, rather than weighing risks rationally (as assumed by neoclassical economics) or irrationally (as determined by behavioural theory that emphasizes specific biases or heuristics).[23]

---

17   Nicola Howell, Therese Wilson and James Davidson, 'Interest Rate Caps: Protection or Paternalism' (2008) Centre for Credit and Consumer Law Discussion Paper <http://www.griffith.edu.au/law/socio-legal-research-centre/industry-partners-collaborators/the-centre-for-credit-and-consumer-law> accessed 25 April 2012.

18   Souichirou Kozuka and Luke Nottage, 'The Myth of the Careful Consumer: Law, Culture, Economics and Politics in the Rise and Fall of Unsecured Lending in Japan' in Johanna Niemi-Kiesilainen, Iain Ramsay and William Whitford (eds), *Consumer Credit, Debt and Bankruptcy: Comparative and International Perspectives* (Hart 2009).

19   Ronald J. Mann, 'Bankruptcy Reform and the "Sweat Box" of Credit Card Debt' (2007) University of Illinois Law Review 375.

20   Nottage and Kozuka, 'Lessons from Product Safety Regulation' (n 1).

21   Quiggin, *Zombie Economics* (n 3).

22   Oren Bar-Gill and Elizabeth Warren, 'Making Credit Safer' (2008) 157 University of Pennsylvania Law Review 1.

23   Dan Kahan, 'Cultural Cognition as a Conception of the Cultural Theory of Risk' (2008) 222 Yale Law School, Public Law Working Paper <http://ssrn.com/

Furthermore, given evidence of significantly divergent world-views affecting risk assessments, he decries the 'cognitive illiberalism' implicit in the approach of behaviouralists.[24] Kahan also argues against a Rawlsian principle of 'public reason' that frames debates towards an 'overlapping consensus' – comprising values allegedly common to all (reasonably held) 'comprehensive views'.[25] Instead, Kahan considers that genuine and empirically grounded liberalism demands 'a new discourse norm, *expressive overdeterminism*, that seeks to contain cognitive illiberalism not by stripping it of partisan social meanings but by infusing it with so many that every cultural group can find affirmation of its worldviews within it'.[26] My previous work suggested that Kahan's approach may provide another contemporary rationale for *why* to regulate commercial risks and consumer credit market risks, as well as *how* to regulate in democratic societies.

This chapter further explores appropriate means of regulating credit, again adopting a multifaceted comparative approach. In particular, I take up the challenge of drawing closer analogies between regulating consumer credit *services* and regulating the safety of tangible consumer *products*. This notion has already helped to establish the CFPB recently in the US, inspired partly by the Consumer Product Safety Commission, which was created in 1972.[27] But section 2 of this chapter suggests that – as with consumer goods safety – our assessments of the probability and extent of harm from consumer lending (including the nature of its target customers) should impact on whether we rely more on markets, private-law redress through the court system, or direct regulation by public regulation. Overall, I argue that public regulation should often play a major role. Yet, section 3 identifies a major gap in the regulation of consumer credit services compared to consumer product safety regulation, even in developed legal systems like Japan and Australia. Just as the latter now require suppliers of goods to notify regulators of serious product-related accidents, I suggest that consumer credit suppliers should disclose abnormal problems arising with their borrowers. One possible trigger for notifying regulators, which might in turn make some of this information available to the public, are suicides by borrowers or personal insolvencies, known to lenders, which are occurring in unusually high numbers by industry standards.

---

abstract=1123807> accessed 30 April 2012.

24   See, for example, Richard H. Thaler and Cass R. Sunstein, *Nudge: Improving Decisions about Health, Wealth and Happiness* (rev edn, Penguin Books 2009).

25   See Dan Kahan, 'The Cognitively Illiberal State' (2007) 60 Stanford Law Review 115, 143, citing John Rawls, *Political Liberalism* (Columbia University Press 1993) and numerous works by Cass Sunstein.

26   Kahan, 'The Cognitively Illiberal State' (n 25) 145 (emphasis added).

27   Elizabeth Warren, 'Unsafe at Any Rate' (2007) 5 Democracy: A Journal of Ideas <http://www.democracyjournal.org/5/6528.php> accessed 1 May 2012. Warren went on to be elected as Senator for Massachusetts in the US election, held on 6 November 2012, as a Democratic Party candidate.

This type of information-disclosure obligation is arguably a prerequisite to a more effective 'regulatory enforcement pyramid'.[28] It is also one that should have broad appeal to policy-makers and citizens adopting diverse economic, political or psychological perspectives on consumer credit problems, including those partial to Kahan's risk cognition approach. Overall, this chapter's more holistic approach to financial markets regulation – open to insights from various product markets, international experiences and theories – offers more hope for avoiding future global economic crises.

2 Three incentive mechanisms for safe products – and safe credit?

The influential study by Bar-Gill and Warren[29] did urge a return to more 'reliance on ex ante regulation rather than ex post litigation' to address pervasive market failures, but it ended with an invitation 'to those more deeply schooled in administrative law and other disciplines to help fill the picture of how such a regulator can optimally be structured'. Earlier, Warren[30] had queried why consumer products (such as toasters) are regulated to ensure minimum levels of safety (so they should not burn down homes) whereas consumer credit services were not (even though they can also lead to people losing their homes). After broadly identifying informational and decision-making problems afflicting consumer borrowers, she went on to propose a 'Financial Product Safety Commission' similar to the US agency established in the 1970s to comprehensively monitor and maintain the safety of tangible consumer goods. Warren suggested that this new regulator:

> ... could develop nuanced regulatory responses; some terms might be banned altogether, while others might be permitted only with clearer disclosure. A Commission might promote uniform disclosures that make it easier to compare products from one issuer to another, and to discern conflicts of interest on the part of a mortgage broker or seller of a currently loosely regulated financial product.[31]

However, although her work did help push the US government into establishing the CFPB in 2010, Warren did not develop detailed analogies with the different forms of consumer product safety regulation. Nor did she set out specifically how those forms might compare or interact with other mechanisms for promoting product safety.

---

28   Ian Ayres and John Braithwaite, *Responsive Regulation: Transcending the Deregulation Debate* (OUP 1992).
29   Bar-Gill and Warren, 'Making Credit Safer' (n 22) 201.
30   Warren, 'Unsafe at Any Rate' (n 27).
31   Ibid.

The starting-point proposed in this chapter is to extend to *credit services* a matrix developed to correlate types of *product* risks with three major forces theoretically capable of providing greater incentives for consumer safety.[32] These mechanisms are markets, the judicial system (especially private law) and the political system (especially direct regulation by public authorities). Thus, despite often higher (direct and indirect) costs to society, public regulation tends to be invoked to address 'Type I' products – with a high probability of harm and grave consequences. Examples would include most pharmaceuticals (example 1 in Table 7.1) or products used every day in or around the home that might contain quite toxic chemicals, such as certain types of wood coatings (example 2a). Likewise, in consumer lending markets, public regulation may be more appropriate for payday or cash loan services generally. It also tends to be feasible for 'Type III' products where adverse consequences are less severe. but risks of them materializing are high, such as cigarette lighters generally (example 3b). This is partly because repeated incidents typically generate media coverage or at least more scope for political attention. Certain types of 'low-doc' mortgages in the US, without all or many of the features associated with high levels of defaults (such as teaser interest rates), would be a good analogy from the field of consumer lending services.

Table 7.1   Risk types versus safety incentive mechanisms

Risks Probability/Severity of Harm		← Severity of Harm →		
			Judicial system (private law) Type 1	
↑ Probability ↓	*Markets* Types I and also III	**Type III** High/Low (e.g. 3b)	**Type I** High/High (e.g. 1, 2a)	*Political system (public regulation)* Type I
		Type IV Low/Low	**Type II** Low/High (e.g. 2b, 3a)	

Market forces can also play a role in encouraging suppliers to make both Type I and Type III products or services safer, as reputation can otherwise suffer. But this will often not be enough – for example, if all or most of the industry becomes entrenched in the ways it effects those supplies. Indeed, such entrenchment can

---

32   Luke Nottage, 'Product Safety' in Geraint Howells, Iain Ramsay and Thomas Wilhelmsson (eds), *Handbook of International Consumer Law and Policy* (Edward Elgar 2010) 260.

readily occur when it is less costly to follow competitors' strategies than to devise a more reputable product, as often tends to be the case in consumer credit markets.[33]

Even more problematic are Type II risks, where the probability of harm is low – thus limiting the scope for reputational effects on firms or impact on the political system – even if the consequences are drastic for particular victims. Cigarette lighters that fall into the hands of children are one example (3a). Another might be low-doc mortgages (even without teaser rates) targeted at particularly vulnerable groups such as the elderly poor. Another Type II product risk could be treated-wood building products professionally installed even in private homes (2b), with limited chances of owners coming into regular direct contact with them – albeit possibly still with devastating subsequent effects, such as cancers. An analogy in consumer lending would be 'payday' or cash loans to well-educated, higher-income earners, where default risks are generally significantly lower but do occasionally materialize with disastrous consequences. For all these Type II risks, however, private-law remedies can often be sufficient to motivate suppliers to take greater precautions. This is because potentially large damages claims can be more credibly asserted by consumers, despite barriers in access to justice through the court system.

Thus, public and private law, as well as market mechanisms, may each be more or less appropriate to incentivize suppliers towards optimal levels of consumer safety, depending on the likelihood of risks eventuating and their consequences. Also relevant in this schematic are the innate characteristics of likely consumers and the situations in which the goods or services are likely to be consumed. Policy-makers should attempt these sorts of risk assessments across various types of consumer credit, following the lead of those interested in the safety of tangible goods, although they may well find that some factors affecting riskiness are more specific to the services field.

Admittedly, the schematic itself is still quite stylized. For example, *public regulation* can comprise administrative law and sanctions, but also criminal law. The latter can provide specific criminal sanctions as part of a targeted regime, incorporated, for instance, within consumer law providing particular product safety requirements, or criminal law can have a more general impact through broader prohibitions found generally in a criminal code. An example from Japan is the offence of 'professional negligence causing death'.[34] This remains a comparatively important incentive mechanism encouraging professionals to take due care in supplying general consumer goods[35] as well as medical services.[36]

---

33   Bar-Gill and Warren, 'Making Credit Safer' (n 22) 18–20.

34   Criminal Code (Law 45 of 1907) art 211.

35   Luke Nottage, *Product Safety and Liability Law in Japan: From Minamata to Mad Cows* (Routledge Curzon 2004) 23–69.

36   Robert B Leflar and Futoshi Iwata, 'Medical Error as Reportable Event, as Tort, as Crime: A Transpacific Comparison' (2006) 12 Widener Law Review 195.

Administrative regulation and criminal sanctions may also be combined, as has occurred in Japan to constrain the most outrageously exploitative lenders.

Within the *private-law* sphere, a traditionally important mechanism has been contract law – imposing duties on sellers to supply 'merchantable' and therefore safe goods. Since the 1970s product liability law (typically characterized as tort law) has emerged to allow strict liability claims for 'defective' or unsafe goods against manufacturers (and usually also importers), even if the harmed user lacks a contractual relationship. This development has generally been welcomed, particularly as a means of addressing Type II risks.

One rough analogy in consumer lending would be Australia's post-global crisis imposition of 'suitability' requirements not only on suppliers, but also on intermediaries such as mortgage brokers, under the new NCCP Act:

> Suitability began in contract ['fitness for purpose' in sales of goods, under 19th century Anglo-Commonwealth common law and codifications]. From an implied contractual term dependent on the acquirer making known the purpose [to the direct seller, before the supply], there is now an affirmative conduct obligation. This obligation arises once the potential borrower may enter a contract. The obligation rests on the credit assistant (broker) and on the credit provider. The person who provides credit assistance (which includes advice) or credit has an obligation to do two things. The first is to discover the objectives and requirements – that is, the purpose – of the prospective acquirer. The second is to suggest or provide only suitable credit. This positive obligation is expressed in the negative. That is, the provider must assess whether the credit is unsuitable. It will be both a civil and criminal offence to provide or suggest an unsuitable credit contract.[37]

Admittedly, my analogy is incomplete not just because of the different definitions of 'manufacturer' (including 'importer' and certain other intermediaries) under product liability legislation (as under Part 3–5 of the Australian Consumer Law) compared to the NCCP Act's definitions of credit provider or assistant. More importantly, product liability assumes no or limited opportunity for direct contact between them and consumers. Accordingly, the requirement to provide goods that are not defective or unsafe derives from the general 'merchantability' requirement implied in contract law (that is, that goods be suitable for common or usual purposes – including safe use), rather than the implied term of fitness for a specific purpose disclosed before the supply. Nonetheless, the NCCP Act does extend a new 'suitability rule' in a consumer services contract setting that can be likened to an attempt to require provision only of 'safe' credit, by mobilizing the private-law system as well as public-law effects. If the borrower ends up with an unsuitable credit contract, the borrower can apply to the courts for an injunction,

---

37 Gail Pearson, 'Reading Suitability Against Fitness for Purpose – The Evolution of a Rule' (2010) 32 Sydney Law Review 311, 331.

seek compensation or a declaration that the contract is void, or seek a contractual variation.[38]

By contrast, the obligation under different Australian statutes to provide other financial services, general services and consumer goods that are 'fit for purpose' still usually only has private-law consequences.[39] However, since the 1970s Australia's general consumer product legislation does assist injured individuals to bring private-law claims if harmed by goods supplied in breach of safety standards or other measures ordered by regulators.[40] There have also been a few cases recently where plaintiffs have brought private law (tort) claims against providers of unsafe goods based on violations of duties imposed by other legislation. It then becomes a matter of statutory intention as to whether or not that other legislation was intended to trigger only public-law consequences.[41]

A clearer dichotomy seems to exist in Japan's legislation re-regulating unsecured consumer loans. Credit suppliers must conduct credit checks (using information from a credit bureau), assess ability to repay, not unduly solicit loans, and not lend if this would bring total indebtedness to more than one-third of gross income.[42] All these are expressed, at least, as merely public-law obligations. In other words, violations attract administrative and criminal sanctions but not necessarily any private-law consequences. Nevertheless, it remains to be seen whether Japanese courts will infer such consequences as well.[43] Although this question also depends on the implied intentions of the legislators, courts in Japan have been very reluctant to allow private-law actions for breaches of consumer protection regulations – particularly compared to German law, which has otherwise generally had a strong influence on both administrative and civil law in Japan.[44] In one respect, however, the situation is

---

38   NCCP Act ss 177–179.

39   See, respectively, ASIC Act 2001 (Cth) s 12ED(2); Australian Consumer Law s 61. This older-style statutory obligation also depends on the specific purpose being disclosed in advance by the acquirer, and the latter's reasonable reliance on the supplier then providing a fit (that is, suitable) good or service.

40   See Australian Consumer Law ss 106(7), 119(3) and 127(3): the harm is presumed to have been caused by the goods supplied in violation of the measure. This reverses the burden of proof in product liability claims under Part 3–5 of the Law, which put the onus on the injured consumer to prove that the goods were defective or unsafe.

41   Jocelyn Kellam and Luke Nottage, 'Happy 15th Birthday, TPA Part VA! Australia's Product Liability Morass' (2007) 15 Competition and Consumer Law Journal 26.

42   Moneylenders Law arts 13 and 13-2. A similar regime is also now applied to credit card issuers and sales credit providers, with certain modifications regarding the maximum permitted amount of credit: Instalment Sales Law (No 59 of 1961), arts 30-2, 30-2-2, 35-3-3, 35-3-4.

43   Andrew Pardieck, 'Japan and the Moneylenders: Activist Courts and Substantive Justice' (2009) 17 Pacific Rim Law & Policy Journal 529.

44   Marc Dernauer, *Verbraucherschutz in Japan* (*Consumer Protection in Japan*) (JCB Mohr 2008).

very clear under the Japanese statutory regime. If a loan contract exceeds the interest-rate cap of 20 per cent per annum, it now always generates criminal-law sanctions for the lender.[45] However, the payment obligation is also void in respect of the excessive interest component (15, 18 or 20 per cent, depending on the amount of the principal), so the borrower has no private-law obligation to pay that component. Thus, the Japanese legislator has also partially mobilized *both* public and private law to incentivize lenders not to supply 'unsafe' credit at particularly high interest rates.

Consequently, the risk-based approach to different forms of intervention (outlined above and in Table 7.1) can be refined and developed in these ways to assess the possibilities and challenges in combining different mechanisms to incentivize suppliers of both consumer credit and consumer goods to take safety measures. In so doing, policy-makers should be conscious of likely divergent risk cognition patterns among different groups within any given society, let alone among different countries.[46] As a further complication, an assessment of the various main mechanisms providing incentives to supply safe goods and services must examine more closely the relative costs and benefits of each mechanism and sub-mechanism, and of their various possible combinations.[47]

It may seem superficially attractive, for example, for governments to expand private-law remedies while reducing direct regulation by public authorities. That was already part of the rationale for enacting Japan's Product Liability Law in 1994. It was envisaged that expanded scope for private-law relief would offset any diminution of *ex ante* regulation. The World Trade Organization Agreements had been signed in 1994, significantly liberalizing trade in goods and expanding the potential for states to claim against others if product safety regulations constituted disguised trade barriers.[48] More broadly, since 2001 the Japanese government has promoted a suite of ambitious justice system reforms, substituting *ex ante* public regulation in favour of more indirect socio-economic ordering achieved through the threat of *ex post* relief pursued by individual claimants. Making such claims credible has meant reforms not only to substantive law, but also to procedural law and many other legal institutions,

---

45   Law on Investments, Deposit Taking and Other Financial Transactions (Shusshi-ho, Law No 195 of 1954), art 5(2).

46   Cf, for example, Dan Kahan et al, 'Geoengineering and the Science Communication Environment: A Cross-Cultural Experiment' (2012) 92 The Cultural Cognition Project Working Paper <http://ssrn.com/abstract=1981907>.

47   See generally Hiroshi Sarumida, 'Comparative Institutional Analysis of Product Safety Systems in the United States and Japan: Alternative Approaches to Create Incentives for Product Safety' (1996) 29 Cornell International Law Journal 79, drawing on Neil Komesar, *Imperfect Alternatives: Choosing Institutions in Law, Economics and Public Policy* (University of Chicago Press 1994).

48   Nottage, 'Product Safety' (n 35) 286–290.

including liberalization of the legal profession and a related system of new postgraduate 'law school' education.[49]

Concern is growing about the overall costs of operating this new system of justice, especially since the global financial crisis. A rather different public–private balance does seem to have emerged,[50] but there now seems little chance of much further diminution in the role of the state in the foreseeable future. In fact, Japan has already re-regulated consumer product safety following a series of major safety failures since 2000[51] and has also introduced stiffer public regulation of consumer credit and other consumer law,[52] rather than further reforms primarily aimed at bolstering private-law remedies and the judicial system. Against that background and, more recently, with the lessons learned from the financial crisis, calls to rely more on market mechanisms to secure safe goods and safe credit are also unlikely to seem very plausible, although corporate codes of conduct and other forms of corporate social responsibility have proliferated in Japan.[53]

3 Public regulation for the safety of consumer goods – and credit?

It is admittedly difficult to add a detailed assessment of relative short- and long-term costs involved in the various major mechanisms that can generate incentives to supply safe goods or services. However, the problem can partially be sidestepped when it comes to considering legislative enactments. This is because statutes themselves typically cost little to create, compared with their implementation – either through regulatory enforcement activity or claims pursued through the courts. It is therefore relatively easy for governments to add regulatory powers in the field of 'post-sale' consumer product safety, for example, because the government is not generally bound actually to enforce them. This rather cynical perspective perhaps helps to explain how quite similar regimes have emerged in Australia, Japan and other major economies (see Table 7.2).[54]

---

49   Daniel Foote, 'Introduction and Overview: Japanese Law at at Turning Point' in Daniel Foote (ed), *Law in Japan: A Turning Point* (University of Washington Press 2007).

50   Luke Nottage, Leon Wolff and Kent Anderson (eds), *Corporate Governance in the 21st Century: Japan's Gradual Transformation* (Edward Elgar 2008).

51   Luke Nottage, 'The ABCs of Product Safety Re-regulation in Japan: Asbestos, Buildings, Consumer Electrical Goods, and Schindler's Lifts' (2006) 15 Griffith Law Review 242.

52   Masami Okino, 'Recent Developments in Consumer Protection in Japan' (2012) 4 UT Soft Law Review 10.

53   Adam J Sulkowski, S P Parashar and Lu Wei, 'Corporate Responsibility Reporting in China, India, Japan, and the West: One Mantra Does Not Fit All' (2008) 42 New England Law Review 787.

54   Nottage, 'Product Safety' (n 35) 269.

Table 7.2   Comparing the introduction of consumer product safety regulations

Feature	US	UK	EU	Japan	Australia
Standards	1972 and 1981	1961	1992	1973	1977
Bans	1972	1978	1992	1973	1977
Warnings	1972	1978	1992	–	1986
General Safety Provision (GSP)	–	(1994)	1992		
Recalls	1972	(2006)	1992 and 2001	1973	1986
Information disclosure	1972 and 1990	(2006)	2001	2006	2010

Thus, all these jurisdictions now have provisions allowing regulators to:

1. set certain mandatory safety standards (requiring goods to meet certain thresholds for physical components or performance, or to provide certain warnings or information to consumers so they can themselves minimize adverse effects from otherwise risky products);
2. ban goods if causing or likely to cause serious harm; and
3. order recalls of such goods.

However, these powers cost much more to invoke than to enact, and so far have been quite infrequently applied by regulators in all these jurisdictions.

A more noticeable divergence relates to information disclosure duties imposed on suppliers, requiring them to inform regulators after becoming aware that goods have caused product-related accidents. The US was quick to impose such an obligation, in its Consumer Product Safety Act 1972 (revised in 1990). Yet it has had reduced practical significance given that nation's unique reliance on (private-law) product liability suits as a mechanism to address and publicize possible safety risks.[55] The EU included a disclosure requirement in its revised General Product Safety Directive (2001/83/EC). It was to be incorporated into the law of each member state by 2004, although the UK only implemented the reform in 2006 (as indicated by parentheses in Table 7.2). That was also the year in which Japan's Consumer Product Safety Law (No. 31 of 1973) added a disclosure obligation on suppliers, albeit more limited in scope. It is triggered by: (a) actual accidents known in fact to suppliers, but not also (as in the EU) all serious risks of accidents reasonably known to suppliers; or (b) certain hazards specified by regulations

---

55   Matthias Reimann, 'Liability for Defective Products at the Beginning of the Twenty-first Century: Emergence of a Worldwide Standard?' (2003) 51 American Journal of Comparative Law 751.

(currently, fires and carbon monoxide emissions), even if, fortunately, no harm ensues. It took Australia until 2010 to enact a disclosure obligation.[56] Furthermore, this is even narrower in scope: limited to known accidents (not mere risks) causing serious injury or illness (excluding slow-onset illnesses).[57]

One explanation for these cross-jurisdictional differences in scope, and delays in introducing them, could lie in the political power of industry compared with that of consumer groups. But another factor is that any such obligations to disclose accident data to the regulators are much more likely to require extra government capacity to deal with the influx of information. In turn, this implies an immediate and readily identifiable extra budget allocation – something that may not have been politically palatable, especially in pre-global crisis deregulatory environments.

Similar considerations could apply even to the General Safety Provision (GSP) introduced in the EU from the 1990s, but not yet in Australia, Japan or the US.[58] A general requirement like this, namely not to supply unsafe goods, would seem more ominous to industry groups compared with duties to comply with some narrowly defined minimal safety standards, but would also tend to create pressure for significantly more resources for regulators to monitor and sanction breaches of the new broad GSP. While some political scientists expect regulators always to welcome and press for more budget and power, even that (controversial) theory would need to acknowledge that other groups (even within government) can often effectively resist 'costly' innovations.[59] This is particularly likely where, as in Australia from the mid-1990s,[60] new regulations are essentially only to be introduced upon proof that the benefits outweigh the costs.

Yet, such practical considerations have not prevented a raft of consumer law reforms in Australia since 2009, outside the product safety field. For example, the Australian Consumer Law adds new regulatory powers such as 'substantiation notices',[61] 'infringement notices'[62] and the possibility of banning businesspeople from directorships.[63] The Productivity Commission's Report[64] that prompted these

---

56   Australian Consumer Law, ss 131–132.

57   Luke Nottage, 'Suppliers' Duties to Report Product-related Accidents under the New Australian Consumer Law: A Comparative Critique' (2011) 25 Commercial Law Quarterly 3.

58   David Harland and Luke Nottage, 'Conclusions' in Jocelyn Kellam (ed), *Product Liability in the Asia-Pacific* (3rd edn, Federation Press 2009) 577–578.

59   Pre-crisis financial markets (de)regulation in the US and the UK are good examples. See Wilmarth, 'The Financial Services Industry's Misguided Quest' (n 5) 46–54; and Ramsay and Williams, 'The Crash that Launched a Thousand Fixes' (n 2).

60   Bronwen Morgan, *Social Citizenship in the Shadow of Competition: The Bureaucratic Politics of Regulatory Justification* (Ashgate 2003).

61   Australian Consumer Law s 219.

62   Ibid s 134A.

63   Ibid s 248.

64   Productivity Commission, *Review of Australia's Consumer Policy Framework* (Productivity Commission Inquiry Report No 45, 2008).

reforms drew partly on the 'regulatory enforcement pyramid' model proposed two decades ago by Ayres and Braithwaite. Derived from game theory, as well as Braithwaite's own experience in Australia's consumer movement, that model emphasizes the need for regulators to respond to a non-compliant firm with a minimum level of sanctions, so that they can escalate to higher sanctions if the firm remains recalcitrant. Restoring and maintaining cooperative relations in this way implies that the regulator should have a panoply of graduated sanctions at its disposal.

This theory also appears to have been influential in corporate and securities law reform. It is also consistent with Australia's credit-law reforms in 2009, which provide for both civil and criminal penalty options for regulators responding to lenders who provide unsuitable credit. The theory is probably attractive to contemporary legislators because it holds out the promise of achieving more effective compliance without regulators actually having to invoke severe (and more costly) sanctions. However, recent empirical research into Australia's recent corporate law reforms suggests that regulators do need to maintain considerable enforcement activity in order to make the model operate credibly and effectively.[65] Moreover, the regulatory enforcement pyramid model also requires good information flows between firms and regulators, so that the latter know when to threaten and even to apply the more stringent sanctions.

Thus, from this perspective, Australia's new obligations on suppliers of goods to disclose product-related accident data are to be welcomed, especially if these requirements are properly enforced and regulators are prepared occasionally to escalate sanctions (for example, by ordering bans or recalls). Yet the same perspective also uncovers a major gap in consumer credit regulation in Australia, Japan and elsewhere. Despite many reforms, nowhere do we find any specific obligation on lenders to disclose information *to regulators* about 'accidents' or risks later befalling their borrowers. Instead, credit regulation remains fixated – arguably, overfixated[66] – on information disclosure direct *to borrowers*, before or when the loan contract is concluded. Yet, if credit suppliers had to disclose information about problematic patterns emerging from their loan portfolios, as product suppliers now generally must do regarding general consumer goods, then regulators could operate a more effective enforcement pyramid and achieve better cooperative relations with regulated firms.

It may appear more difficult to implement this additional disclosure requirement in the case of consumer credit. The problem derives primarily from an unusual feature of credit services compared with tangible goods: the borrower is not only a customer purchasing the service, but also a potential source of costs to the lender as the provider of the service. Thus, on the one hand, the lender will

---

65 See, for example, Michelle Welsh, 'Continuous Disclosure: Testing the Correspondence Between State Enforcement and Compliance' (2009) 23 Australian Journal of Corporate Law 206.

66 Ferran, 'The Reorganisation of Financial Services Supervision in the UK' (n 8) 15.

typically experience any disclosure of its default rates as equivalent to uncovering its cost structure. On the other hand, the borrower will be concerned about his or her privacy if obliged to deliver detailed information about his or her financial performance and other indicators of potential stress, even if this information may be aggregated and reviewed by the lender as part of a reporting obligation vis-à-vis the regulator.[67]

However, the problem should not be insurmountable if the reporting requirement is appropriately limited. Particularly in Japan, for example, a new duty requiring disclosures from lenders to regulators could be triggered by especially high levels of suicides among a firm's borrowers.[68] More generally, disclosure could be required if borrowers experience higher levels of insolvencies than usual in the industry sub-sector or even for that particular lender. Disclosure duties could be made more manageable for credit suppliers by limiting them to quite specific adverse outcomes along these lines, rather than broader 'serious risks' of such outcomes. Thus, in this respect and at least initially, the regime would be closer to the narrower one operating in Japan, or especially Australia, for disclosure of consumer *product*-related data, rather than the regime in the EU.[69]

Admittedly, borrowers may become insolvent or commit suicide for many reasons which might not necessarily be directly related to the features of their loans. However, we can allow for this by limiting the new disclosure obligations to situations where rates are unusually high by historical standards. Similar difficulties can also arise concerning adverse health outcomes that may be associated with unsafe goods, but one compromise is to not require disclosure if the accident is 'clearly' not related to the product.[70] A similar solution could be extended regarding a new duty on suppliers of consumer credit services.

Another practical issue concerns how suppliers would know about serious problems such as suicides or insolvencies as potential triggers for disclosure to regulators. Yet the situation should be simpler for lenders as they are in long-term contractual relationships with borrowers and therefore can know (or readily infer) that something is amiss when they end up having to deal with the borrower's trustee in bankruptcy or the executor of the deceased's estate. By contrast, direct suppliers of consumer goods under one-off sales – let alone the original manufacturers – are much less likely to know that accidents have occurred. However, despite this,

---

67   I am grateful to Professor Souichirou Kozuka for highlighting these points, for our longer jointly-authored article: Nottage and Kozuka, 'Lessons from Product Safety Regulation' (n 1).

68   Mass suicides were also allegedly linked to over-indebted borrowers recently in Andhra Pradesh, prompting many recommendations for reform (including caps on interest): Reserve Bank of India, *Report of the Sub-Committee of the Central Board of Directors of Reserve Bank of India to Study Issues and Concerns in the MFI Sector* (January 2011).

69   Nottage, 'Suppliers' Duties to Report Product-related Accidents under the New Australian Consumer Law' (n 57).

70   As under Japan's Consumer Product Safety Law: ibid.

many jurisdictions now impose disclosure duties on them, either when suppliers become actually aware of accidents (as in Australia and, generally, in Japan), or when they ought to become aware of them (as in the EU).[71] The former approach may provide an incentive for 'wilful blindness'. The latter encourages suppliers actively to seek out and monitor information, but at additional cost and perhaps for little gain in the context of a new duty on credit suppliers. Consequently, it may be better for policy-makers – at least initially – to limit the disclosure obligation to situations where lenders are actually aware of unusually high levels of suicides, insolvencies or other similarly extreme circumstances. However, regulators should bear in mind lenders' growing investments in technologies aimed at analysing borrower behaviour not just in the US,[72] but also recently in Australia.[73]

Overall, new disclosure obligations should help set off warning bells for credit regulators. This should prompt them to scrutinize a firm's (or even an industry's) lending practices and terms more closely, and to enforce more effectively. For example, in Australia civil or even criminal penalties are incurred if lenders turn out to have been providing unsuitable levels or types of credit.

In addition, regulators could make much, or perhaps all, of this disclosed information available to the general public – albeit adding a summary analysis to minimize 'information overload', particularly among non-experts. This would have several benefits. First, consequent extra public scrutiny would encourage regulators to take reports received from lenders more seriously and to undertake follow-up enforcement activities, which recent empirical research (in the corporate-law context) suggests is also necessary to keep the overall regulatory enforcement pyramid working effectively. Second, the regulators' public disclosure of 'accident' reports received from lenders would help put other borrowers 'on notice' about evolving potential risks. Much is now being written, particularly from a behavioural law and economics perspective, about the ineffectiveness of pre-contract disclosure directly from lenders (or intermediaries, like brokers) to borrowers.[74] Part of the problem is that the information or warnings provided tend to be broadly worded. By contrast, allowing borrowers (or consumer groups) to access information about more specific problems, provided initially by lenders to regulators, should help make the risks involved more salient for potential borrowers.

This new information disclosure obligation on lenders would fill a major gap in the regulatory enforcement regime for consumer credit. Yet, even within that paradigm, it may not represent as much of a leap into the unknown as the proposal may seem to entail. After all, in the UK the FSA already requires providers of secured consumer credit to make monthly activity reports, in the context of a

---

71   Ibid.
72   Bar-Gill and Warren, 'Making Credit Safer' (n 22) 23–25.
73   Gough, 'Banking on Finding Your Weak Spots' (n 10); Harrison and Gray, *'Profiling for Profit'* (n 11).
74   Ramsay, 'Regulation of Consumer Credit' (n 7) 386–387.

recently-introduced 'meta-regulatory' obligation to 'treat customers fairly' – or risk escalating sanctions, ending in de-licensing. This, indeed, involves 'a form of ex ante regulation'.[75] Australia's NCCP Act 2009 also already requires all credit licensees to lodge a 'compliance certificate',[76] with the regulator expecting them to keep records of monitoring and reporting. Licensees must also belong to an approved external dispute resolution scheme for consumer complaints (s 47(1) (ii), with regulation 39 requiring schemes to provide for reporting of 'systemic issues'). This may therefore already provide another avenue for regulators to find out about unusual patterns in consumer credit markets.[77]

In addition, the regulatory enforcement regime for consumer credit is drawing much closer to that for consumer product safety in other major respects. First, for example, credit regulation typically already has analogues to mandatory safety standards for goods. Lenders are required to make disclosures directly to borrowers, just as regulators can demand that manufacturers and others affix warning labels or provide specified information when supplying consumer goods.

Second, to maintain product safety, regulators can order that goods include certain components or features, or allow manufacturers to find alternative or additional ways to achieve mandated performance standards. Similarly, credit suppliers may be required to include certain substantive terms in their loans contracts. More commonly, credit regulators specify that other terms *cannot* be included. For example, in loan contracts concluded anywhere in Australia from 2011,[78] and in Japan since 2000,[79] overly one-sided or unfair terms are now void.[80]

---

75   Ramsay and Williams, 'The Crash that Launched a Thousand Fixes' (n 2) 244.

76   National Consumer Credit Protection Act 2009 (Cth) s 53.

77   Australian Securities and Investment Commission, *Annual Compliance Certificates for Credit licensees, Australian Securities and Investment Commission* <http://www.asic. gov.au/asic/asic.nsf/byheadline/Annual+compliance+certificates+for+credit+licensees?ope nDocument> accessed 27 April 2012. For bankruptcies subject to formal proceedings, there also already exists a searchable National Personal Insolvency Index: see Insolvency and Trustee Service Australia, *National Personal Insolvency Index* (17 November 2011) <http:// www.itsa.gov.au/dir228/itsaweb.nsf/docindex/creditors-%3Enpii> accessed 27 April 2012.

78   Jeannie Paterson, 'The Australian Unfair Contract Terms Law: The Rise of Substantive Unfairness as a Ground for Review of Standard Form Consumer Contracts' (2009) 33 Melbourne University Law Review 934.

79   Luke Nottage, 'Consumer Law Reform in Australia: Contemporary and Comparative Constructive Criticism' (2009) 9 Queensland University of Technology Law and Justice Journal 111.

80   Admittedly, the starting-point in both countries is simply that the unfair term is void as between the parties, protecting the consumer if the firm tries to enforce the term. Nonetheless, if a court declares a term to be unfair, continued usage constitutes a contravention of the Australian Consumer Law and therefore attracts further regulatory sanctions. The same is true of terms subject to successful injunction actions under Japan's Consumer Contract Law (No 61 of 2000), if suppliers persist in using such terms.

Moreover, in Australia and Japan, interest rates exceeding specified levels are void – and also attract criminal sanctions.

In addition, inspired by safety regulation particularly in the field of pharmaceutical regulation, Lauren Willis has recently suggested that credit suppliers should be required to present evidence (from field-based testing) that consumers sufficiently *comprehend* features of the credit services they purchase, rather than just making certain specified disclosures to their borrowers.[81] This proposal has parallels with safety regulation that requires general consumer products to achieve certain mandatory performance standards (such as heat resistance) by whatever means devised or preferred by the manufacturer. However, the present Australian regime remains very strict when it comes to mandating the affixing of warnings or instructions; suppliers' attempts at rewording, even if arguably well- intentioned, have resulted in successful prosecutions.[82]

Third, under Australia's new NCCP Act applicable to consumer credit, there is even now an analogue to a GSP provided in some jurisdictions for product safety, although the parallel remains a rough one (as noted already above). Article 3(1) of the EU's General Product Safety Directive requires suppliers to supply only 'safe' goods, while the NCCP Act requires lenders to make loans which are 'not unsuitable'.[83] The same is true with Japan, where the legislative amendments in 2006 generally prohibit lending of 'an amount that will exceed the ability of the borrower to repay'.[84] Indeed, the case of total loans exceeding one-third of the borrower's annual gross income is listed as an example of such 'unsuitable' lending. The latter 'backstop' bright-line rule represents a closer analogue to the GSP available in the case of tangible goods, because the rule essentially defining 'unsafe' credit for an entire category of borrowers (those whose overall indebtedness exceeds one-third of income) even if a borrower's specific circumstances might in fact make loans beyond that threshold manageable or 'suitable'. (Similarly, assessments of product

---

81   Lauren Willis, 'From Disclosure Rules to Comprehension Requirements ... and Beyond' (Powerpoint presentation, Law and Society Association annual conference, Honolulu, 8 June 2012) (available on request).

82   See, for example. *BMW Australia Limited v Australian Competition and Consumer Commission* [2003] FCAFC 167; *Australian Competition and Consumer Commission v Sontax Australia (1988) Pty Ltd* [2011] FCA 1202.

83   However, Pearson, 'Reading Suitability Against Fitness for Purpose' (n 37) does suggest that framing the obligation on credit suppliers in the negative may allow scope for it to be interpreted more narrowly than if it had been phrased simply as an obligation to 'provide "suitable" credit' — as with 'suitable' consumer goods. For a proposal for a general suitability requirement in US consumer credit law, see also Kathleen Engel and Patricia McCoy, 'A Tale of Three Markets: The Law and Economics of Predatory Lending' (2002) 80 Texas Law Review 1259. Cf generally OECD, *Report on OECD Member Countries' Approaches to Consumer Contracts* (OECD 2007) <http://www.oecd-ilibrary. org/science-and-technology/report-on-oecd-member-countries-approaches-to-consumer-contracts_230810708021> accessed 27 April 2012.

84   Moneylenders Law art 13-2(1).

safety take into account the intended and reasonably foreseeable user groups.) A more general 'suitability' requirement, as under Australian consumer credit legislation, does instead focus on the individual circumstances of the consumer.[85]

Even if the parallel is not therefore perfect, it seems ironic that despite the global financial crisis, borrowers in Australia, and especially Japan, obtain better protection regarding the 'safety' of their credit *services* than Australian (and Japanese) users do regarding the safety of general consumer *goods*. In light of this development in consumer credit regulation, the Australian government should revisit the recommendation of its Productivity Commission[86] not to include a GSP within the product safety regulation scheme of the Australian Consumer Law. Meanwhile, however, if Australian regulators do later find consumer goods to be 'unsafe', at least they can ban their supply or order a mandatory recall.[87] Rather similarly, consumer loans found to be unsuitable can already attract civil and criminal penalties under the NCCP Act.

Thus, this chapter's proposal for a new obligation on suppliers of consumer credit to alert regulators about abnormal risks arising after the supply of their services, paralleling duties on many consumer goods suppliers worldwide nowadays, would help bring both regimes closer together. It responds to the more general arguments for such an alignment made by Warren and others over recent years, pointing out many common features of consumer credit services and consumer goods,[88] drawing especially on information and behavioural economics. Inspired also by such research, Willis has recently suggested that credit suppliers might be required to provide evidence that borrowers actually *used* credit appropriately – for example, by making proper payments.[89] That proposal mirrors the one presented here – urging a new duty on credit suppliers to notify regulators about 'abnormal' levels of incidents afflicting their borrowers.

---

85   Gail Pearson, 'Suitable for an Individual or Acceptable for All? A Response to Nottage and Kozuka' (2012) 22(8) Australian Product Liability Reporter 266.

86   Productivity Commission, *Review of Australia's Consumer Policy Framework* (n 64).

87   NCCP Act ss 109, 114, 122.

88   The most important commonality is that consumers in both cases are unable to assess and act on assessments of 'safety', resulting in physical harm and/or economic loss from the goods or services used. This causes a wealth transfer to suppliers that is not based on consumers' informed consent, as well as possible broader negative externalities (such as family breakdown or loss of trust in a market sector). The concerns are not therefore purely distributional, and various regulatory responses seem appropriate, even if some may be more difficult to implement in the context of consumer credit services. Cf Robert Lawless, 'The Limits of Contract as Product' (2009) 157 University of Pennsylvania Law Review 160, 162–164.

89   Willis, 'From Disclosure Rules to Comprehension Requirements' (n 81). This would go beyond even the new obligation she proposes for suppliers to show that consumers *comprehended* the documentation and any warnings issued, at the time the contract was concluded.

Furthermore, adding such a disclosure duty should also appeal on the grounds of cultural risk cognition theory. Specifically, these studies show that:

> Persons with *individualistic* values can be expected to be relatively dismissive of environmental and technological risks, which if widely accepted would justify restricting commerce and industry, activities that people with such values hold in high regard. The same goes for individuals with *hierarchical* values, who see assertions of environmental risk as indictments of social elites. Individuals with *egalitarian and communitarian* values, in contrast, see commerce and industry as sources of unjust disparity and symbols of noxious self-seeking, and thus readily credit assertions that these activities are hazardous and therefore worthy of regulation ...[90]

If similar disparity in risk cognition exists in terms of consumer credit risks, then this chapter's proposed new disclosure obligation might still partly affirm the world-view of 'individualists', especially if regulators disclosed reports to the public after receiving them from suppliers. Yet, in parallel with such a reform, retaining or adding interest-rate caps (even if set at high levels) would help make the overall regulatory scheme more palatable for those holding egalitarian or communitarian world-views, and who therefore adopt different attitudes towards commercial risks (including, arguably, consumer credit risks). This combination of reforms would therefore provide another application of Kahan's empirically-based political theory – that is, 'rather than attempting to cleanse the law of culturally partisan meanings – the discourse strategy associated with the liberal norm of public reason – lawmakers should infuse it with multiple meanings able to affirm a wide range of competing (emotional) worldviews'.[91]

More generally, the proposed reforms could also thereby open up a new avenue for a broader moral discourse in regulatory settings – unconstrained by consequentialist reasoning – aimed only at achieving 'compliance' in a narrow sense. Such a 'compliance trap' may often end up being ineffective for regulators themselves,[92] as well as being dubious from a broader political or societal perspective.

4 Conclusions

This chapter has taken up the challenge, laid down by Warren and others, of teasing out appropriate analogies between regulating for consumer product safety

---

90 Kahan et al, 'Geoengineering and the Science Communication Environment' (n 46) 3 (emphasis in original).

91 Kahan, 'The Cognitively Illiberal State' (n 25) 115.

92 Christine Parker, 'The "Compliance" Trap: The Moral Message in Responsive Regulatory Enforcement' (2006) 40 Law and Society Review 591.

and for the 'safety' of consumer credit services. Useful parallels can be drawn, based, first, on the types of risks found in both spheres. Direct regulation by public authorities, rather than more indirectly through the spectre of private-law litigation and reputation-based or other market mechanisms, is particularly appropriate for high-probability risks.

Moreover, a closer comparison of product versus services regulation highlights one major gap in the consumer credit arena, even after the global financial crisis. Lenders, unlike many suppliers of consumer goods worldwide nowadays, are still not specifically required to disclose serious post-sale problems to regulators. Adding this further information disclosure obligation would significantly enhance the regulatory enforcement pyramid in the consumer credit field, as it already has in other areas of law. Such a reform also seems to be quite plausibly justified on the basis of cultural risk cognition studies, as well as more conventional behavioural economics.

Chapter 8

Bank–Community Development Finance Institution Partnerships as a Means for Addressing Financial Vulnerability

Justin Malbon

1 Introduction

The global economy is presently facing the most significant set of challenges since the great depression of the 1930s. After the October 1929 Wall Street crash a staggering number of bank collapses followed in the US alone.[1] Depositors lost their life savings, which added to the financial shocks and social misery of the times. As a result of the calamity, governments throughout the world were determined to closely regulate banks. Banks were perceived to be the cornerstone of a healthy economy, and consequently bank regulation a matter of utmost national interest. The banks themselves were also anxious to rebuild public trust and confidence. To reinforce an image of solidity and reliability, bank headquarters were invariably housed in stolid stone or granite buildings. A job in the bank was a job for life, reinforcing a sense of stability in the minds of customers and bank employees alike.

By and large, banks saw themselves as playing a special role in society. For one thing, their services were to be available to all (male, white) members of society, unless there was a particular reason not to provide a person with a service – such as a history of loan defaults. To further the ubiquity of banking services, branches were established throughout large cities as well as remote rural communities. A customer's geographical location, for the most part, was not to be a barrier to access to banking services.

Banks were, however, cautious lenders. For most customers, obtaining a bank loan seemed more akin to receiving the grant of a privilege – and one that was only reluctantly bestowed by the bank. In the case of women and ethnic minorities, loans were generally not made available at all, reflecting the remarkable social attitudes of the time. The degree of caution exercised no doubt partly related to the conservative culture that imbued banking organizations after the Great Depression. It may also have been compelled by the blanket of government

---

1   Elmus Wicker, *Banking Panics of the Great Depression* (CUP 1996) 1: the total number of commercial banks in the US was reduced by one-half between 1921 and 1933.

controls and regulations in which they were swathed. In many countries, for instance, governments tightly controlled home loan interest rates. The implicit demand of the electorate was that they be kept as low as possible.

By the 1980s memories of the Great Depression had well and truly faded. During that decade of deregulation, interest-rate caps were lifted and numerous regulatory constraints removed. Banks reimagined themselves (with implicit, and sometimes explicit, government encouragement) as merely businesses like any other. Their mission, just like other non-bank businesses, was to maximize shareholder returns (and, doubtless, increase senior executive rewards). Consequently, this 'shifted the consensus over the importance of banks as quasi-public institutions toward banking as competitive business'.[2] In tandem with these developments, governments pursued regulatory liberalization and the promotion of competition with an almost religious zeal.

The increasing fetishization of profit maximization led banks to comb through their customer lists in search of high-cost, low-value customers. To the consternation of customers in rural and remote areas, along with poorer and more financially vulnerable customers, banks were no longer interested in serving them. Lifelong customer relationships were abandoned, often causing 'economic violence to poorer consumers',[3] with many of the more vulnerable members of society succumbing to predatory lenders, who invariably charged effective annual interest rates of between 300 and 3,000 per cent.[4]

This "liberalization" of bank regulation effectively led to the removal of internal bank cross-subsidizations between lower-cost customers and higher-cost customers that had favoured the latter. Customers often fell within the high-cost category because of their relatively remote geographical location, their relatively low borrowings and deposits or their higher lending risk profile. Pre-liberalization, internalized cross-subsidization offered a longer-term and stable means for providing financial services to higher-cost customers. Liberalization, however, exposed many higher-cost customers to increased financial vulnerability because they were cast adrift by mainstream banks, causing them to be denied access to financial services, given access only to a substantially reduced range of services, or offered services at greater cost to them. By the 1990s those who had limited or no access to financial services began to be recognized as a distinct class of individuals. They were defined as being people who were 'financially vulnerable' or 'financially excluded'. Section 2 of this chapter outlines the ways in which financial exclusion began to be recognized and defined.

---

2   Martin Buttle, 'I'm Not in It for the Money': Constructing and Mediating Ethical Reconnections in UK Social Banking' (2007) 38(6) Geoforum 1076, 1077.

3   Andrew Leyshon and Nigel Thrift, 'Geographies of Financial Exclusion: Financial Abandonment in Britain and the United States' (1995) 20(3) Transactions of the Institute of British Geographers 312, 456.

4   Nicola Howell, Therese Wilson and James Davidson, *Interest Rate Caps: Protection or Paternalism?* (Centre for Credit and Consumer Law 2008).

Put simply, the net impact of liberalization played an important role in markedly increasing the proportion of people who became financially vulnerable and financially excluded. For them, liberalization inhibited their participation in their nation's economic activity, leading, in effect, to an overall economic opportunity cost to society. Those who were financially vulnerable faced an increased risk of falling into a poverty trap, which in turn increased social welfare programme costs, and which in turn placed a greater impost on taxpayers.

Recognition of the existence of a growing class of financially vulnerable people prompted the development of government policies and programmes designed to provide for relatively low-cost access to credit for those who were financially vulnerable. One type of scheme that was developed in a number of countries, including the US, the UK and Australia, involved Community Development Finance Institutions (CDFIs). CDFIs are generally run on a not-for-profit basis and tend to be more costly to operate on a per-customer basis than mainstream financial services. In addition, they cannot source capital from depositors as they are not deposit-taking institutions. Consequently, they often require external funding to maintain their operations and to provide them with sufficient capital for onward-lending. The funding is generally obtained from government agencies and private-sector organizations, including mainstream financial organizations. CDFIs tend to rely on governments maintaining their funding programmes or on banks and other private-sector organizations continuing to fund them, or a combination of government and private-sector support. However, such funding is precarious over the longer term, rendering many CDFIs vulnerable to closure. In a sense, bank–CDFI schemes constitute a (rather limited) form of cross-subsidization between wealthier (bank) customers and poorer (CDFI) customers, without either the degree of pre-liberalization financial support or the longer-term stability that was provided by internal bank cross-subsidization.

Although the overall social and economic losses and benefits of the removal of pre-liberalization cross-subsidization is an interesting topic in itself, this chapter confines itself to considering the sustainability of bank funding and support for CDFIs. Many CDFI schemes, particularly in the UK and Australia, are funded by banks for the purposes of meeting their corporate social responsibility (CSR) targets. CSR developed partly in response to widespread public criticism in the wake of spectacular corporate collapses during and after the 1980s. Scandals surrounding some of the collapses led to the public perception that corporations were moral-less, profit-obsessed organizations that failed to act in the public interest. Many corporations adopted CSR schemes to appease the critics, improve their public image and stave off increased government regulation. CSR activities were often seen by the very corporations that adopted them as undermining, or at least not meaningfully contributing to, the corporation's profit-maximization goals. Consequently, they were relegated to the margins of corporate activity. To some degree, CSR owes its antecedence to the corporate philanthropy movements of the nineteenth and early twentieth centuries, in which some corporations donated (sometimes substantial) funds for community purposes. Although these donations were sometimes very generous and beneficial to the community, they were invariably an act of beneficence, of gift-giving, and tended not to be provided on any sustained or longer-term basis. This was probably less so in the US, where corporate and individual philanthropy tends to be more prevalent and sustained than is the case in many other countries.

The unilateralist nature of beneficence tends to militate against possibilities of mutual, longer-term, commitment to programmes. And so it is with CDFI funding that is sourced from narrowly-based CSR programmes. These propositions are explored in section 3 of this chapter. A possible alternative approach to bank involvement with CDFIs is for the parties to enter into cross-sectoral partnership arrangements. Such partnerships are becoming increasingly popular outside the financial sector, where corporations are entering into partnerships with community-sector organizations for the delivery of products and services to underprivileged communities. Section 4 outlines some of the experiences of the partnerships. The research literature suggests that there are mutual benefits to be gained by the partners. The community-sector organization can gain from the skills and experiences and the sustained commitment of the corporate partner. The corporate partner can gain from enhanced image, developing innovative practices, improved insights and understanding of the marketplace behaviours and needs, and the development of closer links with community networks and locally-based government agencies. The downside is that the corporate partner may skew programmes to better suit its needs, leaving some more vulnerable members of the community underserved, or ignored. The very success of programmes can prompt government to leave the field to the partner organizations, which can lead to it neglecting policy development in the field, or to assume that corporatist models are the best way of meeting social needs. These propositions are explored in section 4.

Finally, this chapter concludes that the experiences of cross-sectoral partnerships can inform bank–CDFI relations, potentially leading to a more stable basis for CDFI programmes. However, the lessons from cross-sectoral partnerships need to be heeded to avoid distortions in programme design and delivery and governments vacating the field.

2 Regulatory liberalization and financial exclusion

The US was the epicentre of the financial services revolution during the 1980s. Many regulations governing financial-market prices and the segmentation of financial product markets that had developed since the Great Depression were eliminated, and an extensive wave of bank mergers followed.[5] Other countries soon followed in the US's wake. Financial regulation and market practices in the

---

5   Gary A Dymski, 'Financial Globalization, Social Exclusion and Financial Crisis' (2005) 19(4) International Review of Applied Economics 439, 448.

UK and elsewhere were rewritten, based on the US model.[6] In the UK, between 1986 and 1999, ten of the 15 largest building societies demutualized, accounting for about 60 per cent of the sector's assets.[7] This left credit unions and CDFIs as the only locally-owned mutual financial institutions in many communities.[8]

Dyminski argues that the changes that occurred from the 1980s led to the global homogenization and stratification of financial practices. This, he says, was the key driver of financial exclusion.[9] It led to more privileged customers gaining an expanded range of investment and debt options, with increased expected returns and lower transaction costs, while customers in less favoured classes were offered fewer savings and investment options and higher transaction costs.[10]

It may be somewhat simplistic to conclude that a clear-line causal link exists between market deregulation and any particular individual's financial exclusion, given that the causes lying behind individual financial exclusion are often complex. Nevertheless, Arashiro's observations are apt:

> The erosion of traditional welfare states, coupled with economic liberalisation, created a context in which the pressure for individualisation of responsibilities and risk coincided with the prevalence of free market rules. These structural transformations resulted in the rise of individual financial vulnerability, without the traditional social safety nets that in the past were assumed as a state responsibility under the terms of the social contract.[11]

Financial exclusion

The consequences of the liberalization of financial regulation on the more financially vulnerable members of society began to be noticed during the early 1990s. Initially, observers become aware of connections between bank closures and the impacts they were having on former bank customers, who no longer had ready access to bank services. The term 'financial exclusion' was initially coined to describe actual physical limitations of access to bank branches.[12] The term was later expanded to encompass barriers of access to mainstream financial services and products. The term now provides a unified way of viewing financial processes

---

6   J Neil Marshall, 'Financial Institutions in Disadvantaged Areas: A Comparative Analysis of Policies Encouraging Financial Inclusion in Britain and the United States' (2004) 36(2) Environment and Planning 241, 242.

7   Marshall, 'Financial Institutions in Disadvantaged Areas' (n 6) 247.

8   Ibid 248.

9   Dymski, 'Financial Globalization, Social Exclusion and Financial Crisis' (n 5) 441.

10   Ibid 443.

11   Zuleika Arashiro, 'Financial Inclusion in Australia: Towards Transformative Policy' (Social Policy Working Paper No 13, Brotherhood of St Laurence and University of Melbourne Centre for Public Policy 2010), 9.

12   Ibid 4.

and comparative institutional arrangements in lower-income and higher-income societies.[13]

During the 1990s deeper insights were offered into the nature and impacts of financial exclusion. Chambers, for example, recognized a distinction between poverty and financial exclusion.[14] He saw poverty as being generally associated with lack or want, and financial vulnerability as arising from 'defencelessness, insecurity, and exposure to risk, shocks and stress'.[15] He concluded that it is the lack of assets to deal with adverse contingencies that leads a person to be prone to financial vulnerability. He also found that interventions to assist those in poverty generally arise after damage to their assets and livelihood has already occurred.[16] The poor, by one measure more recently applied in the UK, includes the 'traditional poor' – those who are out of luck and out of work – as well as the new working poor. These include nursery teachers, cleaners and manual workers. They are low-paid and hold insecure employment.[17]

Kempson and Whyley found that, in many instances, financial vulnerability is not a static state, but rather is one that fluctuates depending on circumstances and events.[18] Financial vulnerability therefore arises from persistent financial hardship, financial insecurity and stress that arise from constant income fluctuations and uncertainty. Dymski describes financial exclusion as the 'failure of the formal banking system to offer a full range of depository and credit services, at competitive prices, to all households and/or businesses', thereby compromising the ability of the financially excluded to participate fully in the economy and accumulate wealth.[19] He adds that:

> Financial exclusion does not mean the absence of credit for a portion of the population: far from it. Those who are excluded need credit, are provided it and pay much more for it, than the financially included.[20]

A generally accepted indicator of financial exclusion is where a person does not hold a basic bank account for daily transactions, along with the lack of

---

13   Dymski, 'Financial Globalization, Social Exclusion and Financial Crisis' (n 5) 441.

14   Robert Chambers, 'Editorial Introduction: Vulnerability, Coping and Policy' (1989) 20(2) IDS Bulletin 1.

15   Arashiro, 'Financial Inclusion in Australia' (n 11) 4.

16   Chambers, 'Editorial Introduction' (n 14).

17   Mick Brown, Pat Conaty and Ed Mayo, *Life Saving: Community Development Credit Unions* (New Economics Foundation 2003) 6.

18   Elaine Kempson and Claire Whyley, *Kept Out or Opted Out? Understanding and Combating Financial Exclusion* (The Policy Press 1999) 14.

19   Dymski, 'Financial Globalization, Social Exclusion and Financial Crisis' (n 5) 440.

20   Ibid 451–452.

opportunity to access appropriate credit, insurance and savings accounts.[21] The denial of access to mainstream financial services may arise because of a person's geographical location, low-income status, temporary or long-term financial hardship from loss of employment, illness or injury, drug and alcohol problems, or a combination of these factors.[22] According to an EC study on *Financial Services Provision and Prevention of Financial Exclusion*, a range of societal factors have been identified as impacting on access to, and use of, financial services, including the liberalization of financial services markets, which have in turn increased the number and complexity of financial products and providers.[23] In any event, it is increasingly recognized that financial exclusion is a significant contributor to socio-economic inequality.[24]

The UK Office of Fair Trading estimated that in 1999 the number of people without bank and building society current or savings accounts was between 6 and 9 per cent (2.5–3.5 million people), with 14 per cent of households not having a current account.[25] A 1998 survey of consumer finances in the UK indicated that 10 per cent of all families were without a cheque or savings account.[26] In Australia about 15 per cent of adults were either fully or severely excluded from access to financial services in 2010, including safe and appropriate credit.[27] Exclusion from access to financial services ranged from full exclusion – where a person had no transaction account, credit facility or basic insurance – to severe exclusion – where a person had only one of these products. Most of the severely excluded lacked access to credit, and 54.5 per cent of the fully or severely excluded could not raise $3,000 in an emergency.[28]

Financial exclusion was addressed by a range of social policy initiatives, including the application of social investment schemes, micro-financing and community financing, or community development financing schemes.[29] In the UK, loans are offered by various vehicles, including credit unions and development trusts.[30] In addition, a lifeline in banking services has been instigated with the two aims of encouraging savings among low-income households to promote

---

21   Arashiro, 'Financial Inclusion in Australia' (n 11) 4.

22   Arthur Affleck and Mary Mellor, 'Community Development Finance: A Neo-Market Solution to Social Exclusion?' (2006) 35(2) Journal of Social Policy 303; Justin Malbon, 'Predatory Lending' (2005) 33(2) Australian Business Law Review 224.

23   European Commission Directorate-General for Employment, Social Affairs and Equal Opportunities, *Financial Services Provision and Prevention of Financial Exclusion* (2008) 40.

24   Affleck and Mellor, 'Community Development Finance' (n 22) 303.

25   Marshall, 'Financial Institutions in Disadvantaged Areas' (n 6) 243.

26   Ibid.

27   Chris Connolly et al, *Measuring Financial Exclusion in Australia* (The Centre for Social Impact 2011).

28   Ibid.

29   Affleck and Mellor, 'Community Development Finance' (n 22) 303.

30   Ibid 304.

asset-based welfare solutions, and of taking a 10 per cent market share from subprime lenders. The largest sub-prime lender in the UK is said to have 1.6 million customers.[31] Indeed, one market-based strategy for impairing the business of sub-prime lenders is to offer competing lower-cost sources of finance.[32]

In the US there has been a dramatic increase in the number of 'community development credit unions', which assist over 600,000 people from the poorest communities. The asset growth of the credit unions has been up to 800 per cent, with some institutions experiencing a 1,200 per cent growth in their financial net worth. Membership of some credit unions has grown by 500 per cent. This spectacular growth has been funded in part by the federal government and other sources, with the injection of funds benefiting around one in three of the 220 community development credit unions.[33]

Community Development Finance Institutions (CDFIs)

Another vehicle for servicing the needs of people who are otherwise financially excluded is the community-based not-for-profit organization – the CDFI. CDFIs specialize in providing financial services to communities not otherwise adequately served by traditional financial institutions. They were developed during the mid- to late 1990s in the UK as part of a government strategy to promote community development. Significant funds were directed towards the so-called 'Phoenix Fund', which mirrored US initiatives to regenerate poorer communities. By around 2005 there were some 80 CDFIs in operation in the UK alone. CDFIs in the US and UK do not necessarily confine their operations to the provision of credit to individuals, and will often provide funds to support small-business activities in marginalized communities.[34]

CDFI lending practices are designed to assist those who are excluded from access to mainstream consumer finance facilities because of poverty (long- or short-term), geographical location, race or some other factor, or a combination of these,[35] and provide a range of financial services, including credit services to individuals.[36] CDFI lending assessments tend to be based on social and economic

---

31   Brown, Conaty and Mayo, *Life Saving: Community Development Credit Unions* (n 17) 5.

32   Therese Wilson, 'Be Careful What You Ask For: What Role Now for Credit Unions in Addressing Financial Exclusion in Australia?' (2005) 15 Griffith Law Review 370.

33   Brown, Conaty and Mayo, *Life Saving: Community Development Credit Unions* (n 17) 5.

34   Christoph Kneiding and Paul Tracey, 'Towards a Performance Measurement Framework for Community Development Finance Institutions in the UK' (2009) 86 Journal of Business Ethics 327, 327.

35   Affleck and Mellor, 'Community Development Finance' (n 22); Malbon, 'Predatory Lending' (n 22).

36   Kneiding and Tracey, 'Towards a Performance Measurement Framework' (n 34) 327.

criteria.[37] In summary, CDFIs differ from mainstream financial institutions in that they: (a) target non-traditional and financially excluded borrowers; (b) provide financial management advice and skills to borrowers; and (c) increase available capital through partnerships with donors, government organizations and mainstream financial institutions.

Unlike other community-sector organizations, CDFIs ultimately seek to be financially self-sustaining – at least to some extent. However, profit-making is secondary to their social purpose, as they seek to serve those underserved populations and households that are either prohibitive or unprofitable for the private market to engage with. Some CDFI schemes are designed to become self-sustaining after initial injections of capital derived from donor bank funds. However, in practice few, if any, schemes ultimately succeed in becoming self-sustainable without continued external capital injections.[38] One difficulty CDFIs face is that, while banks and credit unions can take deposits and are regulated accordingly, CDFIs cannot. In the UK, CDFIs are organized as industrial provident societies or as loan funds.[39] According to Marshall, CDFIs tend to operate on the margins of the existing legal and regulatory system.[40] The claimed reasons for the schemes' dependence on external support include the high overhead costs involved, the low returns on investment obtained and the inherent riskiness of lending to low-income borrowers – although net loan loss default rates in the US are below 1 per cent[41] and micro-finance schemes for low-income Australians report 1 per cent default rates.[42]

A significant source of capital and operational funding for many CDFIs is mainstream banks. This funding, however, tends to be intermittent and unsustained, especially if it is provided on the basis of the donor bank meeting its corporate social responsibility (CSR) targets rather than upon any sustained partnership basis. CSR activities tend to be viewed by corporations as ancillary to their main activities: funding tends to be an act of largess or gifting to enhance the corporation's public image and to mitigate future government intervention, which might compel it to pay higher taxes or to meet government-imposed social objectives. Consequently, the corporation has no real stake in the success or otherwise of the community schemes it funds. These claims can be better appreciated with an understanding of CSR's history.

---

37   Lindsey Appleyard, 'Community Development Finance Institutions (CDFIs): Geographies of Financial Inclusion in the US and UK' (2011) 42 Geoforum 250; Wilson, 'Be Careful What You Ask For' (n 32).

38   Affleck and Mellor, 'Community Development Finance' (n 22).

39   Andy Mullineux, 'The Public Duties and Social Responsibilities of Big British Banks' (2011) 17(4) International Advances in Economic Research 436, 440.

40   Marshall, 'Financial Institutions in Disadvantaged Areas' (n 6) 247.

41   Appleyard, 'Community Development Finance Institutions (CDFIs)' (n 37).

42   ANZ, 'Progress Loans' (2008) <http://www.anz.com/aus/values/community/progress_loans.asp>.

3 A brief history of the rise of corporate social responsibility (CSR)

At about the time banks perceived themselves as essentially no different from any other businesses during the 1980s, other (non-bank) businesses were undergoing transformation. They were becoming increasingly aggressive competitors and more singularly focused on maximizing profits. The 1987 movie *Wall Street*, to an extent, captures the mood of the times. In the movie Michael Douglas plays a fictional character, Gordon Gekko, who is a misanthropic corporate raider. In one scene, which portrays a meeting of the shareholders of the fictional company Teldar Paper that Gekko proposes to raid, he delivers the following speech:

> I am not a destroyer of companies. I am a liberator of them! The point is, ladies and gentleman, that greed, for lack of a better word, is good. Greed is right, greed works. Greed clarifies, cuts through, and captures the essence of the evolutionary spirit. Greed, in all of its forms; greed for life, for money, for love, knowledge has marked the upward surge of mankind. And greed, you mark my words, will not only save Teldar Paper, but that other malfunctioning corporation called the USA.

Implicit in the claims made in the speech is that questions of corporate morality amount to little more than vague and pious platitudes and are of no interest to those who engage in the hard-ball realities of big business. Morality, it suggests, is for philosophers, priests and wimps, and not for big business. As a consequence of these kinds of attitudes and the behaviour they encouraged and supported, corporations met with heavy criticism. Joel Bakan, for instance, famously described large corporations in his book *The Corporation* as legally sanctioned psychopaths.[43]

The combined weight of corporate collapses and scandals began to taint the image of self-centred capitalism. Spectacular collapses during the 1990s included: the Long-Term Capital Management hedge fund, which lost $4.6 billion in less than four months during 1998; Barings Bank which lost $1.4 billion in 1995; the Bank of Credit and Commerce International which lost $13 billion in 1991; and the Pyramid Building Society in Australia, which lost more than $900 million in 1990. Invariably, these collapses involved corporate malfeasance. These and other corporate activities during the 1980s and 1990s that harmed the community (or had the potential to do so) led to growing public disquiet. The activities included:

> ... the Union Carbide gas leak in Bhopal, India [which killed over 3,000 people]; the Exxon-Valdez oil spill; Shell's activities in Nigeria and elsewhere; sweatshop conditions in factories supplying Nike and other brand-name companies; tropical deforestation linked to companies like Aracruz, Mitsubishi,

---

43   Joel Bakan, *The Corporation: The Pathological Pursuit of Profit and Power* (Simon & Schuster 2005).

and McDonald's; Monsanto's promotion of genetically modified organisms (GMOs) and their impacts on small farmers, food security, and consumer health; child labour in the football industry; fires in Asian toy factories; environmental disasters associated with mining companies; as well as the spread of HIV/AIDS, particularly in migrant-labour systems structured by the mining industry.[44]

Activist groups, including consumer organizations, trade unions, shareholder groups and non-government organizations, played an important role in drawing attention to these issues and ran coordinated international campaigns and consumer boycotts, sometimes with spectacular success. They campaigned over issues such as child labour, fair trade, toxic chemicals, oil pollution and deforestation.[45] Large corporations were compelled to take notice because the campaigns increased the threat of regulatory intervention and increased negative consumer sentiment towards their products and services. As a response, many corporations not only acted reactively to neutralize bad publicity, but also increasingly took the initiative by adopting corporate social responsibility (CSR) measures in order to influence, control and lead the agenda of institutional reform.[46]

It is tempting to assume that the idea of corporations having responsibilities to their communities as well as their shareholders originated in the late twentieth century. Business philanthropy is, however, nothing new. For centuries business leaders generously donated funds for building churches and educational institutions community projects. In 1875 the New York store, Macy's, contributed funds to an orphan asylum. George Pullman of the Pullman Palace car company created a community town which was built to housing standards well ahead of their times. The Young Men's Christian Association (YMCA) was established in London in 1844 and quickly established itself internationally. The movement's success owed a lot to considerable financial donations from individuals and companies.[47]

During the early part of the twentieth century, businesses were increasingly providing for hospital clinics, bathing houses, lunch rooms, recreational facilities and profit-sharing.[48] The piano manufacturer Steinway purchased land adjoining its premises and built a church, library and schools for its employees.[49] The chocolate maker Cadbury pioneered the provision of pensions for its workers. In addition,

---

44 Peter Utting, 'Corporate Responsibility and the Movement of Business' (2005) 15(3) Development in Practice 375, 377.

45 Ibid 376.

46 Ibid 375.

47 Archie B Carroll, 'A History of Corporate Social Responsibility: Concepts and Practices' in Andrew Crane et al (eds), *The Oxford Handbook of Corporate Social Responsibility* (OUP 2008) 19, 22.

48 Daniel A Wren, *The History of Management Thought* (5th edn, John Wiley and Sons Inc 2005) 269–270.

49 *Steinway v. Steinway and Sons* (1909) 40 NYS 649; Wren, *The History of Management Thought* (n 48) 110.

a leading member of the company played a key role in planning and funding the development of Bourneville, a model town for its workers.

The motives for such beneficence were often complex. The housing and social programmes for workers in the nineteenth and early twentieth centuries certainly went well beyond minimum legal requirements for protecting employees, yet the benefactors no doubt believed that a happier and healthier workforce would lead to more commitment and loyalty which in turn would serve the company's best financial interests.

The duty of directors and managers to their shareholders

Although many saw these developments as laudable, there were (as there are today) detractors. The central premise of the detractors was neatly put by Nobel economics prizewinner Milton Friedman, who claimed in his 1962 book *Capitalism and Freedom* that 'few trends could so thoroughly undermine the very foundation of our free society as the acceptance by corporate officials of a social responsibility other than that to make as much money for their stockholders as possible'.[50] Objections to corporate beneficence, however, were not limited to ideological claims. It was also claimed that it is unlawful, as managers and the board of directors owe a fiduciary duty to their shareholders, and serving their best interests involves maximizing the value of the corporation.

The legal basis of corporate beneficence has been debated at least since the early twentieth century. Professor E. Merrick Dodd Jr of the Harvard Law faculty, for instance, claimed in an article published in the *Harvard Law Review* in 1932 that the voluntary acceptance of social responsibility by corporate managers runs counter to fundamental principles of law on the basis of two assumptions: that business is private property and that the directors are fiduciaries for the shareholders. He claimed that the assumptions were unsustainable because business

> ... which is the economic organization of society ... is private property only in
> a qualified sense, and society may properly demand that it be carried on in such
> a way as to safeguard the interests of those who deal with it either as employees
> or consumers even if the proprietary rights of its owners are thereby curtailed.[51]

Professor Dodd's statement about businesses as private property only in a qualified sense reflected the 'trustee management' theory of the role of directors which emerged in the 1920s and 1930s.[52] According to this theory, directors and corporate managers were responsible for both maximizing stockholder wealth

---

50   Milton Friedman, *Capitalism and Freedom* (University of Chicago Press 1962) 133.

51   E Merrick Dodd, 'For Whom Are the Corporate Managers Trustees?' (1932) 45 Harvard Law Review 1145, 1162.

52   Carroll, 'A History of Corporate Social Responsibility' (n 47) 23.

and creating and maintaining an equitable balance amongst other competing claims, such as claims from customers, employees and the community.[53] The law recognized and encouraged the existence and operation of a company 'primarily because it is of service to the community rather than because it is a source of profit to its owners'.[54] From this it followed that the manager was the 'trustee' for various groups that related to the company, and not merely as an agent of the company. At that time the notion of acting in the interests of the community was understood as rendering adequate service to its customers, expanding the facilities of the business when called upon by a public authority, charging only reasonable rates and treating all customers alike – which is to say, not doing special deals for privileged customers.[55] Some of these requirements are taken for granted today and would not be considered anything special; nor would they necessarily be categorized as CSR requirements.

Despite the development of the trustee management theory, the proposition that the singular role of directors and managers is to maximize profits for shareholders continued to hold sway and continues to do so today among many economists, lawyers and businesspeople. Although this proposition underlies many economic models of firm behaviour, its legal basis is in fact not particularly strong. Although the law does impose a fiduciary duty on directors and managers to act in the best interests of the company, the courts tend to defer to the 'business judgement' of directors about how that is best achieved. In practice, this provides considerable scope for CSR measures to be adopted.

The broader view of the duties of managers and directors has evolved somewhat since the early part of the twentieth century. A more recent variant on the profit-maximization proposition is the theory that a corporation is a nexus of legal contracts between suppliers of various production factors which agree to cooperate in order to generate monetary returns.[56] These suppliers (including workers, owners of the land on which the firm's production takes place and the owners of relevant intellectual property rights used by the firm) receive set payments for the supply at little risk. Shareholders, on the other hand, supply capital and accept the residual financial risk, for which they receive the residual profits. Under this theory, any profits diverted towards activities such as the social good comes directly from the pockets of the shareholders. On this basis, CSR is close to being theft.[57]

Another theory about the role of managers is the 'operational discretion' theory, in which the law grants managers discretion to comply with social and

---

53 Ibid.
54 Dodd, 'For Whom Are the Corporate Managers Trustees?' (n 51) 1149.
55 Ibid 1149–1150.
56 Forest Reinhardt, Robert N Stavins and Richard HK Vietor, 'Corporate Social Responsibility through an Economic Lens' (2008) Review of Environmental Economics and Policy 6.
57 Ibid.

moral norms, even if it reduces shareholder profits. And, finally, the 'progressive view', which is to some degree consistent with the view proposed by Professor Dodd, holds that the corporation is organized for the benefit of society at large, or, at the very least, the directors' fiduciary duties extend to a wide variety of stakeholders. Under this theory, sacrificing profits in the public interest is entirely legal.[58]

The rise of CSR

Interestingly, Professor Dodd made an observation in his 1932 article that to modern ears sounds much like the nascent form of what we understand today as CSR:

> If we may believe what some of our business leaders and students of business tell us, there is in fact a growing feeling not only that business has responsibilities to the community but that our corporate managers who control business should voluntarily and without waiting for legal compulsion manage it in such a way as to fulfill those responsibilities.[59]

It was not until 1953, when Howard R. Bowen defined the term in his influential book *Responsibilities of Businessmen*, that 'social responsibility' in relation to corporations gained explicit expression. He claimed that public responsibility, social obligations and business morality were synonyms for corporate social responsibility. He defined the social responsibilities of 'businessmen' as the obligations to 'pursue those policies, to make those decisions, or to follow those lines of action which are desirable in terms of the objectives and values of our society'.[60]

In giving effect to these obligations, Bowen called for changes in the composition of boards of directors, greater representation of the social viewpoint in management, use of the social audit, social education of business managers, development of business codes of conduct, and further research in the social sciences.[61] Since then, CSR has been variously defined, two definitions being: 'a set of principles, processes, policies, programs and observable results relative to the relations of the company with society';[62] and as a corporation sacrificing its

---

58   Ibid 7.

59   Dodd, 'For Whom Are the Corporate Managers Trustees?' (n 51) 1153–1154.

60   Howard Rothmann Bowen, *Social Responsibilities of the Businessman* (Harper and Row 1953) 6.

61   Carroll, 'A History of Corporate Social Responsibility' (n 47) 26, citing Bowen *Social Responsibilities of the Businessman* (n 60) 151–13.

62   Ladislao Luna Sotorrío and José Luis Fernández Sánchez, 'Corporate Social Responsibility of the Most Highly Reputed European and North American Firms' (2008) 82(2) Journal of Business Ethics 379, 380.

profits in the social interest. The latter definition implies that there is an inherent conflict between the corporate objective of profit maximization and corporate engagement in activities that may benefit the social interest, which will necessarily reduce potential profit. CSR is therefore framed as a zero-sum game. This stark dichotomy can, however, be relaxed to allow that CSR enables a corporation to pursue its enlightened self-interest by funding programmes that will enhance its reputation, fend off regulatory threats and allow it to learn innovative ways of serving its customers, which will ultimately protect or enhance future profits.

It is unlikely, however, that corporations will pursue CSR objectives at the expense of profits in any significant or sustained way. Reinhardt, Stavins and Vietor identify six conditions under which it would be sustainable for firms to produce goods and services (such as part of goods) that benefit individuals other than their customers. They say that in each case government intervention is required or imperfect competition or both.[63] The conditions arise where the firm undertakes socially beneficial actions because:

1. it is required to by law;
2. they are not costly to the firm (for example, a restaurant donating leftover food);
3. they reduce the firm's business expenses by an amount greater than the cost of the action – for example, introducing energy-saving and climate-friendly technologies that have a short-term cost but longer-term savings;
4. they may yield an increase in revenue – for example, selling 'fair trade'-labelled goods, which attracts socially conscious consumers;
5. it may ward off potential future government regulation;
6. it allows the firm to demonstrate to government the virtues of such actions and allows the firm to lobby government to set standards mandating the socially responsible actions. In this way, the higher standards, if introduced, will provide the firm with an advantage over its competitors which may not be able to meet the high standards, or may only be able to do so at additional cost.[64]

Despite the limited circumstances in which corporations will pursue CSR objectives at the expense of profits in any significant or sustained way, governments appear to be accepting the premise that corporations, or markets, offer the most efficient way of determining social needs and delivering social solutions.[65] This claim, in essence, amounts to saying that corporations are better at dealing with

---

63 Reinhardt, Stavins and Vietor, 'Corporate Social Responsibility through an Economic Lens' (n 56) 13.

64 Ibid.

65 Timothy M Devinney, 'Is the Socially Responsible Corporation a Myth? The Good, the Bad, and the Ugly of Corporate Social Responsibility' (2009) 23(2) Academy of Management Perspectives 44, 48.

social needs than governments. Devinney explains the logic of the corporatist claims as follows:

> First, individuals vote with their feet and pocketbooks. Based on this logic, corporations with more acceptable practices within a society would have more satisfied customers, more satisfied employees, and more satisfied owners and hence would last longer and thrive in more adverse circumstances ...
>
> Second, corporations possess more knowledge than individuals and governments and hence are more likely to be able to use that information to tailor products and services to the appropriate constituencies ...
>
> Third, corporations have a better understanding of trade-offs, technologies, and trends operating within a society and can act on them in a way that is more rational and realistic than governments can ...
>
> Finally, being free of the transparency required of governments and many civil society organizations, corporations can more easily engage in social 'experimentation'.[66]

Devinney warns that a 'naive assumption' underlies CSR – namely that firms are guided by society and do not deliberately manipulate society for their own benefit – adding that '[i]t is the natural vice of corporations that they gravitate toward solving problems from which economic rents can be claimed'.[67] He says that the natural vices of a corporation are to:

1. generate economic returns and not solve societal problems;
2. skew societal standards to their own needs;
3. represent their own interests (which are in essence urban upper-middle-class interests) rather than those of society at large; and
4. behave in a risk-averse and socially conservative way.[68]

A risk that Devinney identifies is the danger of CSR allowing governments 'to abdicate some of their social responsibilities, thus making the delivery of those social services provided by companies less accountable and transparent and more subject to the whims of unelected decision makers'.[69] Paradoxically, corporations are being criticized by some for narrowly pursing profit at the expense of the broader interests of the community and for not sufficiently funding CSR programmes, whilst at the same time there is anxiety amongst non-corporate actors about corporations having undue influence on the design and delivery of social programmes, whether as an aspect of CSR programmes or in some other way. Nevertheless, community organizations and government agencies are increasingly

---

66   Ibid 48–49.
67   Ibid 49.
68   Ibid 49–50.
69   Ibid 51.

engaging with corporations for the delivery of social programmes, which, it is argued, is leading to a 'reinvention of public policy' that is eroding the central core of governments and shifting from a hierarchical system of policy support to a system involving multiple organizations arranged in networked systems, resulting in the 'hollow state'.[70]

All this suggests that community-sector and government-agency engagement with CSR-funded programmes should be entered into by all parties with eyes wide open. Caution should be exercised to ensure that the interests of the ultimate beneficiaries of such programmes are clearly identified and their needs properly assessed, in order to ensure there is no skewing of programmes away from meeting those needs. The observations made about CSR funding and engagement offers important insights for the better development of bank–CDFI programmes. Additional insights for ways of improving and maintaining bank–CDFI relationships can be gained from cross-sectoral partnerships that are being increasingly embraced by corporations outside the financial sector.

4 Social partnerships

The formation of partnerships with not-for-profit community organizations to deliver goods and services to meet social objectives is becoming increasing popular among corporations outside the financial sector. These partnerships are variously described as social alliances or strategic partnerships,[71] or as 'cross-sector social-oriented partnerships'.[72] They involve cross-sector organizations jointly addressing challenges such as community capacity-building, economic development, education, health care and poverty alleviation.[73] The partnerships are often either transactional – that is, short-term, constrained and largely self-interested – or integrative and developmental – that is, longer-term, open-ended and largely common-interest-oriented.[74]

Proponents claim these partnerships are an organizational imperative[75] and are leading to a 'stunning evolutionary change in institutional forms of governance'.[76] Governments have also joined the 'partnership craze' and are engaging with

---

70   Brent C Smith, 'The Sources and Uses of Funds for Community Development Financial Institutions: The Role of the Nonprofit Intermediary' (2008) 37 Nonprofit and Voluntary Sector Quarterly 19, 19. Smith refers to governments increasingly contracting out policy implementation and the provision of public services to non-profit and for-profit organizations.

71   John W Selsky and Barbara Parker, 'Cross-Sector Partnerships to Address Social Issues: Challenges to Theory and Practice' (2005) 31 Journal of Management 849, 850.

72   Ibid.

73   Ibid.

74   Ibid.

75   Ibid.

76   Ibid 849.

community organizations, in many instances for the purposes of service delivery.[77] Community partnerships may well offer a more stable, sustained and longer-term basis for the operations of CDFIs than obtaining bank funds in non-partner arrangements. However, the potential costs and benefits of proposed bank–CDFI partnership relationships can be better assessed in the light of the experiences of community partnerships more generally.

Studies aimed at understanding the nature and dynamics of the partnerships and measuring their success or otherwise have created a virtual cottage industry for academics. Many studies adopt a particular framework for understanding the relationships. One framework posits that the partnerships are a mechanism for solving problems that cannot effectively be addressed by a single organization. Another posits that they are an instrument for a larger search for alternative methods of governance.[78] Some studies find that the parties maintain sectoral distinctions, thereby 'minimizing interorganizational dependencies and preserving the organization's autonomy'.[79] Studies within this frame tend to focus on ways in which partnership activities can be best implemented and sustained. The focus here is on examining the ways in which the partners build, maintain and govern their relationships, and apply their managerial strategies. Issues such as trust, power and stakeholder relations are also examined within this frame.[80] A broader conception of the partnership relationship, however, sees that the partnership creates new relationships between governments, businesses and civil society organizations, which blur the boundaries between sectors or 'spheres'.[81]

The motivations for party engagement in these partnerships have also been studied. The studies show that the community organizations' motives tend to be altruistic, whereas the business partner tends to pursue its self-interest. The extent to which businesses are motivated by pure self-interest is an issue on which the literature reaches differing conclusions. A number of studies suggest that, in many cases, a blend of self-interest and altruism exists.[82] Assessments of the success of these partnerships tend to be measured at three levels: direct impact on attaining the objectives; the impact on building capacity, knowledge or reputational capital, which may attract new resources; and influence on social policy or system change.[83]

There are a range of claimed benefits accruing to the business partner from the relationship, including improved networking with community and government

77   Ibid 855.

78   Smith, 'The Sources and Uses of Funds for Community Development Financial Institutions' (n 70) 22.

79   Barbara Gray and Donna Wood, 'Collaborative Alliances: Moving from Practice to Theory' (1991) 27 Journal of Applied Behavioral Science 3, 7.

80   Selsky and Parker, 'Cross-Sector Partnerships to Address Social Issues' (n 71) 856.

81   Ibid 853.

82   Ibid 863.

83   Ibid 858.

groups. In the early twentieth century both Marshall and Schumpeter recognized the value of these networks for harnessing interdependent and specialized organizations to enable economies of scale in distributing resources and information.[84] These networks are now seen to allow firms to enter into 'unusual domains' with established actors in the field so as to extend the firm's network 'to aggregate small markets into more attractive, larger ones, reduce costs (e.g., lower advertising expenses), and lead to increased sales'.[85]

The partnerships are also seen to offer firms the potential to innovate. They provide creative organizational models to offer innovative solutions to complex and persistent social problems.[86] The partnerships, it is also claimed, enable firms to gain easier access to developmental projects and resources to enable the integration of existing logistics and the collaborative pooling of established resources and competencies.[87] Various studies suggest that even further benefits accrue to businesses from the partnership relationships, including:

- an improvement in the trustworthiness of the firm as perceived by members of the community and government;[88]
- an enhancement of the firm's corporate image, garnering the firm social capital, which might lead to better sales of its products and the attraction, motivation and retention of desirable employees;[89]
- the capacity to develop closer links to a community, which allows for a number of further benefits, including:
    - the ability to identify new sources and forms of innovation, test new technologies in the community and reassure the business partner about the existence of unmet community needs[90]

---

84   Alfred Marshall, *Industry and Trade: A Study of Industrial Technique and Business Organization* (Macmillan and Co 1919); Joseph Alois Schumpeter, *The Theory of Economic Development; An Inquiry Into Profits, Capital, Credit, Interest, and the Business Cycle* (Harvard University Press 1934); Smith, 'The Sources and Uses of Funds for Community Development Financial Institutions' (n 70) 21; Clodia Vurro, M Tina Dacin and Francesco Perrini 'Institutional Antecedents of Partnering for Social Change: How Institutional Logics Shape Cross-Sector Social Partnerships' (2010) 94 Journal of Business Ethics 39, 46.

85   Ibid.

86   Ibid 39.

87   Ibid 46.

88   Francesco Perrini and Clodia Vurro, 'Corporate Sustainability, Intangible Assets Accumulation and Competitive Advantage' (2010) 2 Emerging Issues in Management <www.unimib.it/symphonya> accessed 26 June 2012.

89   Selsky and Parker, 'Cross-Sector Partnerships to Address Social Issues' (n 71) 855.

90   Perrini and Vurro, 'Corporate Sustainability, Intangible Assets Accumulation and Competitive Advantage' (n 88); Rosabeth Moss Kanter, 'From Spare Change to Real Change: The Social Sector as Beta Site for Business Innovation' (1999) 77 Harvard Business Review 122.

- an improved capacity to manage community expectations, and for the firm to better manage its social context of reference[91]
- improved organizational practices that provide managerial or market gains;[92]
- the capacity to gain additional insights into market behaviour and conditions, leading to product and service innovations for the business;[93]
- the capacity to lower transaction costs by using the community sector's networks and organizational arrangements;[94] and
- the attainment of other intangible benefits, leading to competitive advantage.[95]

One example of mutual benefits arising from a cross-sectoral partnership is M-Pesa (Mobile Money), a mobile banking service operated by Safaricom, a Vodafone subsidiary in Kenya. The service allows subscribers to deposit, withdraw and transfer funds using mobile phones.[96] The service was developed in partnership with the non-profit sector. Another partnership involves Nestlé and the Rainforest Alliance in which both parties seek to improve the sustainability of coffee farmers' processes in various developing countries.[97]

Businesses, unsurprisingly, tend to be more attracted to 'direct-impact partnerships' that can demonstrably improve education, environmental sustainability or job development, rather than relationships leading to 'indirect impacts' such as advocacy or good governance.[98]

Various studies also suggest that community organizations' expectations about the relationship can differ markedly from that of the business partner. For instance,

---

91   Sandra Waddock and Samuel B Graves, 'The Corporate Social Performance: Financial Performance Link' (1997) 18(4) Strategic Management Journal 303.

92   Francesco Perrini and Antonio Tencati, 'Sustainability and Stakeholder Management: The Need for New Corporate Performance Evaluation and Reporting Systems' (2006) 15 Business Strategy and the Environment 296.

93   Selsky and Parker, 'Cross-Sector Partnerships to Address Social Issues' (n 71) 852.

94   Perrini and Vurro, 'Corporate Sustainability, Intangible Assets Accumulation and Competitive Advantage' (n 88).

95   Jordi Surroca, Josep A Tribò and Sandra Waddock, 'Corporate Responsibility and Financial Performance: The Role of Intangible Resources' (2010) 31 Strategic Management Journal 463.

96   Vurro, Dacin and Perrini, 'Institutional Antecedents of Partnering for Social Change' (n 84) 46.

97   Gabriela Alvarez, Colin Pilbeam and Richard Wilding, 'Nestle' Nespresso AAA Sustainable Quality Program: An Investigation into the Governance Dynamics in a Multi-Stakeholder Supply Chain Network' (2010) 15(2) Supply Chain Management: An International Journal 165, 170.

98   Selsky and Parker, 'Cross-Sector Partnerships to Address Social Issues' (n 71) 853.

members of community organizations might see the term 'governance' as connoting intense, personal and immediate engagement, whilst the business does not.[99] Despite some scepticism about business motivations, community organizations tend to see these partnerships as a necessary means to achieve their social goals. Nevertheless, they tend to fear reputational damage should the partnership fail to achieve its goals or the business partner engages in unsavoury activities unrelated to the partnership, thereby reflecting poorly upon the community organization's judgement.

Despite the celebratory accounts of cross-sectoral partnerships, there is considerable scepticism about the longer-term social benefits to be gained from business partnerships with community organizations to attain social objectives. However, despite some commentators' concerns about the risks of misallocating resources that may arise from programmes being skewed in favour of the interests of the corporate partner, a large number of studies nevertheless suggest that a positive relationship exists between social and economic performance, which belies those concerns.[100]

5 Bank–CDFI partnerships

Because many CDFIs are not deposit-taking institutions and are high-cost operations on a per-client basis, they tend to be reliant on external sources of funding. These sources of funding often derive from government programmes or from philanthropists and banks. The CDFIs tend not to focus on profit-making, but rather on servicing the needs of financially excluded members of the community. As a consequence, sustaining their existence or the programmes designed for financially excluded people is a constant challenge.[101] Early schemes designed to serve the interests of financially excluded people involved donor funding to community-sector organizations that did not have prior lending experience. As a consequence, many of these schemes were unsustainable.[102]

One way of placing CDFI operations on a more sustained basis is for the institutions to enter into partnership arrangements with banks, more or less in line with arrangements in corporation/community-sector organization partnerships

---

99   David Billis, 'What Can Nonprofits and Businesses Learn from Each Other?' in David Hammock and Dennis Young (eds), *Nonprofit Organizations in a Market Economy* (Jossey-Bass 1993) 319, 325.

100   Perrini and Vurro, 'Corporate Sustainability, Intangible Assets Accumulation and Competitive Advantage' (n 87) 6.

101   National Australia Bank, *Do You Really Want to Hurt Me? Exploring the Costs of Fringe Lending – A Report on the NAB Small Loans Pilot* (NAB 2010).

102   Simon Blake and Esther de Jong, 'Short Changed: Financial Exclusion: A Guide for Donors and Funders' (New Philanthropy Capital 2008) <http://www.unlock.org.uk/upload_pdf/Short%20changed%20summary.pdf>.

more generally. For CDFIs, such partnerships can offer potential benefits such as: longer-term operational stability; a more reliable source of funds; less time and effort consumed in continually seeking ongoing funds from new sources; and the opportunity to learn and adapt lending practices from the bank partner.

The potential benefits for the bank partner include gaining an improved capacity to develop deeper and richer linkages and relationships with local and regional economies. CDFIs generally have close associations with local businesses and community organizations, as well as with government agencies that serve local needs.[103] These linkages can benefit a bank by leading to increased trust from, and strengthened relationships with, stakeholders, as well as by offering it opportunities to identify new sources of innovation and differentiation from banking competitors.[104]

Studies suggest that some banks are actively engaging with non-profit organizations such as CDFIs to gain access to low-wealth borrowers. In some instances, CDFIs are product-delivery agents for the public sector, enabling capital to be provided to the communities. A bank partner can potentially be engaged with, and learn from, this delivery process. In this way, a bank can benefit from the CDFI's community connections.[105] The partnerships can therefore offer a means for a 'two-way signalling', thereby reducing information asymmetries between funding banks and local communities.[106] This may in turn provide knowledge and ideas for developing new and innovative ways of delivering existing bank products or developing new ones.

Bank–CDFI partnerships can also present considerable challenges to the parties. The CDFI partner can face a number of difficulties, as Rubin notes:

> Adopting a 'business mindset' can be very difficult for a nonprofit ... it can move a nonprofit organisation's activities away from its social mission and potentially even harm the individuals the organisation was created to serve.[107]

Problems of this nature also confront community-based organizations engaged in cross-sectoral partnerships outside the banking sector. Indeed, many of the risks inherent in non-bank partnerships, such as the skewing of programme objectives and delivery in ways that better serve the interests of the corporate partner, may well also be faced in partnerships involving banks. In other words, the benefits,

---

103   Smith, 'The Sources and Uses of Funds for Community Development Financial Institutions' (n 70) 20.

104   Perrini and Vurro, 'Corporate Sustainability, Intangible Assets Accumulation and Competitive Advantage' (n 88).

105   Smith, 'The Sources and Uses of Funds for Community Development Financial Institutions' (n 70) 23.

106   Ibid 20.

107   Julia Sass Rubin, 'Adaptation or Extinction? Community Development Loan Funds at a Crossroads' (2008) 30(2) Journal of Urban Affairs 191.

costs and risks arising in non-bank partnerships are likely to parallel those that will arise in partnerships involving banks.

6 Conclusion

The liberalization of banking regulation that began during the 1980s removed internal bank cross-subsidizations that favoured relatively high-cost customers. Servicing these customers often involved greater cost because of the customers' relatively remote geographical location, their higher risk profiles or the low return gained from them because they kept small accounts. The removal of cross-subsidization exposed many of these former bank customers to increased financial vulnerability. Various government and community organization programmes were developed during and after the 1990s to address financial vulnerability. Some programmes promoted the development of CDFIs which were designed to provide finance to people and businesses in financially deprived areas and regions. Because CDFIs are not deposit-taking institutions, and because they are primarily designed to service the needs of otherwise financially excluded people rather than for profit-making purposes, these institutions invariably require external subsidization.

In many instances, funds are sourced from banks, which often provide funds as part of their CSR programmes. Funding based on meeting narrow CSR objectives tends to be fickle, which makes it difficult for CDFI organizations to plan and operate strategically. As a consequence, this can impact on their longer-term viability. These problems can be mitigated by CDFIs entering into partnerships with banks. There is a growing volume of research into the nature and viability of corporation/community-sector partnerships that can inform the future development of bank–CDFI partnerships. This chapter has identified a number of potential benefits from such partnerships, along with potential risks for the parties and, indeed, for the community as a whole.

Whichever way these partnerships are developed and promoted, they are unlikely to offer a sufficient longer-term basis for reducing financial vulnerability because they are unlikely to develop to the necessary scale. Second, the partnerships are unlikely to address the needs of some types of financial vulnerability because these will never attract the interest of the bank partner. Bank–CDFI partnerships are therefore unlikely to be a panacea for financial vulnerability. Public policy therefore needs to pursue options and processes that more fundamentally tackle financial vulnerability, rather than simply rely on schemes such as CDFI–bank partnerships.

Chapter 9

Mortgage Racketeering: The American Home Mortgage Foreclosure Crisis and the UN Convention Against Corruption

Christopher L. Peterson[1]

1 Introduction

The dominant world-narrative of the American mortgage financial crisis has been economic. Most journalists, scholars, regulators and political leaders have used financial and economic ideas to describe and explain the crisis. Most especially, the leading metaphor of the financial crisis has become 'a bubble', whereby rapid mortgage refinancing artificially inflated housing prices at variance with intrinsic value. Indeed, some believe that both in the US and in many other countries around the world, the rise in house prices was 'the biggest bubble in history'.[2] From this perspective, the mortgage financial crisis is presented as a result of changing conditions as though the crisis were nothing other than the result of interaction of disembodied supply and demand trends. Professor Steven Schwarcz, a leading American law professor on the topic of mortgage securitization, has argued that the mind-numbing complexity of securitization markets was one key cause of the crisis because investors and rating agencies had difficulty spotting the risks of mortgage-backed securities.[3] Others have pointed to the Federal Reserve Board of Governors' monetary policy, arguing that low prevailing interest rates created yield spreads on mortgage-backed securities that were simply too tempting to resist.[4] In this paradigm the long-standing and consistent growth in American housing values created irrationally exuberant faith in the sustainability of housing prices, which in turn led to a painful market correction. The foreclosure crisis is characterized as something akin to economic weather: a naturally occurring phenomenon of market forces. At its core, this paradigm has great difficulty recognizing crime.

---

1   This chapter was produced for a Griffith University symposium held in January 2012. The opinions and views expressed in this chapter are exclusively Professor Peterson's.

2   'The Global Housing Boom: In Come the Waves' *The Economist* (18 June 2005) 65.

3   Steven L Schwarcz, 'Disclosure's Failure in the Subprime Mortgage Crisis' (2008) Utah Law Review 1109.

4   Edmund L. Andrews, 'Greenspan Concedes Flaws in Deregulatory Approach' *New York Times* (24 October 2008) B1.

A smaller narrative of the American foreclosure crisis focuses on personal greed and dishonesty. Some internet bloggers, newspaper columnists and many middle- and working-class Americans have called the financiers responsible for originating, packaging and servicing residential mortgage-backed securities crooks, criminals and even 'banksters'.[5] While this populist rhetoric is a common sub-theme in press accounts of the crisis, neither most academics nor mainstream policy-makers have seriously examined such name-calling.[6] Law enforcement in the US and around the world has initiated only a handful of criminal prosecutions that are dwarfed in comparison to the magnitude of the financial crisis. It is also unclear how criminal explanations of the crisis fit within the dominant market-force-based paradigm. There is no place for a criminal *mens rea* in the American *uber*-metaphor of 'the bubble'.

This chapter explores the influence of corruption on residential mortgage finance by comparing the industry with the archetypal American criminal organization: the American Mafia. Many caveats are in order. This chapter does not argue that the American Mafia has infiltrated mortgage securitization markets. Nor does it does argue that participants in mortgage securitization and servicing are somehow morally equivalent to Mafia racketeers. Moreover, this chapter does not argue that public authorities should treat mortgage market participation law enforcement similarly to Mafia investigations. Most importantly, the mortgage markets are distinguishable from racketeering by the immensely beneficial value and well-being created for society by mortgage lending under ordinary circumstances. Mortgage lenders, servicers and investors should, generally speaking, be tremendously proud of the role they play in facilitating families' acquisition of shelter and all the personal and communal benefits that go along with it. In comparison, mafia syndicates rarely do anything useful for anyone but themselves. Yet, having said all this, this chapter does suggest a limited, yet still provocative, point: the recent organization of the American mortgage origination, investing and servicing markets has some profound similarities to the organization of criminal Mafia syndicates. Furthermore, this chapter briefly considers the UN Convention Against Corruption as a comparative touchstone that points to several corruption-prone features in the American mortgage finance markets. Overall, the objective here is to provide an additional perspective that may help scholars, policy-makers, and the financial industry itself understand what went so terribly wrong in the American mortgage foreclosure crisis.

2 Beyond the mafia mystique

Throughout much of the twentieth century a loosely affiliated group of organized crime families with cultural roots in southern Italy, popularly known as the

---

5 Dylan Ratigan, *Greedy Bastard$: How We Can Stop Corporate Communists, Banksters, and Other Vampires from Sucking America Dry?* (Simon & Schuster 2012).

6 Ian Crouch, 'MSNBC's Ratigan Rails Against Waste and Greed' *Boston Globe* (20 January 2012) 5.

American Mafia, exerted significant influence on the American economy. Also referred to as La Cosa Nostra, the American Mafia at various times controlled America's largest port; exercised dominion over the garment industry that produced most of America's clothing; infiltrated some of America's most important labour unions; and engaged in sophisticated bid-rigging and securities scams, milking billions from working Americans and the US government. In the mid-twentieth century 'the wealth of the national syndicate was greater than the richest Fortune 500 corporation'.[7] Although the American mafia passed the zenith of its wealth and power several generations ago, American law enforcement has continued to successfully prosecute American Mafia crime families in recent years.[8]

Although the American Mafia has wielded considerable power, the cultural stereotypes that have emerged in its wake arguably dwarf reality. Thoughtful reflection on corruption and organized crime must always contend with and move past what Herbert Alexander and Gerald Caiden called 'the Mafia mystique'.[9] Scores of Hollywood films – well over a hundred – use gangsters as a vehicle for entertainment or artistic purposes.[10] Most prototypically, Mafia protagonists personify a spectacular rise-and-fall trajectory of a tragic hero following a path of successful enterprise, ending in a precipitate failure born of overindulgence.[11] These stories, which range from reminiscences of Greek tragedy to whimsical farce, to mindless celebrations of pop culture, to violent indulgence, have left an indelible imprint on American culture.[12] Because of the international market for US cinema and pop culture, the American Mafia stereotype has even, to a degree, moved beyond American shores. Perhaps because gangsters embody a 'nightmare vision of our own desires and ambitions run amok', the genre has endured and thrived for a century.[13] Today, this fictional imprint colours how we perceive actual crime and criminal law. Indeed, this genre of entertainment has erected a cultural

7   Thomas Reppetto, *American Mafia: A History of its Rise to Power* (Macmillan 2004) xi; Herbert Alexander and Gerald Caiden, *The Politics of Organized Crime* (Rowan & Littlefield 1985) 1.

8   Frank Donnelly, 'Staten Island Business Owner, A Reputed Capo, Sent to Prison in Mob Gambling, Loansharking Ring' (*Staten Island Advance*, 8 July 2010) <http://www.silive.com/news/index.ssf/2010/07/staten_island_business_owner_a.html> accessed 15 January 2012.

9   Alexander and Caiden, *The Politics of Organized Crime* (n 7) 1.

10   George S Larke-Walsh, *Screening the Mafia: Masculinity, Ethnicity and Mobsters from The Godfather to The Sopranos* (McFarland 2010) 233–237.

11   Robert Warshow, 'The Gangster as Tragic Hero' in *The Immediate Experience: Movies, Comics, Theatre and Other Aspects of Popular Culture* (Anchor Books 1946) 83–88; Jack Shadoian, *Dreams and Dead Ends: The American Gangster Film* (2nd edn, OUP 2004); Larke-Walsh, *Screening the Mafia* (n 10) 233–237.

12   Lee Grieveson, Esther Sonnet and Peter Stanfield, 'Introduction' in *Mob Culture: Hidden Histories of the American Gangster Film* (Rutgers University Press 2005) 1–10.

13   Marilyn Yaquinto, *Pump 'Em Full of Lead: A Look at Gangsters on Film* (Twayne Publishers 1998) xiii.

barrier one must surmount in order to apply the label 'organized crime' to anything other than La Cosa Nostra.

It is important to note that the potency of the American Mafia stereotype has forced Italian-Americans to face an unfair and inaccurate stigma. The gangster caricature has allowed a small group of criminals to influence the larger public perception of an ethnic origin that has nothing whatsoever to do with organized crime. Ironically, many Italian-Americans, both ordinary citizens and law-enforcement officials, have been among those who have most aggressively pursued organized crime.[14] But, because their stories do not fall within the racially charged stereotypical narrative, they have wrongly resonated less in the public consciousness.

Nevertheless, the popular perception of the American Mafia continues to exert considerable influence over how Americans think about, and respond to, organized crime. Most prominently, it is no coincidence that the most important American federal organized crime law, the federal Racketeer Influenced and Corrupt Organizations Act, is nicknamed the 'RICO' statute after the anti-hero of a famous 1930 gangster film. *Little Caesar* spotlights the rise and fall of Rico 'Little Caesar' Bandello, a poor Italian-American who, hoping to become 'a somebody', moves to the city, 'where things break big'.[15] After a lucrative but short career of robbery and murder, Rico is penniless when police gun him down in a deserted street. The federal statute that takes his name facilitates both criminal prosecution of and private civil suits against the leaders of 'corrupt organizations' by attributing the crimes of individuals to a larger criminal enterprise.[16]

Thoughtful reflection on corruption and organized crime must recognize the American Mafia caricature for what it is: a stereotype. Such a caricature has as much potential to mislead as to accurately describe. Stereotypes can be useful because they draw a simple and potentially incisive account of identity around which groups can consolidate shared purpose. But the simplicity of stereotypes can also provide camouflage to mislead and conceal important truths. With the decline of power of the American Mafia over the past several decades, one inescapable truth is that there is significant diversity in organized criminal activity in the US and around the world. Misha Glenny's research, for example, has exposed a vast and complex web of criminal enterprises and networks that are interwoven across the global market.[17] The common thread of all forms of criminality is the criminal activity itself. Nevertheless, for the typical American, laying the label of 'organized crime' at the doorstep of large financial institutions is intuitively apocryphal because of the cultural preconceptions at the core of the Mafia

---

14   Humbert S Neli, *The Business of Crime: Italians and Syndicate Crime in the United States* (University of Chicago Press 1981) 42.

15   *Little Caeser* (Warner Bros 1931).

16   18 USC § 1961 *et. seq* (2012).

17   Misha Glenny, *McMafia: A Journey Through the Global Criminal Underworld* (Knopf 2008).

mystique. An objective evaluation of the allegations of widespread criminality in the American mortgage financial crisis must leave these preconceptions behind.

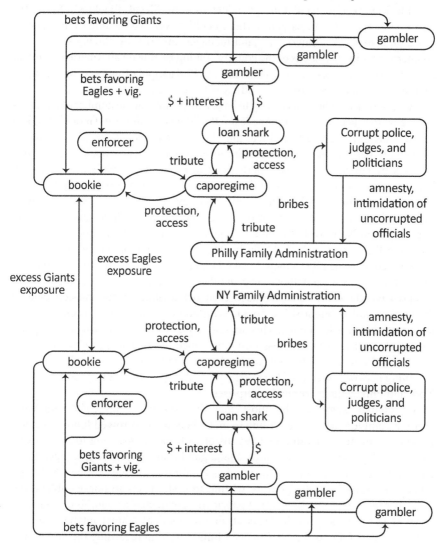

Figure 9.1   Organizational structure of a typical American Mafia sports-betting operation

A more thoughtful account of organized crime must look beyond the cinema-driven Mafia mystique to the organization of the Mafia as a business enterprise, or a series of related business ventures. Taking one classic American Mafia business venture as an emblematic example, Figure 9.1 graphically represents a mid-twentieth-century sports-gambling operation. Because sports gambling was (and continues to be) illegal in most of the US, the American Mafia serviced this black-market demand through a network of illegal 'bookies'. Since the outcome of sporting events is uncertain, bookies were vulnerable to unexpected game outcomes. The American Mafia managed this risk by 'laying off' bets to counterparties in other areas of the country. Taking betting on an American football game between the New York Giants and the Philadelphia Eagles as an example, Figure 9.1 shows how bookies would lay off excess exposure to losses.

A New York area bookie is likely to have a disproportionate number of gamblers betting on the success of their home team: the Giants. As more and more bets come in, the New York bookie would fear that the Giants might exceed his estimate of their likely performance, exposing him to large losses. The bookie could hedge this risk by contacting another sports book in Philadelphia and placing his own bets that also favour the Giants. If the Giants do exceed the bookie's expectations, then the New York bookie collects sufficient payout on his pro-Giants bets with the Philadelphia bookie to soften his losses on bets he made against the Giants with his local New York customers. Equally, the Philadelphia bookie is doing the same thing, so that both Mafia bookies are hedging against an unexpected game outcome. This allows them to take in more foolish bets by fans who naively favour their home team without exposing themselves to large losses on bets made to unreasonably lucky fans. Because each bet includes a commission paid to the bookie, called 'vigorish', a bookie with good nationwide connections could attempt to balance his books. This strategy tends to make the outcome or point spread of a particular game less important since the bookie's profits are driven by the 'vig' rather than betting tactics. By facilitating balanced books, intercity gambling networks increased the overall profitability and stability of both the New York and Philadelphia criminal enterprises.

Of course, some of the most lucrative sports-betting customers were chronic gamblers who were willing to make bets with borrowed funds. Because legitimate financial institutions have historically been unwilling to make loans to fund highly speculative ventures, Mafia gambling operations developed loan-sharking operations to finance the purchase of their gambling services. Although American Mafia loan sharks were willing to make loans to non-gamblers, the bulk of Mafia loan-sharking was historically connected to gambling rackets.[18] Loan sharks typically made loans at simple nominal annual interest rates of 250 per cent.[19] Of course, the absence of underwriting regarding the ability and willingness of borrowers to repay their gambling related debts exposed Mafia families to default risks. This, in turn, necessitated the use of the enforcers,

---

18   Mark H Haller and John V Alviti, 'Loansharking in American Cities: Historical Analysis of a Marginal Enterprise' (1977) 21 American Journal of Legal History 125, 147–148.

19   Christopher L Peterson, *Taming the Sharks: Towards a Cure for the High-Cost Credit Market* (Akron UP 2004) 11.

usually called *piciottos*, who have often dominated the public consciousness of Mafia operations. The American Mafia would use violence and the threat of violence to collect debts.

Gambling, usury and assault were all illegal in the mid-twentieth century, generating the most unquantifiable and difficult-to-manage risk of the operation: public law enforcement. American Mafia families, or *borgata*, dealt with the threat of law enforcement through a complex system of relationships. The basic unit of a *borgata* was a crew of roughly ten men, called a *decina*. Each crew was headed by a lieutenant called a *caporegime* or sometimes *capodecina*.[20] Members of a crew could include both soldiers and associates. A soldier (*soldato*) was a member of the Mafia admitted, or 'made', through an admission ceremony that require a vow of loyalty to the organization. Once an individual became a soldier, he was entitled to the protection of the *borgata*. As the primary work force of the *borgata*, soldiers were expected to find profitable business opportunities, including both legal and illegal activities. An associate was not a member of the *borgata*. Akin to an independent contractor, associates worked for the criminal organization and were in an important sense 'connected' to it, but nonetheless were not entitled to the same degree of loyalty or protection under the family's organizational norms.

Each *caporegime* traditionally interacted with a central family administration. Mafia family central administration typically included an operational director called the underboss (*capo bastone* or *sottocapo*), a counsellor (*consigliere*) and a chief executive (*capo crimini*). The *sottocapo*, the second-highest-ranking member of a *borgata*, was the point of contact between the *caporegimes* and the administration. The underboss was responsible for managing the daily operations of the organization. In contrast, the *consigliere* was an advisor to the boss who specialized in mediating disputes and consulting on organizational strategy. Finally, as the leader of the organization, the boss was responsible for managing relationships with other criminal organizations as well as influencing government leaders, law enforcement and the judiciary. Access to this network is one of the most valuable resources of a *borgata* because these relationships provide protection for members and associates.[21] In the context of a typical sports-betting venture, the central administration provided *caporegimes*, bookies, loan sharks, and enforcers access to Mafia families from different territories that were crucial in laying off risk. Moreover, the presence of the central family administration provided each of the front-line gambling network operators the confidence that their contracts would be enforced, despite their illegality.

---

20   Stephen L Mallory, *Understanding Organized Crime* (2nd edn, Jones & Bartlett Publishers 2011) 125.

21   Diego Gambetta, *The Sicilian Mafia: The Business of Private Protection* (Harvard UP 1993) 8–9.

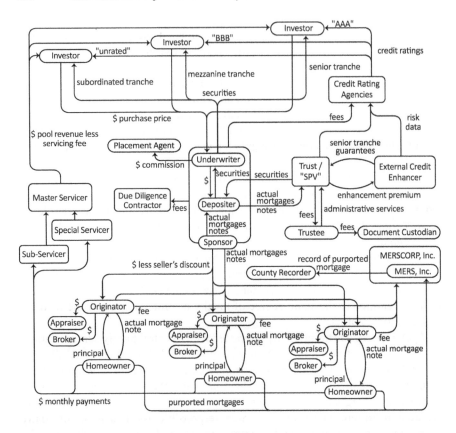

Figure 9.2   Organizational structure of a typical private-label residential mortgage-backed securitization conduit

3 What is a bank robber? Parallel organizational characteristics in American Mafia sports betting and residential mortgage lending

While the American Mafia engaged in many different legal and illegal businesses, the sports gambling rackets provide a useful foil for drawing some provocative comparisons with the American residential home mortgage business. Like sports-betting operations, financial institutions used the residential mortgage-backed securities market to channel investment. Figure 9.2 provides a graphic representation of typical private-label residential mortgage securitization during the 'bubble'.[22] In American residential mortgage securitization conduits, the front-

22   Figure 9.2 draws upon and updates similar graphics from my prior work including Christopher L Peterson, 'Foreclosure, Subprime Mortgage Lending, and the Mortgage Electronic Registration System' (2010) 78 University of Cincinnati Law Review 1359,

line participants included mortgage brokers, loan originators, property value appraisers and loan servicers. Mortgage brokers identified potential borrowers through a variety of marketing approaches, including direct mail, telemarketing, door-to-door solicitation and television or radio advertising. Loan originators and brokers worked together to sell prospective borrowers loans that would consolidate other debts, refinance a pre-existing home mortgage, or possibly fund the purchase price of a home. Home appraisers estimated the value of homes to provide assurances that there would be sufficient collateral value to cover losses in the event of foreclosure. At the loan closing some brokers funded the loan directly using their own money or a warehouse line of credit, while other brokers acted as an agent, using the originator's capital to fund the loan.[23]

In typical securitized mortgage loan conduits, originators quickly resold their loans to a larger financial institution, usually called a sponsor, which in turn deposited many loans into a pool.[24] Investment banking firms often outsourced the due-diligence review of mortgage loans purchased for securitization.[25] These due diligence contractors were typically smaller, thinly capitalized companies.[26] Pooled loans were held by business entities called special-purpose vehicles (SPVs) established by sponsoring investment banks. Investment banks typically set up SPVs as trusts under New York law. These trusts had no other assets, employees or function beyond the act of owning the mortgage loans. Under the pooling and servicing agreements that transferred mortgage loans into the trust, the trust sold beneficial participations in itself to investors in the form of residential mortgage-backed securities (RMBS).[27] In a typical transaction, an underwriter who was affiliated with the seller purchased all the trust's securities and then employed placement agents, working on commission, to sell these securities to a variety of investors including pension funds, mutual funds, insurance companies, financial institutions and governments. The securities were issued in a variety of risk categories called tranches, each of which received some form of credit rating from one of the major credit-rating agencies. Credit-rating agencies were paid significant fees by investment banking firms that pooled the loans in exchange for their rating services.[28] Those tranches that received the

1372; Christopher L. Peterson, 'Predatory Structured Finance' (2007) 28 Cardozo Law Review 2185, 2208.

23   Kurt Eggert, 'Held Up in Due Course: Predatory Lending, Securitization, and the Holder in Due Course Doctrine' (2002) 35 Creighton Law Review 503, 546, 538.

24   Frank J Fabiozzi, *Handbook of Structured Financial Products* (John Wiley and Sons 1998) 1–3; Steven L Schwarcz, 'The Alchemy of Asset Securitization' (1994) 1 Stan J L Bus & Fin 133.

25   Len Blum and Michael A Mattera, *Finance Company Transactional Due Diligence*, in Fabiozzi, *Handbook of Structured Financial Products* (n 24) 53, 56.

26   Paul Muolo and Mathew Padilla, *Chain of Blame: How Wall Street Caused the Mortgage and Credit Crisis* (John Wiley and Sons 2010) 228, 293.

27   Fabiozzi, *Handbook of Structured Financial Products* (n 24) 1–3.

28   Gerald Caprio Jr, Ash Demirguc-Kunt and Edward J Kane, 'The 2007 Meltdown in Structured Securitization: Searching for Lessons, Not Scapegoats' (2008) *World Bank Policy*

highest credit ratings usually included credit enhancement promises which often took the form of a third-party guarantee from an insurance company on losses from mortgage defaults and prepayments.[29] While, for the sake of simplicity, Figure 9.2 shows only three tranches, between six and 15 tranches were in fact common.[30]

In pooling and servicing agreements, mortgage loan servicing companies also purchased pool servicing rights obligating them to collect monthly payments, correspond with borrowers and foreclose when necessary.[31] Servicers also typically maintained mortgage loan escrow accounts and forwarded property taxes to local governments. Either in the pooling and servicing agreement or through separate sub-servicing contracts, master servicers often subcontracted servicing obligations with separate companies that may specialize in terms of geographical area or type of loan.[32] For example, a master servicer could have had management responsibility for the entire loan pool, while subcontracting out primary servicing responsibility to a sub-servicer and collection of defaulting loans to a special servicer.[33] Servicers were compensated by taking a servicing fee of between 25 and 50 basis points out of collected monthly payments prior to forwarding those payments to the SPV and investors. Additionally, servicers made money on the 'float' – that is, the interest paid on borrowers' escrow accounts and the servicer's own deposit accounts which hold payments prior to forwarding. Finally, servicers also typically retained the right to collect ancillary fees, such as late payment fees and kickbacks for insurance purchased by the servicer but paid for by the borrower, as well as foreclosure-related fees.

Mortgage Electronic Registration Systems, Inc., or MERS, is a shell company used by financial institutions to circumvent recording mortgage assignments with, and paying fees to, county governments.[34] Traditionally, every county government in the US maintains property records of all land-ownership interests, including mortgages and usually assignments of mortgages. In most jurisdictions this included recording an assignment of a mortgage whenever a promissory note was negotiated to a new buyer. This protected the buyer of the note from losing its priority claim on the land and also provided a transparent, public record of what entities had a stake in the ownership of the land. These ownership interests were

---

Research Working Paper 4756, 14–15 <http://papers.ssrn.com/sol3/papers.cfm?abstract_id=1293169> accessed 15 January 2012.

29   Daniel Singer, 'Securitization Basics' in Frank J Fabiozzi, *Accessing Capital Markets Through Securitization* (John Wiley and Sons 2001)13, 17–18.

30   Nomura Fixed Income Research, 'Mbs Basics' (2006) 22–23 <http://www.securitization.net/pdf/Nomura/MBSBasics_31Mar06.pdf>.

31   Adam Levitin and Tara Twomey, 'Mortgage Servicing' (2011) 28 Yale Journal on Regulation 1.

32   Ibid 24.

33   Jason H P Kravitt, *Securitization of Financial Assets* (Aspen 1997) para 16.05[A] [6].

34   Peterson, 'Foreclosure, Subprime Mortgage Lending, and the Mortgage Electronic Registration System' (n 22) 1359, 1403.

tracked by individual and business names in grantor–grantee indexes maintained by government offices, usually called a county recorder or register of deed. However, when financial institutions began to securitize mortgage loans, the multiple transfers of each loan necessitated recording several different mortgage assignments. This took some personnel time and necessitated paying county governments modest fees of typically about $35 for each assignment. Instead of following customary practices, the industry began to record mortgages listing MERS as the mortgagee 'in nominee capacity'. The industry's plan was for MERS to remain listed as the mortgagee in the public records for the life of the loan and thus avoid the need to update the records with the true owner of the loan.[35] In addition, MERSCORP, the parent company of MERS, maintains a competing, private database on which mortgage market participants can register ownership and servicing rights if they choose to do so. MERSCORP has about 50 employees, but MERS has no employees. Instead, MERS relies on the employees of other financial institutions, law firms and servicing companies to process loan-related business in the name of MERS. About 20,000 employees of other companies represent that they are vice presidents and assistant secretaries of MERS, even though they receive no compensation and have no formal employment relationship with MERS. About 60 per cent of American mortgages are now recorded in the name of MERS.[36] Since the financial crisis began, courts have struggled to deal with the repercussions of MERS' claim to own mortgages under the property laws of each of the 50 states.

Stepping back from the details of the residential mortgage business, the organizational roles and services provided in mortgage securitization conduits bear some interesting basic similarities to the organizational roles and services seen in the classic sports-gambling operation illustrated by Figure 9.1. In particular, there are at least six key institutional parallels seen in the organizational, product line and management features of both Mafia sports-betting operations and residential mortgage securitization.

First, American Mafia sports-gambling operations used expendable soldier and associate classes for actual criminal activity. A *borgata* expected its bookies, enforcers and loan sharks – all of whom were drawn from the ranks of soldiers and associates – to serve occasional jail and prison sentences without complaint when caught. The *borgata* made reasonable efforts to avoid this through bribery, extortion and aggressive criminal defence litigation. But, nevertheless, periodic jail and prison sentences were considered an occasionally unavoidable part of *borgata* life. Soldiers and associates were simply expected to be prepared to absorb this organizational friction. Indeed, many American Mafia members considered minor prison sentences for soldiers and associates an important rite of passage. Minor periods of incarceration among the expendable provided an opportunity for

---

35   R K Arnold, 'Is There Life on MERS?' (1997) 11 Prob & Prop 32, 34.

36   Kate Berry, 'Foreclosures Turn up Heat on MERS' *American Banker* (10 July 2007) 1.

criminal indoctrination and education as well as a chance to prove loyalty. Indeed, ironically embodying this expectation of periodic incapacitation, the common American Mafia euphemism for prison sentences was being 'away at college'.[37]

Of course, there is no expectation that mortgage brokers, originators, servicers, sub-servicers, appraisers or other front-line mortgage finance workers go to prison. Nevertheless, mortgage appraisers, brokers, originators and due-diligence contractors were expected to commit or abet fraud, violate sound underwriting practices, and ignore or undermine consumer protection statutes. As law-enforcement claims and bad debts accumulated, the collective understanding was that mortgage originators and brokers would shed their corporate identity through insolvency – doing their time so to speak – only to reappear in another business form. Both after the 2008 crash and for many years preceding it, both large and small mortgage lending and brokerage companies consistently and periodically declared bankruptcy.[38] Securitization allowed these thinly capitalized companies to 'churn' out loans in a volume far exceeding their own assets.[39] As government regulators and private attorneys representing borrowers gradually caught up with originators and brokers, the bankruptcy of these thinly capitalized companies allowed the industry to absorb liability without threatening the overall structure of the business venture. Similar to the periodic incapacitation of American Mafia soldiers and associates, the boom-and-bust cycle of mortgage originators allowed the home finance industry to discard mortgage origination companies that attracted the attention of law enforcement. Originator and broker insolvency absorbed and deflected government sanctions, preserving the vital link to world capital markets provided by the large investment banks. While there are many differences, both the Mafia and the residential mortgage securitization business share this common feature: both relied on the periodic incapacitation of front-line workers to deflect liability away from the organizational core.

A second and related shared organizational feature of American Mafia families and private mortgage securitization conduits was the use of cellular groups to conduct illegal activity. The illegal business operations of an American Mafia *borgata* were generally undertaken within crews of about ten men. Each crew was large enough to accomplish difficult tasks, but still small enough to keep a relatively tight distribution of information. This cellular organizational structure created natural firewalls limiting the distribution of information and shared criminal liability. This, in turn, tended to prevent infiltration by law enforcement.

The mortgage business, of course, did not use ten-person crews, but the disaggregation of lending business functions produces some similar results.

37   Scott M Deitche, 'Mafia Lingo' <http://www.netplaces.com/mafia/mafia-lingo/> accessed 15 January 2012.

38   Erick Bergquist, 'Preparing for a Bad-Loan Boom' *American Banker* (6 October 2000) 1; Robert Julavits, 'Warehouse Lenders Struggle Through Merger Boom' *American Banker* (23 October 2000) 9A.

39   Eggert, 'Held Up In Due Course' (n 23), 546.

Financial institutions always have the relatively simple option of originating, servicing and holding loans within their own portfolio. Financial institutions that use this strategy tend to enjoy benefits from process discipline, preserved business knowledge, data security and broad accountability for regulatory compliance. Nevertheless, private-label securitization markets generally disaggregated lending business functions into a cellular structure in which different tasks were assigned to legally distinct companies rather than to departments within a larger more cohesive entity. Brokers relied on independent appraisers to produce inaccurate home value appraisals. Originators relied on independent brokers, who did not have liability for Truth in Lending Act violations, to communicate with borrowers. Sponsors relied on independent due-diligence contractors, who lacked the regulatory scrutiny that comes with significant capital, to engage in anaemic and illusory due diligence.[40] Trustees relied on credit-rating agencies, which received handsome fees for granting overgenerous credit ratings based on specious assumptions, to create a seal of approval on residential mortgage-backed securities.[41] And underwriters relied on servicers, who have strong incentives to generate servicing-related fee revenue rather than optimal investor returns, to collect the money from and foreclose upon borrowers.[42] At every level of private-label securitization there were strong conflicts of interest built into the design of the system. Each of these conflicts of interest created a defence of plausible deniability where one participant could blame each other rather than accepting accountability for the production of loans that should never have been made and the subsequent failure to properly service those loans. Each of these conflicts of interest allowed the principal to 'bargain down due diligence' by selecting the agent least likely to raise objections to moving loan volume through to unsuspecting investors.[43] The natural firewalls separating each independent actor within the system created an almost impenetrable opacity that still confounds courts, regulators, homeowners and investors.

A third organizational feature is the parallel roles played by the *omerta* oath and the bankruptcy remote true sale doctrine in American law. A primary organizational norm in American Mafia families was the shared commitment to the infamous oath of *omerta*. This oath is a vow of silence and loyalty that prevents soldiers from directing law enforcement inward towards the organizational leadership.

---

40   Kathleen C Engle and Patricia A McCoy, *The Subprime Virus: Reckless Credit, Regulatory Failure, and Next Steps* (OUP 2011) 46.

41   Kia Dennis, 'The Ratings Game: Explaining Rating Agency Failures in the Build Up to the Financial Crisis' (2009) 63(4) University of Miami Law Review 1111, 1145–1146.

42   Levitin and Twomey, 'Mortgage Servicing' (n 31) 1.

43   Kurt Eggert, 'Beyond "Skin in the Game": The Structural Flaws in Private-Label Mortgage Securitization That Caused the Mortgage Meltdown', Prepared Statement for the Financial Crisis Inquiry Commission Hearing entitled The Impact of the Financial Crisis at the Ground Level – Greater Sacramento, California (2010) 16 <http://fcic-static.law.stanford.edu/cdn_media/fcic-testimony/2010-0923-Eggert.pdf> accessed 15 January 2012.

The long-term sustainability of organized crime families depended on the *omerta* oath because it prevented (or at least minimized the risk of) accountability for the institution's many crimes from being visited upon the organization's command-and-control centres.

In securitization, the 'true sale' of residential mortgage loans is, of course, very different from a secrecy oath. Nevertheless true sales serve a parallel organizational function in that, like the *omerta* oath, true sales prevent accountability from being visited upon a securitization conduit's organizational core. When a mortgage loan originator declares bankruptcy, its creditors will seek to gather all the assets of the originator and sell them off to pay the creditor's debts. In order to securitize mortgage loans, the loans must be sold by the originator through a 'true sale' that will withstand the efforts of the originator's creditors to seize those assets. Moreover, credit-rating agencies typically required an opinion of legal counsel that mortgage loans deposited into a special-purpose vehicle would not constitute property of a sponsor's bankrupt estate under Section 541 of the Bankruptcy Code.[44] The US Bankruptcy Code, in turn, usually defers to state law to define what commercial transactions constitute a true sale.[45] The true sale doctrine in American bankruptcy law dictates when an asset can be recaptured by a bankrupt debtor's creditors. When law-enforcement efforts pursue thinly capitalized originators and brokers, the securitized assets churned out by these soldier-class financiers have already been sold to bankruptcy remote trusts that own nothing other than the right to receive loan payments from borrowers. This means that the insolvent mortgage loan originator's creditors – including even fraud victims – cannot normally recapture the assets that were produced through fraudulent underwriting. Although securitization does not involve a secrecy oath, true sales are organizationally similar to *omerta* in that they create an organizational barrier that prevents soldier-class liability from migrating deeper into the organization.

Fourth, in both American Mafia gambling rackets and mortgage securitization the most profitable organizational leadership positions do not have an ownership stake in the assets created by the business. The *borgata* administrations typically did not place bets or collect unpaid gambling debts. This allowed the criminal enterprise's administration to remain relatively unexposed to criminal prosecution for the operation's primary illegal activities. Instead, bookies and loan sharks paid regular tribute to their *caporegime*, who in turn paid tribute to the family administration. Prior to the federal RICO statute it was difficult to prove that accepting these tribute payments was a criminal action. The RICO statute criminalized participating in an ongoing criminal enterprise, including accepting the cash proceeds of a gambling operation. But even after this important legal change, RICO prosecutions of American Mafia leaders remained complex and expensive cases. Mafia family administrators remained relatively insulated from losses and liability, but not from profits.

---

44   Kravitt, *Securitization of Financial Assets* (n 33) 7.03[C].
45   Uniform Commercial Code para 9–318.

Although there are many differences between Mafia gambling enterprises and the securitization of mortgage loans, financial institutions did design private-label mortgage securitization to minimize their 'skin in the game'. Similar to the way in which the Mafia *borgata* administrators do not take an ownership stake in gambling receivables, securitization allowed sponsors and underwriters to profit even though they did not retain economically meaningful ownership stakes in securitized mortgage loans. The originate-to-distribute model of mortgage lending created a powerful incentive to cut corners, ignore traditional underwriting practices and engage in outright fraud, because these financial institutions intended to shed the risk of non-payment from their balance sheets by selling mortgage-backed securities to investors. Moreover, trustees only received fees in exchange for providing limited administrative services, but did not stand behind promised returns to investors. The fact that sponsors and underwriters did not own mortgage loans themselves made it much more difficult to find assignee liability-based theories for holding them accountable for fraud or other violations of consumer protection law. Moreover, the relatively narrow scope of pooling and servicing agreement representations and warranties, along with collective action problems faced by investors, made it difficult for investors to impose liability on sponsors for underperforming securities.

Fifth, both Mafia gambling operations and private-label residential mortgage-backed securitization profited from linking to relatively naive or irrational groups. For example, in Figure 9.1 the gambling operation profits by taking bets favouring the New York Giants from New Yorkers as well as bets favouring the Philadelphia Eagles from Philadelphians. Many gamblers are sentimental, excessively rely on the advice of false experts, overestimate the effect of momentum and disproportionately favour teams they are familiar with.[46] While there are certainly some highly expert gamblers, 'the pool of money bet by the unsophisticated public dominates the pool of money bet by knowledgeable handicappers'.[47] Moreover, because each bet carries a vigorish payment, the likely rationality of the public's bets varies inversely with the ability of bookies to efficiently build the prospects of each teams' success into point spreads and odds. Moreover, insofar as bookies can lay off excess risk by pitting betters against one another, the bookies' profits can originate exclusively from the vigorish.

Although purchasing a residential home mortgage is a very different financial transaction from sports gambling, the two markets share the fundamental similarity that both markets include many irrational participants. A growing body of social science suggests that the traditional characterization of financial services markets

---

46   Christopher Avery and Judith Chevalier, 'Identifying Investor Sentiment from Price Paths: The Case of Football Betting' (1999) 74 *Journal of Business* 493.

47   John Gandar, Richard Zuber, Thomas O'Brien and Ben Russo, 'Testing Rationality in the Points Spread Betting Market' (1988) 43 Journal of Finance 995, 1007.

is highly inaccurate.[48] Mortgage lending, like sports betting, is a target-rich environment for those who seek to profit from poor decision-making. Moreover, as with the mortgage market, there is a great deal of evidence demonstrating the limited rationality of investors. The reoccurrence of price bubbles – whether in real estate,[49] Internet company stocks[50] or tulips[51] – is surely well documented at this point in human history. In traditional mortgage loan underwriting, finding overoptimistic, unqualified borrowers was never a challenge. Indeed, for generations loan officers have spent much of their time turning away borrowers who lacked the credit history, income or assets necessitated by responsible mortgage underwriting. Securitization facilitated the approval of many more of these loans than in years past because financiers could, like bookies, lay off the excess risk of loan default on other investors who were naively willing to bet on borrowers' ability to repay.

Finally, one hopes that the most important distinction between Mafia sports-betting operations and private-label residential mortgage securitization is the unwillingness of the financiers to resort to violence to enforce debts and intimidate whistleblowers. Many American Mafia *borgatas* employed brutal sociopaths that used torture and murder as a tool of business. There is no question that this was profoundly different from anything seen in structured finance of residential mortgages. Nevertheless, it is also true that the structured finance of sub-prime and exotic mortgages continues to disproportionately rely on another form of violence that is disturbing in its own right. Foreclosure on family homes relies on the very real threat of state-sponsored violence to expel insolvent families from their homes, by force, if necessary. In the foreclosure crisis there have been many stories of the police dragging families from their homes.[52] Public respect for the rule of law

---

48   Peterson, *Taming the Sharks* (n 19) 156–198; Patricia A McCoy, 'A Behavioral Analysis of Predatory Lending' (2005) 38 Akron Law Review 725; Lauren E Willis, 'Decisionmaking and the Limits of Disclosure: The Problem of Predatory Lending: Price' (2006) 65 Maryland Law Review 707; Hooman Estelami, 'Cognitive Drivers of Suboptimal Financial Decisions: Implications for Financial Literacy Campaigns' (2009) 13 Journal of Financial Services Marketing 273; Debra Pogrund Stark and Jessica M Choplin, 'A Cognitive and Social Psychology Analysis of Disclosure Laws and Call for Mortgage Counseling to Prevent Predatory Lending' (2010) 16 Psychology, Public Policy and Law 85.

49   Robert M Hardaway, *The Great American Housing Bubble: The Road To Collapse* (Praeger 2011).

50   David L Western, *Booms, Bubbles, and Busts in U.S. Stock Markets* (Routledge 2004).

51   Mike Dash, *Tulipomania: The Story of the World's Most Coveted Flower and the Extraordinary Passions it Aroused* (Random House 2001).

52   Chris Morran, 'Woman Forcibly Removed from Home, in Spite of Restraining Order Against Citibank' (*The Consumerist*, 21 June 2012) <http://consumerist02.wpengine. com/2012/06/woman-forcibly-removed-from-home-in-spite-of-restraining-order-against-citibank/> accessed 24 June 2012; 'Man, Police Exchange Fire During Eviction' (*Columbia*

and deterrence ensure that police who are enforcing court ejection orders are only infrequently forced to turn to actual violence. Nonetheless, the threat of violence is quite real and casts a shadow across the decision-making and well-being of American families and their children. The physical and emotional harm suffered by families who have lost their shelter is no less real if produced by threat of force rather than by actual force. Indeed, sociologists and public-health scholars have long known that there is high morbidity associated with the loss of family homes. People who are expelled from their homes suffer such stress and sense of loss that they become much more susceptible to disease, including depression and suicide.[53] The children of defaulting debtors also suffer profoundly from credit trouble. Residential instability is associated with hunger, emotional, behavioural and academic problems in children, as well as increased risk of teen pregnancy, early drug use and depression.[54] The heart-wrenching stories of homeowners who kill themselves on the eve of foreclosure should dispel any notion that reckless mortgage finance has no victims.[55] Both organized crime and home mortgage foreclosure rely on violence.

Daily Tribune Missouri, 7 June 2012) <http://www.columbiatribune.com/news/2012/jun/07/man-police-exchange-fire-during-eviction/> accessed 24 June 2012; Steven Rosenfeld, 'Dozens of Police Evict Georgia Family at Gunpoint at 3am' (*Alternet*, 5 May 2012) <http://www.alternet.org/story/155292/dozens_of_police_evict_georgia_family_at_gunpoint_at_3am?ak_proof=1&akid=8725.47561.tAOB5N&rd=1&t=2> accessed 24 June 2012; Kari Huus, 'Marine Takes Last Stand in Foreclosed Home' (*MSNBC*, 22 February 2012) <http://usnews.msnbc.msn.com/_news/2012/02/22/10472579-marine-makes-last-stand-in-foreclosed-home?lite> accessed 24 February 2012.

53   Carolyn C. Cannuscio et al, 'Housing Strain, Mortgage Foreclosure, and Health' (2012) 60 Nursing Outlook 134; Janet Currie and Erdal Tekin, 'Is the Foreclosure Crisis Making Us Sick?' *NBER Working Paper No 17310* (August 2011); K A McLaughlin et al, 'Home Foreclosure and Risk of Psychiatric Morbidity During the Recent Financial Crisis' (2010) 42 Psychological Medicine 1441; Craig Evan Pollack and Julia Lynch, 'Health Status of People Undergoing Foreclosure in the Philadelphia Region' (2009) 99 American Journal of Public Health 1833.

54   Margot B Kushel et al, 'Housing Instability and Food Insecurity as Barriers to Health Care among Low-Income Americans' (2006) 21 J. Gen Intern Med 71; Deborah A Frank et al, 'Heat or Eat: The Low Income Home Energy Assistance Program and Nutritional Health Risks Among Children Less than 3 Years of Age' (2006) 118 Pediatrics 1293; T. Jelleyman and N. Spencer, 'Residential Mobility in Childhood and Health Outcomes: A Systematic Review' (2008) 62 *Journal of Epidemiology and Community Health*, 584, 584–592; Robert Haveman, Barbara Wolfe and James Spaulding, 'Childhood Events and Circumstances Influencing High School Completion' (1991) 28 *Demography* 133, 133–157.

55   'Foreclosure Threat Drives Some to Suicide: Economic Crisis Turns Even More Grim as Two Philadelphia Homeowners Take Own Lives Before Evictions' *CBS News* (New York, 24 March 2010); Frank Juliano, 'Foreclosure Notice Leads to Suicide of "Nice Lady"' *Connecticut Post* (3 January 2010); 'Ohio Woman, 90, Attempts Suicide After Foreclosure' *Reuters* (New York, 3 October 2008); Michael Levenson, 'Facing Foreclosure,

4 Corrupt mortgage finance in perspective: Article 12 of the UN Convention Against Corruption

Similarities seen in organizational, service and management characteristics of American Mafia syndicates and residential mortgage finance suggest that corruption is a necessary concept in understanding the causes of the home mortgage crisis. Unfortunately, a survey of the scholarly literature focusing on corruption is well beyond the scope of this short chapter. Although much has been written about corruption, in recent years it is a concept that is perhaps most typically applied to the public institutions of developing nations or the pockets of organized criminality in industrialized economies.[56] For example, Transparency International's oft-cited perceived corruption index ranks nation-states according to their perceived levels of public-sector corruption by aggregating assessments and opinion surveys on the prevalence of bribery, public procurement kickbacks, embezzlement of public funds and the effectiveness of public anti-corruption efforts.[57] Although no region or country is immune to the effects of corruption, Transparency International's index suggests that lesser developed countries tend to have greater levels of perceived public-sector corruption.[58] This perception is reinforced by the UN Convention Against Corruption, which states in its opening passage that corruption is an 'evil phenomenon [that] is found in all countries – big and small, rich and poor – but it is in the developing world that its effects are most destructive'.[59] While this might be true, many of the same principles adopted in the UN Convention have surprising relevance for the American home mortgage foreclosure crisis.

In particular, Article 12 of the Convention provides an interesting lens through which to view American residential mortgage finance. This Article requires that:

> In order to prevent corruption, each State Party shall take measures, in accordance its domestic laws and regulations regarding maintenance of books and records,

---

Taunton Woman Commits Suicide' *Boston Globe* (23 July 2008); Cheryl McDermott, 'Elderly Prineville Couple's Suicide May be Linked to Mortgage Foreclosure' *Bend Weekly* (Oregon, 24 October 2007).

56   Kofi A Annan, 'Preamble', *UN Convention on Corruption* (United Nations 2004) iii.

57   Transparency International, 'Corruption Perceptions Index 2011' <http://cpi. transparency.org/cpi2011/results/> accessed 15 January 2012.

58   Mohsin Habib and Leon Zurawicki, 'Corruption and Foreign Direct Investment' (2002) 33 Journal of International Business Studies 291, 291–307; H Kevin Steensma, Laszlo Tihanyi, Marjorie A Lyles and Charles Dhanaraj 'The Evolving Value of Foreign Partnerships in Transitioning Economies' (2005) 48 Academy of Management Journal 213, 213–235. But see Danielle E Warren and William S Laufer, 'Are Corruption Indices a Self-Fulfilling Prophecy? A Social Labelling Perspective of Corruption' (2009) 88 Journal of Business Ethics 841, 841–849 (arguing that corruption index may serve to reinforce, rather than reform, corruption in developing economies).

59   Annan, 'Preamble' (n 56) iii.

financial statement disclosures and accounting and auditing standards, to prohibit the following acts carried out for the purpose of committing any of the offences established in accordance with this Convention:

(a) The establishment of off-the-books accounts;

(b) The making of off-the-books or inadequately identified transactions;

(c) The recording of non-existent expenditure;

(d) The entry of liabilities with incorrect identification of their objects;

(e) The use of false documents; and

(f) The intentional destruction of bookkeeping documents earlier than foreseen by the law.[60]

There are troubling echoes of each of these corrupt actions in the American mortgage finance crisis. For example, while the drafters of the UN Convention probably did not intend to include securitization within the scope of the term 'off-the-books', it was precisely the off-balance-sheet nature of securitization that enabled thinly capitalized originators to churn out so many ill-advised loans. Moreover, finance industry critics have harshly criticized mortgage loan servicing companies for charging a host of unearned fees for non-existent or overpriced servicing-related expenditures.[61] Mortgage origination settlement statements incorrectly identified the object of borrower liabilities by failing to reveal the quid-pro-quo nature of mortgage brokers' yield-spread premium payments.[62] Lenders secretly gave brokers these payments to compensate brokers for convincing borrowers to agree to higher interest rates than borrowers qualified for on the basis of lenders' own underwriting guidelines.[63] Bankers' use of false foreclosure documents led to the largest joint federal-state settlement ever obtained.[64] The five largest mortgage servicers agreed to pay over $25 billion to settle a lawsuit alleging that they had systematically lied to judges on an industrial scale.[65] And the public recording of mortgages in the name of MERS, rather than the names

---

60   UN Convention Against Corruption (2003) art 12, para 3.

61   Gretchen Morgenson, 'Dubious Fees Hit Borrowers in Foreclosures' *New York Times* (6 November 2007) A1; Katharine Porter, 'Misbehavior and Mistake in Bankruptcy Mortgage Claims' (2008) 87 Texas Law Review 121, 182.

62   Howell Jackson and Laurie Burlingame, 'Kickbacks or Compensation: The Case of Yield Spread Premiums' (2007) 12 Stanford Journal of Law, Business and Finance 289, 358.

63   Peter J Hong and Marcos Reza, 'Hidden Costs to Homeowners: The Prevalent Non-Disclosure of Yield Spread Premiums in Mortgage Loan Transactions' (2005) 18 Loyola Consumer Law Review 131, 132–133.

64   Department of Justice, 'Press Release: Federal Government and State Attorneys General Reach $25 Billion Agreement with Five Largest Mortgage Servicers to Address Mortgage Loan Servicing and Foreclosure Abuses' (9 February 2012) < http://www.justice. gov/opa/pr/2012/February/12-ag-186.html> accessed 10 February 2012.

65   Barry Ritholtz, 'The Robosigning Deal: A Useless Embarrassment' *Washington Post* (26 February 2012) G06.

of the real parties in interest, amounts to an intentional destruction of public land ownership bookkeeping documents in a way not contemplated by the law.[66]

The most important limitation of the UN Convention Against Corruption, like many international treaties, lies in its unenforceability.[67] In particular, the Convention provisions on private corruption have a non-mandatory framework that only requires signatories to take measures to prevent private corruption in accordance with their own pre-existing law. Still, the greatest strength of international treaties can be found in what they may teach signatories about themselves. Perhaps the US should more seriously draw upon the private-sector anti-corruption efforts of other signatory states as it considers how to reform American mortgage financial practices.

5 Conclusion

American cinema has portrayed, and American culture has been preoccupied by, the greed and violence of the American Mafia. While the history and continuing influence of the Mafia is certainly an important topic, its salience has detracted from the ability of the American public to clearly see and respond to other forms of organized corruption. The American Mafia survived, in part, because of an organizational structure that allowed it to keep profits while minimizing the risk of accountability. Likewise, the American mortgage lending industry developed an organizational structure that mimics some of the accountability-minimizing tactics seen in Mafia syndicates. This is not to say that *every* loan churned out of the mortgage boom years was predatory, or even that the *average* mortgage loan was in some way unfair. It is certainly not to say that all mortgage finance professionals bear the same culpability as mobsters. Rather, the point of this chapter is to emphasize that financiers deployed corruption-prone organizational structures that allowed the origination and securitization of many – indeed *millions* – of commercially unreasonable loans with an unjustifiable risk of default and foreclosure. And now, more recently, this same organizational structure has compounded its catastrophic underwriting failures by replicating similar corruption-prone practices in the servicing, foreclosure and loss mitigation associated with those loans.

Of course, there is no evidence that leading financial institutions consciously decided to emulate the organizational structure of the Mafia. Nevertheless, both of these industries existed within similar environments and acted with similar

---

66   Christopher L Peterson, 'Two Faces: Demystifying the Mortgage Electronic Registration System's Land Title Theory' (2011) 53 William and Mary Law Review 111, 125–128; David E Woolley and Lisa D Herzog, 'MERS: The Unreported Effects of Lost Chain of Title on Real Property Owners' (2012) 8 Hastings Law Journal 365, 388–392.

67   Philippa Webb, 'The United Nations Convention Against Corruption: Global Achievement or Missed Opportunity?' (2005) 8 Journal of International Economic Law 191, 228.

goals that sparked processes of organizational evolution, resulting in comparable strategic plans. If the Hollywood gangster mystique is indeed a window into essential human ambitions run amok, perhaps it should not be so surprising that legitimate financial institutions would replicate Mafia-like organizational solutions to resolve comparable institutional pressures.

Index

For Product Safety Concerns and Information please contact our EU
representative GPSR@taylorandfrancis.com Taylor & Francis Verlag GmbH,
Kaufingerstraße 24, 80331 München, Germany

Printed and bound by CPI Group (UK) Ltd, Croydon, CR0 4YY
01/05/2025
01858359-0006